SEEING, KNOWING, AND DOING

SEEING, KNOWING, AND DOING

A Perceptualist Account

Robert Audi

OXFORD
UNIVERSITY PRESS

Oxford University Press is a department of the University of Oxford. It furthers the University's objective of excellence in research, scholarship, and education by publishing worldwide. Oxford is a registered trade mark of Oxford University Press in the UK and certain other countries.

Published in the United States of America by Oxford University Press
198 Madison Avenue, New York, NY 10016, United States of America.

First issued as an Oxford University Press paperback, 2025

Library of Congress Cataloging-in-Publication Data
Names: Audi, Robert
Title: Seeing, knowing, and doing : a perceptualist account / Robert Audi.
Description: New York, NY, United States of America :
Oxford University Press, 2020. |
Includes bibliographical references and index.
Identifiers: LCCN 2019044697 (print) | LCCN 2019044698 (ebook) |
ISBN 9780197503508 (hb) | ISBN 9780197802342(pb) |
ISBN 9780197503522 (epub) | ISBN 9780197503539
Subjects: LCSH: Perception (Philosophy) | Knowledge, Theory of.
Classification: LCC B828.45 .A93 2020 (print) |
LCC B828.45 (ebook) | DDC 121/.34—dc23
LC record available at https://lccn.loc.gov/2019044697
LC ebook record available at https://lccn.loc.gov/2019044698

Paperback printed by Marquis Book Printing, Canada

CONTENTS

PREFACE

This book provides an account of perception leading to partial accounts of knowledge, justification, and the connection of both to action. Perception and its epistemological roles are center stage. Here the book has the further aim of showing the extent to which an account of perception and perceptual justification can enhance understanding of the a priori—my second major topic. There is a great deal of empirical literature on perception, and I have sought to accommodate much that I have learned from it. But I have not tried to bring recent empirical findings centrally into my own account. In my view, the philosophy of perception should accommodate, even at times explain, certain empirical data and should aim at compatibility with any plausible empirical hypotheses that can be anticipated. It need not, however, aim to mirror empirical theories by (for instance) adapting philosophical vocabulary to their major elements. That tendency can lead to an intellectualist account of perception, as where perception is considered inferential, conceptual, belief-entailing, or all of these.

The book resists a kind of intellectualism both natural for philosophers and common in contemporary literature. It also resists a related tendency to view philosophy as mainly concerned with interpreting and defending the leading scientific picture of human beings and their world. On my view, philosophy is an autonomous discipline with its own standards. It is not (in terms used by Quine in describing epistemology) a kind of empirical discipline, and even the philosophy of perception is not, as he might have thought, a branch of psychology. But philosophy also does not have the luxury of being a wholly a priori and abstract field with the limited responsibility to common-sense reflection that may be appropriate to purely formal theorizing.

The structural, phenomenological, and normative parallels between belief and action have not been adequately explored by philosophers, and I will present a theory encompassing both in relation to the respects in which they are parallel—a theory that treats the theoretical and the practical as, in an important way, counterparts of each other and brings both into an integrated conception of human persons.

At least implicitly, I present some ideals for intellectual life. They concern understanding evidence, reasons and reasoning, rationality in action, and critical assessment of beliefs and actions. In appropriate places, I indicate connections to my previous work, which supports many points made here. But I have minimized repetition of points previously established and have refined and built on my earlier theories of justification, knowledge, and action. In the general theory of rationality, my *Architecture of Reason* (2001a) is a major statement of my overall theory of rationality as it then stood; in action theory, *Practical Reasoning and Ethical Decision* (2006) is a comprehensive treatment of such reasoning in historical perspective and with applications in the moral realm; and, in both these areas and others, many of my papers written in the decade after the latter book deal with one or another issue addressed here. References to my previous work are often included to indicate where anyone interested can find some of the many arguments for my view that are not repeated here.

The book takes account of existing literature but is not a study of it, nor is it concerned with all the pertinent discussions in the journals. It is meant to be both empirically and historically informed but, in content, neither historical nor empirically oriented. The effort is to achieve a kind of philosophical adequacy that takes account of some major elements in the empirical literature and leaves room for the kinds of developments we might expect from the experimental work of recent decades. I have also sought to be as brief as clarity allows and, through using numerous illustrations, as concrete as possible. Readers who do not know the philosophical and psychological literature on perception should find the book self-contained; readers who do know that literature will often see connections with it that go beyond those indicated in the notes.

ACKNOWLEDGMENTS

In addition to my books just cited, I should say that I have drawn substantially on—though also revised and extended—my "Perception and Cognition: Structural and Epistemic Elements," first given as the Muenster Lecture in 2016 and published in *Robert Audi: Critical Engagements* (2018); "Understanding, Self-Evidence, and Justification," *Philosophy and Phenomenological Research* (2018c); "Intuition and Its Place in Ethics," *Journal of the American Philosophical Association* (2015); and "On Intellectualism in the Theory of Action," *Journal of the American Philosophical Association* (2017).

For valuable discussion and in some cases very helpful comments on earlier versions of some segments of this book, I am very grateful to many colleagues, students, and audiences. What follows is a list of many (I fear far from all) readers and conversation partners who have contributed to my thinking in the book: Robert Merrihew Adams, Maria Alvarez, Karl Ameriks, Alexander Arnold, Paul Audi, Heather Battaly, John Bengson, Salim Berker, Paola Bernardini, Patricia Blanchette, Paul Blaschko, Lawrence BonJour, John Broome, Bartosz Brozek, Lara Buchak, Anjan Chakravartty, Elijah Chudnoff, Earl Conee, Roger Crisp, Dustin Crummett, Brian Cutter, Jonathan Dancy, Marian David, Claudio DeAlmeida, Mario De Caro, Michael DePaul, Julia Driver, Elizabeth Fricker, Matthew Frise, Berys Gaut, Sanford Goldberg, Alvin Goldman, John Greco, Scott Hagaman, John Heil, Brad Hooker, Elizabeth Jackson, Zoë Jenkin, David Kaspar, Ralph Kennedy, Christopher Kulp, Jennifer Lackey, Clayton Littlejohn, William Lycan, Anna-Sara Malmgren, Kevin McCain, Sarah McGrath, Alfred Mele, Christian Miller, Paolo Monti, Johannes Müller-Salo, Samuel Murray, Saumel Newlands, Nikolaj Nottelmann, the late Derek Parfit, Carlotta Pavesi, Michael Quante, Michael Rea, Baron Reed, Sonja Rinofner-Kreidl, Blake Roeber, Benjamin Rossi, Rachel Rupprecht, Susanna

Siegel, William R. Smith, Marta Soniewicka, David Sosa, Ernest Sosa, Jeffrey Speaks, Scott Stapleford, Leopold Stubenberg, Eleonore Stump, Richard Swinburne, Artur Szutta, John Tasioulas, Joshua Thurow, Mark Timmons, Raimo Tuomela, Ted A. Warfield, Abigail Whalen, René van Woudenberg, and Linda Zagzebski. For extensive discussion or painstaking comments I am especially grateful to Nevin Climenhaga, E. J. Coffman, Garrett Cullity, Peter J. Graham, Thomas Grundmann, Thomas Kelly, Timothy Williamson, and, particularly, Declan Smithies and Matthias Steup.

Special thanks go to the Australian Catholic University. As an ACU Professorial Fellow in recent years I have benefited much from collaboration with Wayne McKenna and James McLaren and from seminars and conversations in the ACU Institute for Critical Inquiry and, more recently its new Dianoia Institute in Philosophy, where interactions with (among others) Stewart Braun, Richard Colledge, Stephanie Collins, Stephen Finlay, David Killoren, Ole Koksvik, David Newheiser, Tyler Paytas, and Richard Rowland were of particular help. I also want to acknowledge the benefit of comments by anonymous readers, and no such book comes to fruition without assistance and advice from editors. I thank Allison Nespor for preparing the index (which is quite comprehensive apart from generally not listing many of the terms prominent in the detailed table of contents), and Deepti Agarwal for overseeing the laborious process of production. I am also grateful to my Editor, Peter Ohlin, who has been of great help in contributing both to the development of the book from an early stage and through to its publication.

INTRODUCTION

Perception is basic for human knowledge, but as familiar as it is, it poses a multitude of challenges to philosophy. It defies sharp definition. It takes many subtly different forms. It bears complex relations to thought. It guides our actions in countless ways. It provides the mind with raw materials for reflection that ranges far beyond the physical realm. If perception gives us a kind of representation of the physical realm, it also provides a ladder—or the footing of a ladder—to the abstract realm. Human knowledge begins at the perceptual level, but it rises to understanding and knowledge of matters that go far beyond that—indeed extending to all possible worlds. I refer, of course, to a priori knowledge. A distinctive aim of this book is to clarify a priori knowledge partly on the basis of an understanding of perception and perceptual knowledge.

If perception governs our receptivity to the world, it also enables our acting as we do within and upon that world. What we see, hear, touch, taste, and smell enables us to find paths to what we seek. Perception is a reliable source of information about such paths. How its reliability is to be understood, how, given that reliability, perception yields knowledge of these paths, and how the mind acquires the know-how to follow the paths are questions that pose still further challenges to philosophy. The theory of perception developed in this book is aimed at meeting these challenges too.

Part One presents a theory of perception that centers on its causal relation to its objects and its representational capacities regarding them. Its six chapters explain the principal forms of perception, the kinds of content it has, its structure in terms of more and less basic levels, and the way in which deliverances of the senses provide grounds for justification and knowledge. Perception is shown to be a basis for belief and knowledge without being taken to entail actually forming beliefs or producing knowledge. Perception is conceived as non-inferential and, in relation to that, shown to be not essentially "theory-laden" in several senses of that elastic term. Beyond this, *grounds* of perceptual justification and knowledge are distinguished from *reasons* that justify perceptual belief. Perceptual justification, even when characterizing true beliefs, is shown to differ from perceptual knowledge in ways that go beyond the point that justified true beliefs need not constitute knowledge.

In Part Two, with the theory of perception and a partial account of knowledge and justification before us, perception is viewed as a basis for understanding intuition, which may be seen as, in central cases, intellectually responsive to its non-physical objects much as perception is responsive to its physical objects. Apprehension of abstract entities is significantly analogous to perception. The central chapter of Part Two shows how apprehension of abstract entities can rise to understanding of self-evident propositions and thereby yield a basic kind of a priori justification and knowledge. For achieving a philosophically adequate account of a priori justification and knowledge, self-evident propositions are the central kind we must understand. In very broad terms, self-evident propositions are to apprehension much as clearly perceptible empirical truths are to perception.

Part Three concerns practical knowledge, which encompasses knowing *how* to do various things, as distinct from knowing what one should do to achieve various ends. In particular, we need an account of how knowledge, especially as an achievement of the intellect, should guide the will. We must also ascertain whether everyday action, at least if rational, must be guided by practical reasoning and, if so, whether rational actions must be based on sound reasoning and intentionally performed. This raises a further question, also pursued in Part Three: What constitutes rational action, and might the range of behavior it encompasses extend to action that is not intentional?

The overall aim of the book is to provide a perception-centered—"perceptualist"—account of the most basic kind of empirical knowledge; a related theory of a priori knowledge; and a conception of practical knowledge that explains how it is guided by perception but does not burden agency by treating it as dependent on beliefs we need not form in realizing our aims or on inferences we need not perform. The emerging conception of the human person as perceiver, knower, and agent respects our natural place in the world, but it does not reduce us to physical systems that are merely integrated parts of the world or seek to capture our distinctive character by intellectualizing knowledge and action.

SEEING, KNOWING, AND DOING

PART I

PERCEPTION

1

PERCEPTION AND PERCEPTUAL BELIEF

Seeing and Knowing the Physical World

I am seated under a canopy of maples, copperbeach, and hemlock. Shafts of morning sunlight coming through the trees warm my face. On the ground, a mason's wall beneath a flat badminton court stretches out before me. To my right, a dry retaining wall curves down the hill. A whisper in the grass reveals a chipmunk scurrying along the line of shrubbery to the dry wall, which it enters between large stones. My perceptions fill my consciousness. Reflecting on this experience, I find no reason to doubt that these perceptions are true to the sights and sounds around me. Indeed, I simply cannot doubt that there really are trees before me, a wall across my field of vision, a chair beneath me, the sound of the wind in the upper branches, the smell of newly cut grass, and the taste of coffee. All five senses are receptive to my surroundings: I see, feel, hear, smell, and taste familiar things. These experiences are paradigms of perceptions. We need not take them to be the only possible kinds of perception; but if there are other perceptual modalities, we would expect them to bear important similarities to these. This chapter provides a preliminary account of perceptions of these kinds.

I. Perception Broadly Conceived

The perceptions that guide daily life illustrate something quite general. Perception is experiential. If you are hearing something, you are having

Seeing, Knowing, and Doing. Robert Audi, Oxford University Press (2020). © Oxford University Press.
DOI: 10.1093/oso/9780197503508.001.0001

an experience, and it is distinctive as compared with experiences in the other perceptual modes. Some perceptual experiences are highly variegated. A piano you are playing can have a look, a sound, and a feel, but these three are very different. I take experiences to have a phenomenal character. The green that fills my visual field when I view maple trees in full foliage is distinctive. It has a character of its own, and it contrasts, in a transitional way, with other colors and, in a cross-categorial way, with the feel of the cool metal arms of my lawn chair.

To say that experiences have a phenomenal character is compatible with taking experiences themselves to be properties of persons. There is something it is like for me to see print unfolding here. I assume that it is like what you experience in viewing similar print, but that comparative point does not indicate what I mean by saying there is something it is like for me to see the printed words. I also assume that others understand what I mean here, but no definition will indicate this clearly for anyone who lacks the kind of experience in question. Still, we need not deny that there is something my experience itself may be said to be like: I find it like seeing black lines drawn on white paper, not like seeing red ones drawn on it. The likeness and unlikeness in question is phenomenal, not comparative. There is a comparative sense of 'like', but though it is related to the phenomenal sense it is different and plausibly considered less basic. If my experiences of red and of green—in the sense of visual responses to those colors on surfaces of things I observe—were alike phenomenally, I would not visually discern the difference between red lights and green lights.

Phenomenal properties have an intrinsic character. This may be described by attributing higher-order properties to them, such as the green in my visual experience of maple foliage. The term 'quality' is natural for this aspect of my experience, partly because it indicates a contrast with highly similar experiences. But we need not take that quality to belong to something other than me. If I have the experience of seeing green leaves, this green partially characterizes my experience, but in doing so it also characterizes me. It should not be taken to describe a distinct object, such as a mental image that has a green color "in its own right." Visual experiences may have many other kinds of properties, for example being vivid, static, fuzzy, or marked by sharply distinct trees lining a quiet pond.

The epistemological importance of perception is unquestionable. Perception is our basic way of knowing the world around us and the people in it. This is one reason why seeing, touching, hearing, tasting, and smelling are crucial for the normal development of concepts and the formation of beliefs in which they figure. This does not entail that there can be no other perceptual modes, but these five are ample material for theory and essential elements in any comprehensive philosophical treatment of perception. Even seeing—perhaps the most richly informative of the five—is sufficiently representative and important to serve as subject-matter for a quite broad understanding of perception, and it will be the main perceptual mode I discuss. The other modes, however, must be considered in appraising any comprehensive account of perception and the knowledge it provides, and we must bear them in mind. No single work can provide a detailed, fully comprehensive account of perception, but this book aims at sufficient comprehensiveness for an understanding of perception that captures the elements central for seeing its overall structure, its experiential character, and its relation to belief, knowledge, and action.

Perception as Experiential

Our perceptions are responses to the world. We also have an awareness of states of our own body, such as the position and movement of our limbs, and that awareness is at once similar in character to "outer" perception yet not dependent on the five senses. Here I set aside such inner perception, though its parallels to "outer" perception are well worth exploring.[1]

One element common to perceptions of any kind, including inner ones, is their status as kinds of experience. Perception—as understood in terms of the ordinary notions of seeing, hearing, touching, tasting, and smelling—requires a kind of consciousness and in that way is experiential. Nothing experienced, nothing seen. One might think that such phenomena as "blindsight" falsify this claim. There, though people report having no visual image (or anyway not seeing anything), visual stimulation yields beliefs (or conjectures or impressions) about the relevant objects. These are more likely to be true than they would be by chance. In my view, however, the data making 'blindsight' seem applicable to special cases of cognition can be best accommodated in relation to stimulation of the visual system (which receives light rays) and resulting cognitions of the patient. These two kinds of variable are

1. The analogy between perception and introspection is developed in some detail in ch. 5 of my 2010. But (as noted there) introspection is not the only possible case of inner perception. For an extensive survey of inner perception, see Ritchie and Caruthers (2017).

uncontroversially important in understanding perception, but their joint presence in blindsight does not undermine the also important truth that there is something it is like to see. One way to understand what this phenomenological expression means is to consider standing before a landscape painting and closing, then opening, one's eyes. The change from darkness to color and shape is experiential. Viewing the painting is a visual experience in the sense relevant here. It may be momentary, but that does not prevent its having a qualitative character and representational content. A glimpse can be like a snapshot; it may be almost instantaneous yet may record a great deal of information. Some of the information may be recoverable by memory long after the fact, and some may be utterly forgotten.

Among the first things to be said in understanding how blindsight may work is that knowledge of the visible need not be visual knowledge. This is obvious given that testimony can yield knowledge of the unobserved, but the point may also be illustrated by blindsight—if it is fully blind, as opposed to a case in which subjects misreport their visual experience. To be sure, if we think of blindsight as perception, then the very fact that perception has a representational character may lead us to posit unconscious representation rather than seeing without visual consciousness. This would be a representational state one could not describe in terms of what it is like to have it but only in terms of its content and the behavior it enables or tends to produce. Positing unconscious representation (a notion that is at best puzzling) is not, however, the only possible response to the case.[2] Another is that in some way the object of blindsight causes belief-formation (or some cognition) by a process in the "visual system" that, like some purely testimony-based beliefs whose content describes color and shape, bypasses visual phenomenology. I leave these options open and take them to call for experimental investigation.

The possibility of pure blindsight (an idealized case I call *pure* because it embodies no visual experience) brings out something

2. In Prinz (2017), we find a case for countenancing unconscious perception, which he characterizes as "unconscious transduction of information that is in someone [some way?] useable by the organism that transduces it" (p. 373) and later as "perception without the benefit of a frontal cortex" (p. 386). I do not see that the case is inconsistent with describing the phenomena he cites from the literature, as I would, in terms not entailing that perception occurs without the instantiation (in consciousness) of any of the kinds of phenomenal properties I view as essential to it.

important. The notion of seeing may be *both* partly tied to the notion of acquisition of visual knowledge, or at least of visual beliefs of the kind that characteristically constitute knowledge, and partly tied to their acquisition through the eyes. If pure blindsight became common and we could understand how the eyes play a crucial role, the term 'blindsight' might become common, and we might treat it as a kind of seeing that contrasts with ordinary, "visual" seeing.[3] We might then usefully speak of action-guiding consciousness of one's environment by contrast with phenomenal consciousness of it, as where one experiences the colors of a painting one is viewing.

Note, however, that if there should be no sensory experience as an element in the "seeing," we would not expect the subject (*S*) to have the kind of memory of seeing that is normal for recalling, in visual imagination, what was seen. *S* might remember how to get to the library without recalling visual details of the route. If there should be such apparent recall, this might suggest that there had been (unacknowledged) visual experience after all. There are other imaginable possibilities, but perhaps enough has been said to indicate that whatever the possibilities of visual knowledge without ordinary seeing, that common phenomenon is matter enough for a theory of perception as we normally know it.

A more important point for this book is that although every visual perception is a visual experience, the converse does not hold. The vocabulary common among epistemologists can obscure this point. Hallucinations can (in principle) be robustly visual, yet still not perceptions of anything. I use 'sensory experience' for the wider sensory category that includes hallucinations as well as perceptions, but some writers on perception have included hallucinations (often only implicitly) in the category of perceptual experience. In some philosophical writings, hallucination is contrasted with "veridical perception." I prefer to avoid this terminology, though it does rightly suggest that hallucinations are not "truthful" perceptions, and I grant that, broadly speaking, hallucinations are perceptual phenomena. Nonetheless, by invoking the thought that veridical perception is simply

3. For John Locke, this would likely be too strong a concession: he held that perception is not only in consciousness but also entails a sensory "idea": "[W]*herever there is sense,* or *perception, there some* idea *is actually produced*" ([1689] 1986: 57) Cf. Burge's view (also usefully compared with Prinz's), which allows that in blindsight, although there are "perceptual constancies—including motion, location, and size . . . consciousness is missing" (2010: 374).

non-hallucinatory, non-illusory perception, the term 'veridical perception' can invite assimilation of merely sensory experience to perception.

Whatever our terminology, should we call a perfect visual hallucination of, say, an approaching bear seeing? I think not. Should we consider it a kind of perception that would be veridical if there were an approaching bear producing the experience? I would resist this. Genuinely seeing, I take it, is intrinsically veridical in some sense. It is, in a referential way, *factive*, i.e., fact-entailing: it entails the existence of an object seen—and so cannot be hallucinatory. Consider illusions, such as seeing a partially submerged stick as bent. These must be considered veridical with respect to existence but not with respect to shape. Here we have referential factivity together with visual error. There is a stick in the water, but it is not bent.

A further complexity is that we can properly speak of someone struck on the head as "seeing stars," and drugs can induce "seeing" snakes. These are non-factive uses of 'see'. They seem metaphorical or, at best, to indicate a weaker sense of 'see'. If there are no snakes, then no one actually sees snakes. Even if we take 'seeing' to have some literal use in the hallucination case, positing seeing something whose existence one would truly deny is at best not a case central for the theory of perception.

If having a sense-experience entails being conscious of something—at least representationally conscious of something phenomenally presented—then contrary to the views of some students of the subject, perception, given its experiential character, cannot be unconscious. This holds at least if 'unconscious' has the common strong sense in which it allows that, for instance, the subject sees or hears something without *anything's* occurring in consciousness that indicates a sight or sound. Countenancing pure blindsight is one possible source of the idea that seeing is possible without visual consciousness of anything. Another possible source is the behavioral effect of subliminal advertising, as with 'Have a Coke' flashed quickly on a screen. There is no question that behavior may be affected in both cases in a way it would not be if the eyes were closed, and perhaps there is a fleeting visual experience in such cases that is simply not remembered. Suppose, however, that subliminal advertising can show that visual stimuli unaccompanied by *any* visual experience can provide information that influences behavior. This causal relation might hold in any case for someone who *never* has visual experiences of the kind characteristic of seeing as normally understood. In terms of the mental life of the agent, simply receiving visual stimuli via light affecting the retina and brain need not differ from the relevant information's reaching the brain directly through suitable wiring and affecting behavior in the same way.

People may also misreport or forget a visual experience or, conceivably, suffer from a disconnection between the visual experience and the normal mechanism enabling us to report it. An intermediate case would be that of the constant noise of traffic on a distant roadway. There is some inclination to say that one is not conscious of it at all until, as where an accident blocks the road, it stops. But this comment is best understood as meaning that (for instance) one does not notice it, is not attending to it, or is not *focally*, as opposed to peripherally, aware of it. Those possibilities are compatible with one's having (as seems normal) an overall auditory experience that has mixed humming and tire-rubbing characteristics that are jointly an element in one's experience.[4]

Some of what I am implying regarding vision can be illustrated with respect to hearing. As with seeing, if you are hearing something, you are having an experience of a distinctive kind as compared with experiences in the other perceptual modes. Granted, a rose can have *both* a look and a smell, but the two are very different. Again, it will be evident that I take experiences to have phenomenal aspects that may be variously described. When, for instance, I look at maples in full foliage, I have the property of experiencing greenly (to put it adverbially). We might also say that I have the property of its (visually) seeming to me as if there is something green there, though not necessarily of its seeming to me *that* there is something green there (the latter locution, construed as conceptual, will be considered shortly). The relation of such properties to their external counterparts is controversial, but here the point is simply that positing such phenomenal properties does not require denying that there *is* an external property I see, one that contrasts both with

4. Prinz cites Ned Block as using a similar example, air-conditioner noise, and holding (in Prinz's words) that "we can be phenomenally conscious of a stimulus while lacking access consciousness to it" (2017: 375). As I see such cases, in them we do not in fact "access" our consciousness, but normally can. I grant, however, that consciousness of something does not *entail* the ability to describe or even report it. I disagree with Prinz's view that "To notice something we have to classify it" (374). As to his using 'unconscious perception' to refer to "unconscious transduction of information that is . . . useable by the organism that transduces it" (373), this neurological view makes it easy to see how perception can be considered sometimes unconscious assuming (plausibly) that the brain, apart from our experiences (and certainly without our noticing), can receive information that can guide purposive action.

other color properties and with properties accessible to non-visual perceptual modes, say the coolness and hardness of the metal arms of my lawn chair.

The Sensory Aspect of Perceptual Experience

In speaking about experience, we quickly encounter a duality of reference: there is the coolness actually possessed by the arms of the chair and (at least on a realist view of color) the green of tree leaves. Experiencing these is relational. But there also is the experiential coolness—felt coolness, we might say—and the visualized green. Could the same experience not occur by virtue of a qualitatively identical hallucination, where the experience is non-relational?[5] Again there is a duality of reference: in what we might call the strict everyday sense of 'experience,' you cannot experience the brilliant sound of a particular Steinway piano unless you actually hear that sound; but you could have an auditory experience just like that under conditions of (say) artificial stimulation in the absence of any piano. Suppose machines that produce such experiential replicas of perceptions became common. One can imagine marketers saying that with their recreative devices you can experience in your own home any musical piece you choose.

A natural way to this duality has been foreshadowed: we may speak of *perceptual experiences* where *S* is really seeing, hearing, and so forth for the other perceptual modes, and of *merely sensory experiences,* say visual experiences, where *S* is not seeing or otherwise perceiving but, phenomenologically, *S*'s experience is either qualitatively identical with or sufficiently like what one experiences in the corresponding perception. Not all sense-experiences, to be sure, are qualitatively identical (in phenomenal properties) with any actual instance or kind of perceptual experience. One might, in a nightmarish daydream, have a sensory experience as of an approaching bear. The experience could be much less vivid than a counterpart perception, but the possibility of identical vividity seems undeniable and is significant for understanding perceptual experience and its role in providing knowledge and justification.[6]

5. Some disjunctivists appear to deny this, but their views (which will be discussed in chapter 6) are highly variable. See, e.g., Fish (2010) and Prichard (2012). Valuable critical discussion of disjunctivism is provided by D. Sosa (2011).

6. For Susanna Schellenberg (2017), who does not distinguish perceptual and sensory experience as I do, the same "perceptual capacity" is exercised in both. This suggests that a Cartesian or brain-in-the-vat scenario, in which there

Why should we speak of *merely* sensory experiences when, although one is not really perceiving, one is having a familiar-seeming experience of an apparently external reality? The answer is certainly not that sense-experience not embodied in perception is unimportant—hallucination can produce important actions and beliefs. The answer is (in part) that perception, though it embodies sense-experience, is not constituted by it and implies much more. Perception implies all that goes with having an external object. Seeing a maple in full (green) foliage, for instance, includes the sense-experience of its distinctive shade of green but also entails the existence of the tree itself.

Some philosophers might describe this perceptual experience (misleadingly, in my view) as one of awareness of "phenomenal green." A better way to put this phenomenological point is to say that there is something it is like to see a maple in full foliage, and one could have a merely sensory experience that, visually, is qualitatively just like that yet is not a case of seeing one. That experience might be hallucinatory, but this possibility does not entail that between genuine perceptual experiences and just *any* corresponding hallucinatory ones—those with the same ostensibly perceived external object—there is always a "common factor" that is precisely the same in both cases. Such precise commonality would occur only in cases of exact qualitative similarity, which might be idealizations never approximated. Shall we say, then, that perceptual experiences *have* phenomenal properties (or qualities, in some uses)? One might say this, but it is misleading. Perceptual experiences are a relation between a perceived object and a perceiver, and ascribing phenomenal properties to such relations is at best a way of indicating that they entail a sense-experience in which the perceiver has those properties. If I hallucinate a birch tree, *I* have the property of "experiencing birchly." There is also some question whether we should conceive having sense-experiences as *identical* with the subject's *having* certain phenomenal properties or, more cautiously, as *equivalent to* having those properties by the experiencing subject (such instantiations may be events, processes, or states, and I leave open how these are to be analyzed). It is true that we must be able to attribute experiences to persons, hence to treat experiences as a kind of property—a relational property for many uses of 'experience'. But in the uses of 'experience' central here, experiences are non-relational phenomenal

is sensory experience intrinsically like perceptual experience, is not possible. I do not foreclose that possibility but take perceptual experience to be *both* sensory and relational.

properties. My concern here is sense-experience, which can occur apart from perceptual experience and so, on that count, at least, is not relational (at least not a relation to any physical object). I conceive having sense-experiences simpliciter as the property of having a set of phenomenal properties of a certain kind: both sense-experiences and phenomenal properties are properties of persons, but to instantiate the former properties is to instantiate each property in a set of the latter.

To be sure, not all phenomenal properties are sensory: silently reciting Donne's "A Valediction Forbidding Mourning" is both experiential and phenomenal, as is simply imaging a giant redwood. Moreover, there are questions about whether hearing a Bach Invention while seeing green trees is one experience or two, but there is no need to settle this, since either view leaves untouched the idea that (sensory) experiences are properties consisting in the subject's instantiating certain phenomenal properties.

The Discriminative Responsiveness of Perception

Perception is not just any causal relation between an experiencing subject and a perceptible object. It is not even just a relation in which the object causes an appropriate sense-experience. In a special way that is difficult to capture, perception represents the object and does so through a non-deviant causal relation (more will be said about non-deviance below).

How accurately representational must perception be? There may be no simple answer, and, for different senses, there may be differences in the degree of inaccuracy allowable by the concept of perception through the sense in question. But one general point is evident regarding vision. Suppose I see a plane in the distance. It may appear to me as a slow-moving speck that disappears into a distant cloud. Suppose it is moving and to my right, but it is not black, as it appears to be, nor simply an oblong winged object, as it also appears to be. Still, I can discern its path and approximate location; and, in addition, my responsiveness to it is such that if it changed course, or speeded up significantly, or exploded, or turned bright red, I would see this. In short, I have a (perceptual) *discriminative responsiveness* to it, such that I am causally connected with it in a way that assures that my visual phenomenal properties representing it will vary depending on at least certain of its visible properties.[7] This

7. I take causal connections to imply certain counterfactuals but do not consider them analyzable simply in terms of counterfactuals (I leave open here

notion of responsiveness is vague, but so is the notion of seeing, and in much the same way. I can see it, as I can see a cat walking across the room, even if I would not visually register *every* change in its speed; but I cannot actually see either of them if (other things equal) I would not register *any* change in them.

To say that perception of something entails a discriminative responsiveness to it does not commit one to taking perceiving something to require actual discrimination regarding it. Encased in a seamless green sphere, I could see nothing but, e.g., green surrounding me, with no borders or variations to be represented in an "exercise" of discrimination. Yet I would still tend to notice a change in it if it darkened. The point is not just that I need not *do* anything describable as discriminating; it is that my experience may not *represent* any differences: seeing the uniform field of green is a perception regardless of whether any variations in it are seen at the time.[8]

Perhaps it would be fair to say this: for a sense-experience to be genuinely perceptual, the experience must in some way represent *something* true of the perceived object at least approximately right, though it need not represent the whole object perceived, and, second, it must be in some way discriminatively sensitive to changes in at least some of the perceptible properties of the object. But there is room both for limitation in accurate information and for a good deal of misinformation. Compare picking up (or touching) a skillet. You must grasp (or touch)

whether actual causal connections are conceptually primitive). A related qualification is this. Where there is a time gap, as with seeing distant stars, the best option seems to be to suppose that we see them as they *were* at a certain time, and that this requires that we have whatever discriminative responsiveness is appropriate to seeing the properties they had by which we see them. Strictly, there may always be a gap between the time of seeing and the time at which the information-bearing light waves leave the object seen (and similarly for any other connecting process there may be, since seeing is not conceptually dependent on light); but where the gap is imperceptible we normally do not and need not speak of seeing the object as it was.

8. By contrast, "On the enactive view . . . to have genuine representational content—the perceiver must possess and make use of *sensorimotor knowledge*" (Noë 2004: 17). Schellenberg draws a different contrast, viewing a comparably encased subject as "discriminating the part of the uniformly colored wall to her right from the part of the wall to her left" (2018: 27). There is a difference between looking to one's left and looking to one's right, but I doubt this makes any difference in the color seen. In any case, one would surely see the green surface upon merely staring straight ahead.

some part of it, even if just the tip of the handle. Some parts, to be sure, give more leverage than others, but this depends on both you and the skillet.

Perceptual Reliability

There is a related variable we must take into account in understanding perception: the reliability of the process by which the perceived object's instantiating a set of perceptible properties produces a set of representational phenomenal properties in the perceiver sufficient to qualify the perceiver as seeing it. This is roughly a matter of whether there is a high (perhaps better than even) probability of a certain kind of discriminative response to the object under the relevant conditions. Suppose that a distant plane's speeding up by even 100 percent would not affect my visual experience of it. This does not prevent my seeing it—as opposed to bearing on how *well* I see it—if I would respond to a change in direction and to its hovering in midair. But suppose that (other things remaining equal) I would not discern any such changes in its movement. This makes it doubtful that I still see it. Suppose, however, that I would respond to a change in its color. Do I not then see it, even if less well?

It turns out that to determine whether I see the plane, we need a good deal of information; and even given that information, there will be borderline cases. It may be that there is a certain kind of reliability built into the causal condition on seeing: we presumably cannot see at all something that in no way causes us to have a visual experience that is, in an appropriate sense, *of* it. Moreover, not just *any* way a plane causes me to have a clear visual impression of it entails my seeing it. I do not see the plane at all if there is an opaque object between me and it but my visual impressions are caused by a machine that, unlike reliable prosthetic devices, accidentally enters a state which, by a further accident, produces the appropriate visual experience in me by using a photographic representation of the plane to stimulate my brain so as to give me the right aeronautic "vision." (This would be a "deviant" causal chain.) Granted, causal determinists would take it that the connection is in principle capturable by a universal law. I am assuming only that positing causal connections of the kind required for perception implies at most a lawlike connection of a weaker kind. Perhaps the connecting generalization might be probabilistic or a tendency statement.

As the aeronautic example shows, we should not take mere causation of a sensory state by an object, even one whose causal impact on the subject yields a detailed and accurate representation of it, to entail perceiving it. Here is a different example. Suppose a ball is dropped in a closed room next to the one I am in but it accidentally triggers a machine which then causes me to hallucinate a ball just like this moving exactly as this does. I may then have true quasi-visual beliefs about the ball, though it does not causally affect me (at least not in the right way) and I do not see it.

It could be, however, that I am caused to see a distant object by light rays reaching me accidentally and producing a visual impression of the kind I would have if I saw it in the normal way. Imagine that a machine with revolving mirrors produces the impression in me at a time it was supposed to be turned off, but my visual impression is just what it would have been had the light rays not been bent toward me through the machine but instead reached me in the normal way. The object causes my impression, which would vary with changes in its color or motion, so that I can identify it, though it is not where I take it to be. We might call this *lucky seeing*: I am lucky that I see the object, but although the *way* I see it is highly improbable, the causal connection between it and me is close enough to normal to permit our saying (for instance) that I got a lucky glimpse. The process by which the object produces my experience is one that only luckily occurs; but *given* all the variables in place when it occurs, it is not by luck that I see it. I see it just as I would in a stationary mirror that I control and am accustomed to using to see around corners. This is a kind of genuine though indirect seeing.

The kind of reliability we have been considering might be called *identificational reliability*. It is a matter of whether the process by which the object (appropriately) produces the relevant sense-experience conveys the object's properties with sufficient accuracy for that experience to count as seeing, hearing, etc., where we can (in principle) refer to the object in relation to *some* property of it. One reason to speak of identificational reliability here is that we can rely on the experience to give us the information that there is something there, even if we can know little about it. This is, to be sure, *minimal* identification, as opposed to the usual cases with familiar kinds of objects in which we identify them as something in particular.

One might think we can be in a position in which we can know nothing about an object we see—being mistaken in *any* property-ascription we can make regarding it (at least any we are disposed to make). We need not, for example, see it by seeing any particular property of it. One reason to think this is that we can refer to a thing when all our beliefs—at least all our *de dicto* (roughly, propositional) beliefs—about it are false, as on direct reference theories of proper names. Recall the aeronautic example. On a direct reference theory, I can be wrong about the size, speed, color, and shape of the plane and still see it. But if I see it, I must at least be discriminatively sensitive to *some* property of it, even if only a relational property such as that it is changing location relative to surrounding clouds. I need not *believe* any such thing. I can be mistaken in all my beliefs that are "directly" about it; but without a visual thread connecting me to it which *can* yield knowledge or at least belief about it, I do not see it. This is parallel to the point that, even if all my beliefs "directly" about, say, Homer, are false, I *could* know that Homer is the person spoken about by (for instance) T. S. Eliot in a certain place. If perception is factive and connects us with reality in the way it appears to, perceptual knowledge will be possible, even if it never arises.

There is, however, another dimension of perceptual reliability. Here the question is not the reliability with which, for a perceiver to see or otherwise perceive it, an object must produce some phenomenal representation in the perceiver, but rather the reliability of sensory representations in correctly identifying properties of the object. This dimension of perceptual reliability is roughly the probability that an object has a property, *F*, given the process by which, in the circumstances, the object produces a sense-experience representing it as being *F*. Suppose there is a fog and I easily make out the plane through it, but in most cases of a plane of that kind under these conditions it would be obscured by clouds and I would not make it out. This might be lucky seeing: I am lucky to see it, but, given my seeing it, would not be lucky to have the true belief that it is before me, and I can visually know something about it. Now suppose that I see the plane as blue and thereby believe that it is blue (which it is), but that it is rare for the color of a plane like this to show through a fog of this kind and I have hit upon a scarcely darkened spot. Lucky seeing is now combined with lucky accuracy: I am lucky to have believed it to be blue when I saw only a dark color. Here my belief is like a guess and does not seem to be a case of knowledge. We might say here that relative to the property in question, being blue, the perception lacks *representational reliability* (though this might not hold given further specification of the case, e.g. the addition of sunlight on the plane coming through a break in the clouds). I might, however, know it to be moving westward. Relative to movement, the perception is representationally reliable. This is also a kind of *epistemic reliability*, the kind needed for the basis of a true belief to be such as to render it knowledge. The difference is roughly this: one kind of reliable process is needed for us to see the object at all; another kind is needed to see it *well enough* to go significantly beyond mere identification. This difference is related to that between conditions for reliable reference and those for reliable predication. Both are important achievements made possible by perceptions.

II. Four Structurally Distinct Cases of Visual Perception

Vision is an especially good focus in the epistemology of perception because of how much information it typically provides. This, in turn, may be partly owing to its uniqueness among the senses in the way it registers, in a kind of constitutive way, both primary and secondary qualities.[9] By this I mean that both kinds, say shape and color, are characteristically presented in seeing. The object seen appears as, e.g., shaped and colored, with determinates of these represented, say being square and blue. Touch might indicate the secondary quality heat as well as, e.g., hardness and shape, but in its normal functioning it need not yield either any shape perception, as is typical of visual experience, or an apparent temperature.

Compare tasting and smelling. These do not by their nature present any primary quality, nor are these presented by the mere presentation of a primary quality.[10] Touching a rose might cause one to have a sense of its distinctive odor, as smelling it might cause one to have a sense of its shape; but this is perhaps by way of some association, and it contrasts markedly with the way in which the flowery shape qualities of the rose are presented to touch. Similarly, hearing a bell represents the primary qualities, such as being metallic, indirectly: by the character of the sound as an indication of metal, whereas, in seeing, colors and shapes are presented in a direct way. Granted, seeing a colored object need provide no sense of a *particular* shape. Imagine awakening in a global chamber with its entire interior surface seamlessly painted green. There need be no sense of a particular shape, since no borders or discontinuities would be present. But extension is still represented. Shape would be too if a patch with determinate borders were blackened.

There are apparently four (structurally) basic cases of seeing. In calling these basic, I am not implying that they are in no sense analyzable. My point is that none of the four is reducible to any other or some combination of them, though (as will be explained) this is compatible

9. I offer no account of the distinction between primary and secondary qualities and simply presuppose the usual inclusion of certain ones on each list. A historically informed treatment that adds clarity is Simmons (2017).

10. This is compatible with holding that if there *is* nothing tasted or smelled then one is having a merely sensory experience.

with some of them being required for others, and in that sense *more* basic in the order of perceptual kinds, than others.

The first three factive cases are seeing *an object*; seeing an object *to have a property*, say seeing a rose to be yellow; and seeing *that* some fact holds (say, that some "observation" proposition holds), for instance that a rose is swaying in the wind. I call these *simple perception*, *attributive* (or *predicative*) *perception*, and *propositional perception*.[11] These are all factive in the following ways. First, our seeing an object, *x* (having an "object perception," in some terminologies), entails the existence of *x*: there *is* in fact an *x* that we see; this is *referential* factivity. It might also be called veridicality (at least where there is no illusion or comparably distorted impression). Secondly, if we see *x* to be silver-grey, there is an *x* we see *and it is sliver-grey*; this also illustrates *attributive* factivity (we could also call this kind of factivity *objectual* to avoid the unwarranted suggestion that there need be any mental act of attribution). Thirdly, if we *see that x* is sliver-grey, that proposition is true (equivalently, it is a fact that *x* is silver-grey); this is *propositional* factivity. Normally, we also *know that* the proposition holds. This last point may be plausibly taken to illustrate that propositional perception exhibits another important kind of reliability in perception, a kind that simple perception, as we have seen, need not have: a kind of *attributive representational reliability*.

These points about the factivity of perception are apparently conceptual, though their status is obscured if we do not set aside such phenomena as "seeing stars" when the head is struck or "seeing snakes" in cases where they inhabit the hallucinatory visual field of an alcoholic with *delirium tremens*. It also seems to be a conceptual truth that seeing is *hierarchical* in this sense: seeing that *x* is *F* (where *F* is a perceptible property) entails seeing *x* to be *F*, and that in turn entails seeing *x* simpliciter. The converse entailments apparently do not hold. Even if one can see a thing only *by* seeing some property of it, say *F*, one need not see it to be *F* (at least in cases requiring a concept of being *F*). Moreover, one can see a thing to be *F*, say see a ship's hull to be black, without seeing that (hence believing that) the hull is *F*. Propositional perception requires conceptualizing of the object (beyond conceiving of it as the thing that is *F*), something not needed for simply seeing it to have a property.[12] Idiom easily obscures this point. We can loosely say of

11. Here and in discussing perception in some other parts of the chapter, I draw on (but also refine) ch. 1 of my 2010 and later work, including 2013a.

12. It is not self-evident that seeing *x* by seeing its *F*-ness does not entail seeing it to be *F*, but if we grant that it *positions* one to see it to be *F*, we may then plausibly claim that whereas seeing *x* by seeing its *F*-ness requires somehow

a prelingual toddler with no concept of electricity that she sees that an electrical box is smoking when our meaning is that she sees it (which she could refer to only pointing at it) to be smoking.

A fourth case we must consider is seeing *as*. This is a hybrid: in perceptual uses—as opposed to intellectual cases in which 'see' is equivalent to 'view' in its descriptive uses—seeing *as* is factive as to what is seen, but not regarding what it is seen *as*. It is, then, referentially factive but, by contrast with seeing to be, not predicatively factive. Using structural language, we might say that, as in the case of simple seeing, the position of 'x' in 'S sees x as F' is referentially transparent (and so not under a veil of intensionality), so that if $x = y$, then seeing x as F is (in part) seeing y; but the position of 'F' in 'S sees x as F' is neither factive nor transparent. In this second way, seeing *as* is like seeing *to be* in the non-transparency of the predicate position. Seeing someone as rushing toward one does not entail that the person is doing so. Here aspectual seeing is not factive, and similarly, neither seeing something as circular nor seeing it to be circular entails seeing it as having the shape of a figure whose circumference is pi times its diameter, even if these properties should be equivalent. Both aspectual seeing and attributive seeing exhibit non-transparency. One reason for this is that not all who have the concept of a circle believe that the circumference of circles is pi times their diameter. Seeing a shape to be circular entails its obeying the theorem, but does not entail one's *seeing* or believing it to obey it. Granted, someone might in such a case infer, from properties of the shape we see, that it has the property entailed by the theorem, but I am conceiving perception as non-inferential (I will return to this issue.)

Seeing *as* is not always a matter of seeing something as having a property, such as being circular. One can also see something as identical with or as an instance of another kind of thing. In Shakespeare's *A Midsummer Night's Dream* we find, in a passage about the work of the imagination in influencing aspectual seeing:

> Such tricks has strong imagination
> That . . . in the night, imagining some fear,
> How easy is a bush supposed a bear.
>
> (*A Midsummer Night's Dream,* act 5, scene 1)

responding to the property, F, seeing x *to be* F requires more, at least if the seeing is conceptual, since that entails conceptualizing F in some way. If it is not conceptual, it entails at least attributing F-ness, where this attribution requires a kind of focal consciousness of F, even if not any attributive event.

Here the perceiver is represented as seeing a bush and also seeing it *as a bear*. One might take this as a matter of seeing the bush as having the property of being a bear, but the most natural description of the case calls for describing it as one of seeing it as *a bear* or, equivalently, visually taking it to be a bear. Neither locution presupposes believing that there is a bear before one, though that might be natural here.

It should be clarifying to indicate how we might construe certain camouflage cases. You might look right at a haystack in which a stock-still hen is directly before you. If you are looking for it, you might come away saying you did not see it. Here 'see' can have roughly the sense of 'notice'. But clearly you have an experience that represents the hen—though you do not see the hen *as* such. You would, however, notice it if it moved; you see the spot it occupies to be a bespeckled brown; and if you were to draw exactly what you see, you would accurately draw the hen except for indicating its borders with the surrounding hay. On the first count, given your ability to see various movements the hen may make, you have a discriminative *responsiveness* to it, though you do not *discriminate* it from its environment, which explains why you do not notice it. On the second count, you discern certain of its properties, since you see it (as the relevant area in the haystack) to be a bespeckled brown; and on the third, in being able to draw it accurately, your "perceptual content," at least given adequate attention, exhibits a correct and highly detailed representation of the hen apart from its borders—unless perhaps you see them simply *as* part of the pattern(s) you discern in a large part of the haystack you see.

The case seems, then, to be one of simple seeing with only limited predicative seeing, without propositional seeing (at least without seeing that there is a hen), and without aspectual hen-seeing: seeing the hen as such. There is even potential noticing; one would tend to notice (in the relevant area) the same changes that one would notice if one did see the hen as such. Given these points, I do not believe we should take the basic cases of simply seeing to require actual noticing.[13] It may be best to recognize differences in judgment on the applicability of 'see' in such cases and note that my point could be applied to seeing simpliciter as opposed to what we might call *delineational seeing* or perhaps *segmentational* seeing. I am inclined to hold that seeing as such

13. The hen case is drawn from Maddy (1980: 171). She there seems content to say that in a "strict sense" one does not see the hen. More extensive discussion of such cases is provided by Siegel (2006). See also Tye (2010).

need not be delineational, even if there are kinds of things, such as shadows, that can be seen only delineationally.[14]

In the light of these examples, let us look more closely at the metaphysical question of the representationality of perception.

III. The Representational Character of Perception

It is widely assumed that, as our examples illustrate, perception is in *some* sense representational. This view needs analysis. If perception is indeed factive in the ways illustrated, the natural assumption would be that it represents its object: the thing that is (for instance) seen and seen to have some property, or heard and heard to have some property. The perceiver may also see *that* it has a property. Perceptual representationality is confirmed by the functional dependence—a kind of discriminative dependence—of the phenomenal element on the object perceived. Normally, if someone approaches us head on, our visual impressions vary accordingly; and if leaves are burning nearby, our olfactory sensations intensify as the wind brings the smoke toward us and wane as it angles off. The sensory elements I refer to are phenomenal and are the main determinants of what the perceptual experiences in question "are like."[15] But we should not infer that we see observable properties of objects by *seeing* corresponding phenomenal properties (as opposed to having them). "Outer seeing" is not a kind of inner seeing and does not entail it.

I assume here that in everyday perception we see physical properties. It is natural, moreover, to think that seeing (or otherwise perceiving) a physical property entails seeing an object that has it. But what of seeing a flash of light in empty space? Must we consider some chunk of space to be an "object"? This is not incoherent, but it may be useful

14. For detailed discussion of such fascinating cases see Sorensen (2018) and (2008). The former takes up the role of photographability in perception. Space does not permit discussion of the many "perceptual ephemera" a fully comprehensive account of perception should provide, but much valuable discussion is provided by Crowther and Cumhaill (2018).

15. The sense in which phenomenal properties are representational seems to presuppose understanding the representationality of physical properties. I have anyway assumed that we may describe the former as if we had some kind of acquaintance with the latter. If a Cartesian demon world is possible, we must take such acquaintance to be possible in the absence of physical objects instantiating the properties. This possibility seems real, but is controversial.

to compare such seeing with, for instance, smelling the scent of roses when none are nearby (or even exist). Must this be hallucination? That seems doubtful—at least if, as is usual, 'hallucination' implies visual sensory or perceptual abnormality, even if we are hard pressed to determine what (if anything) has the scent when there are no roses suitably near. If I alone had such experiences under circumstances in which it would be normal for others to have them—as where you are looking toward the same patch of space or sniffing the same air—I might take myself to be hallucinating or somehow deluded. But it does not follow that I am. I could be seeing what for some reason others cannot. This illustrates the kinds of possibilities skeptics are fond of pointing out. In both cases, however, even skeptics tend to grant that if perception is indeed occurring, it is relational and factive.

What the flash case shows is that the physical (as with a light beam) need not be material (in any natural sense). This distinction raises difficult metaphysical questions we need not settle here.[16] What we need to see now is that on the sketch of representationality so far provided, seeing physical properties entails *instantiating* certain phenomenal properties. We *see* color and shape, as opposed to merely acquiring knowledge of the presence of them, when the entity having those properties causes us (in a certain way) to have visual experiences in which appropriately corresponding phenomenal properties are instantiated in us (or anyway by us). In basic cases of seeing, these properties represent to us how the object looks. In non-basic cases such as seeing anger or wrongdoing, the object of perception is represented by virtue of the representation of the crucially indicative properties.[17]

In speaking of the phenomenal properties "corresponding" to the physical ones seen, I am leaving open whether there is a sense in which, say, phenomenal red is conceptually or in some other way prior to physical red. I do not doubt that, developmentally, sensorily encountering physical properties is needed for instantiating the phenomenal properties we think of as corresponding to them, in the way

16. Presumably a region of physical space can instantiate the quality of flashing, and we can then develop either a trope-theoretic account of the object of perception or defend construing spatial regions as non-material physical objects. Ontological aspects of sense-experience are considered further in ch. 3.

17. How this higher-level representation takes place without being pictorial is explained in my 2013, esp. chs. 2 and 3. For a related and extensive treatment of the role of phenomenal properties in perception see Smithies (2019).

being appeared to redly corresponds to the red of an apple, or feeling smooth corresponds to the smooth surface of a windowpane. My main epistemological purposes do not require settling these difficult conceptual and semantic issues, and I leave open plausible views of both. On any such view, a central element will be the functional dependence that is crucial for the phenomenal properties to play the representational roles they do.

Phenomenal properties are, in various ways illustrated so far, important for understanding challenges in both the philosophy of mind and epistemology, for instance regarding the basis and status of our beliefs ascribing such properties to ourselves. Given the widely recognized representationality of perception and given the typically rich information apparently provided by phenomenal properties, it has become common to speak of both perceptual representation and phenomenal properties in terms of perceptual "content."[18] This terminology needs—and will receive in later chapters—more clarification than (so far as I can tell) it has received in recent philosophical work on perception.

Perception is experiential, relational, and representational. In broad terms, it is a phenomenally representational, discriminative, nondeviant causal relation to an object. In seeing, we have visual experience; in visual experience that is perceptual and not merely sensory, as with hallucinations, some object is visually represented as having certain properties; and genuinely seeing that object entails that it exists. Given its relational element, this view of perception is a version of realism. It is realistic both about the objects of perception and about the phenomenal properties we instantiate in perceptual experience. This is not to say that the view entails a philosophy of mind embodying an irreducibly mentalist conception of phenomenal properties; it leaves open their ultimate ontological status. Those properties, however, must be understood to have a character that enables us both to experience what, phenomenologically, it is like to see and what, externally, the things seen are like physically. Perception, perhaps most clearly with seeing, has a kind of content. Visual content is our next main topic.

18. Much detailed discussion of such content is provided by Susanna Siegel in *The Contents of Visual Experience* (2010) and in *The Rationality of Perception* (2017b). The notion is also treated in many of the papers in Matthen (2015).

2

DIMENSIONS OF PERCEPTUAL CONTENT

The notion of perceptual content is not an everyday one, but philosophers have found it important for discussing perception. Is there a non-technical point of departure? We understand the notion of the contents of ordinary containers such as boxes and bureaus, briefcases and barrels. On the semantic side, we understand 'the contents of sentences', and similarly for paragraphs, even whole articles. Here contents are, roughly, what they say. (This is rough because an article may also contain diagrams and pictures, and because there is a question whether certain propositions not asserted in an article but self-evidently entailed by what is clearly asserted in it are also part of its contents.) But, especially because perception is a relation, we are entitled to be puzzled by the idea of its contents. Do we even conceive relations as having content, as opposed to elements ("terms")? Might the contents of a relation, such as *taller than*, include its terms, say a spruce and a dogwood? We can so stipulate, but, at least for perception, say for a person's seeing an object *x*, that seems ad hoc, especially since only one term, the object, would be an eligible candidate for the content of the relation. We can, however, speak of what is *in* an experience, and this is perhaps how the idea of speaking of the content of perceptual experience can seem natural. Let us explore it.

I. Three Categories of Perceptual Content

Suppose I see a rose in the garden. I might be said to be having a visual experience *of* a rose, and the rose might be said to be something *in* my experience of the garden. But should we call the rose itself the content

Seeing, Knowing, and Doing. Robert Audi, Oxford University Press (2020). © Oxford University Press.
DOI: 10.1093/oso/9780197503508.001.0001

or part of the content of my experience? Or is it preferable to say that the content is simply a *representation* of that flower? Are the *properties* I see the rose to have that content, or part of it? Does the *proposition* that the rose is yellow and swaying in the wind (if I see this color and movement) belong to the content? Are all of these elements together the content?

Cases like this call for an element of stipulation, particularly given the diversity of philosophical terminology regarding content. A reasonable constraint here is that, at least if content is mainly or wholly a matter of what a perceptual experience represents to the perceiver, then its content in one important sense should be the same as that of any sense-experience qualitatively identical with it. It would then in one clear sense represent the same thing to the subject. This is why Shakespeare's Macbeth might have reached for the dagger he hallucinated and expected to have the tactual sensations normal for grasping a dagger. Behavior can be produced in this way by such experiences even apart from their having no external object. This is one reason to approach content—of one kind, at least—in the light of this constraint.

Many philosophers talk as if perceptual content is propositional, though there are differences in the way they conceive propositions.[1] Perhaps the only uncontroversial point here is that if we see a thing, *x*, by seeing a property *F* that it has, such as being green, then it is true that *x* is *F* and also that we are in a good position to have perceptual knowledge that it is *F*, in which case we must have some concept of *being F*. But, secondly, even if we see *x* by seeing its *F*-ness, we need not know or believe that it is *F*. Indeed, just seeing (hearing, etc.) *x* by seeing some property of it does not entail even being a 'conceptual' agent, much less exercising a concept in the way required by *x*'s figuring as such in a (*de dicto*) belief we form about it.

This second point implies that perceivers need not understand or even have the capacity to understand the content of their perceptions as construed propositionally and that, thirdly, where they can understand such content, they need not believe any proposition corresponding

1. See, e.g., Siegel (2010: 28–30) and related parts of (2017a) and (2017b); and Speaks (2015), whose view is that "the contents of visual experiences are Russellian propositions" (p. 76), as they might perhaps be for D. Sosa (2011a): "[I]t's because your visual state is *about* Booker [the book you see] that the content of that state is that Booker is bound" (p. 482). A different propositionalist view—on which 'to see' is intensional—is proposed by Brogaard (2017: 55–72).

to or constituting one of the contents.[2] The second point indicates a puzzle: how a proposition can be in one's experience without one's having even a capacity to understand it. Would this possibility be like having in mind a sentence one cannot understand? Or is it better conceived as experiencing something *describable* by a proposition one cannot understand? This seems the better conception, in which case the possibility adds nothing not implicit in plausible non-propositional views of perception: we can certainly see things (truly) describable by propositions we cannot understand. A small child could see a parent's embarrassment but be unable to conceptualize it.

The second point—that perception does not entail the ability to understand all the propositions that express its propositional content—may receive some confirmation from the fact that sense-perceptions are not properly called true or false, as propositions are, and as are propositional attitudes, such as beliefs, that have truth-valued contents as objects. Beliefs are called true or false derivatively from the truth value of the propositions that are their content. Perceptions are not called true or false (at least in the same way). It appears, moreover, that just seeing a thing does not entail seeing *that* it has a property. Contrary to an apparent commitment of the propositional view of content, then, even a perception with propositional content—such as a simple perception—need not be a propositional perception. (This matter will be considered further in relation to "seeing is believing.")

It seems preferable and most plausible to say that if we seek to make theoretical use of the notion of the content of a simple perception (the most basic case of perception), then we should probably view its content as constituted by all the properties phenomenally represented in the perceptual experience—or (if this is different) at least in the sense-experience that is embodied in the perception. This makes good sense of the idea that the content of an experience is *in* it, since these properties at least partly determine what it is like to see the object. Moreover, we can still say that the experience has a *corresponding* "propositional content" and that this content is *accessible* to a perceiver with

2. This might be thought not to apply to Russellian propositions, comprising (in these cases) mainly the object perceived and the property in question. But here it seems that believing such a proposition comes to no more than believing the object *to have* the property. If believing the Russellian proposition comes to this, it is not by itself true or false, but rather adequate or inadequate to the object, depending on whether or not the property it predicates is *true of it*. This much seems correct.

adequate conceptual capacity. This correspondence is significant and may capture much of the motivation for construing the content of perception propositionally. Given conceptual adequacy for understanding the propositions in question, *S* can form beliefs ascribing one or more of the properties constituting the representational property content, and normally a subset of these can constitute perceptual knowledge.

In any case, we can distinguish several elements in perception that might be considered contentual. One element might naturally be described as follows. For a perceptual experience, we might call the perceived object its *object content*—this would be a kind of external content but is "in" the experience, provided this experience is conceived as relational. This parlance is analogous to speaking of experiences in the light of presupposing their entailing a relation to something external, such as an advancing tornado: if we see it, it is in, and in *that* way a content of, our experience.

There is, however, an unfortunate consequence of calling the perceived object a content of the experience. Suppose I am viewing a dogwood when a machine wired to my brain causes me to hallucinate precisely that tree just as a second machine blocks any perception of it. I will have no sense of a change at all, yet we would have to say that the content of my visual experience has changed. Similarly, if two people view exactly similar balls under the same conditions, then although their experiences might be qualitatively identical phenomenologically, they would differ in "content" owing to their different objects. Intuitively, this is not a difference in what it is natural to call the content of their perceptual experiences—conceived as *in* them and phenomenally represented—but in the objects they see: in the objects of their perceptions, what their experiences are externally *of.* They would not describe their experiences differently, even if they were answering, e.g., 'Describe the content of your perception' and were entirely accurate regarding what, in a purely visual way, they are acquainted with. Moreover, if we assume, plausibly, that a qualitatively identical hallucinatory experience has the same content as their perceptions, then again the object view of content has what seems an implausible result: intuitively, content is in what possesses it, not something external to it to which it bears a relation. Given that 'content of perception' is a philosophers' term, we may simply call such "object content" external and distinguish it from the other kinds noted here.

A more plausible notion of perceptual content is suggested by the point that we do not perceive an object without perceiving some property of it and in typical cases of seeing we perceive a number of properties.

Call the perceived properties of it the *minimal property content* of the perceptual experience.[3] We might then speak of the *propositional content* of the experience in reference to the property-ascriptive propositions that, given adequate concepts, the perceiver can, under normal conditions, perceptually know (non-inferentially) on the basis of the perception. The reference to concepts is necessary on the plausible assumption that one cannot know that *x* is *F* without having a concept of being *F* (and some concept under which one can have *x* appropriately "in mind"). If we abstract from conceptual capacity, then the *total* propositional content of a perceptual experience will be both all of the propositions ascribing to the relevant object(s) some set of properties presented to the perceiver—call this set the *presentational property content.* Call the set of propositions entailed by the instantiation of those properties (an infinite set given a broad notion of a property) the *full propositional content* (an idealized notion inapplicable to finite beings).[4]

This terminology can mislead if we do not take account of a difference between representational and propositional content. The former, but not the latter, is *phenomenally actual*: if my perception of a wooden railing has the railing's supporting dowels in its content, I will have a visual experience (with a visually representational content)—being appeared to "dowelly"—whereas corresponding propositional content, e.g. *that* the railing is supported by dowels, is phenomenally actual only if the proposition(s) in question are present in consciousness, as when occurrently believed. In the former case, no additional experience, such as a propositional thought (e.g., *there must be two dozen dowels there*) is required for my visual experience of the railing to have this dowelly phenomenal content. There is, to be sure, a *path* from visual representation of properties seen to occurrent beliefs whose propositional objects

3. This is the minimal property content because there can be properties represented in a perceptual experience that do not belong to the object—ranging from the ellipticality that the mouth of a glass can seem to have when viewed from an angle to the properties of a hallucinated face of a rival of a distraught man, which he might "see" in the middle of an abstract painting he is actually seeing. We might term the set of all the properties represented (phenomenally as opposed to intellectively) in a perceptual experience its *full* property content. A further distinction is between what is basically represented (the ellipticality) and what is non-basically represented—the roundness, which, for those whose vision "corrects" for angular distortion, is seen through visually experiencing "elliptically."

4. This implication apparently accounts for Hagaman's conception of perceptual content in its widest sense (2015).

encompass (some of) the phenomenal content visually represented (where *occurrent* belief does require instantiating some phenomenal property). Perception in itself, however, does not require our traversing that path. We can see the dowels supporting a railing without believing, or even having the propositional thought, that it is dowel-supported.

Seeing the dowels in a railing is much like seeing a speckled hen—a case much discussed since Chisholm brought it to prominence.[5] We can have twenty dowels in our visual field even in a glance, but of course we need not see the railing *as* having twenty dowels, any more than one need see a speckled hen one views (even delineationally) as having (say) thirty speckles. In principle, if our visual impression were unchanging during an attempt to count, we might make an accurate count. But can it be unchanging in normal cases? And if it can be, can we know that it is, given the possibility of unnoticed change? Surely it can in principle be unchanging; we could even have evidence of an unchanging visual state over a period of time given sufficient knowledge of the brain and on the assumption that phenomenal properties are strongly enough correlated with identifiable brain properties. The important philosophical point here is that a property, such as unchanging shapes, can be visually present without being seen as the property it is. Evidence for this is our discriminative sensitivity to changes of even minor kinds. If, e.g., a dowel disappeared from my visual impression of twenty in a row, I might notice that change (or some gap) even if I had not focused on that particular dowel. Such sensitivity is even possible at the level of sense-experience that occurs in hallucination.

Using this terminology, we can now say that the *presentational property content* of a visual experience, even if hallucinatory, can be the same as that of a perception embodying the relevant sense-experience. A similar point applies to other perceptual modes: tactile, gustatory, auditory, and olfactory. But whereas a significant proportion of the corresponding propositions—those ascribing the relevant properties to an object—will be true where there is an actual perception, they need not be true for sense-experiences not embodied in perceptions. We can also say that the phenomenal content of a perceptual experience is the presentational property content of the embodied sense-experience. There are of course further discriminations to be made regarding content, but these should suffice for our purposes here.

5. See Chisholm (1942). For a detailed contemporary discussion see D. Sosa (2011b: 297–99); Smithies (2019, esp. ch. 10 on luminosity); and Pace (2017).

This presentationalist sketch of an intuitive notion of content contrasts with an intentionalist one. If we take intentionalism to be the view that the phenomenal content of a perception is determined by its intentional content, where that is a kind of propositional content, then intentionalism invites one to think of propositional "information" received as more basic than properties phenomenally presented. Presentationalist views tends to go in the other direction. The former emphasis may derive from the idea that perceptual content is constituted by Russellian propositions.[6] Let us explore this idea.

II. Singular Reference and the Possible Role of Russellian Propositions

Singular reference is a special challenge. It occurs in expressions of *de dicto* beliefs, given that they can be about particular objects, and in their propositional objects (or at least in uses of sentences expressing such propositions). Perhaps in part to accommodate both singular reference and the intuitive idea that propositions are true or false, Russell posited what are now called "Russellian propositions." He was apparently motivated by the principle of acquaintance: "Every proposition which we can understand must be composed wholly of constituents with which we are acquainted."[7] As usually conceived, Russellian propositions are "structured, abstract entities capable of being true or false. They all contain properties or relations, and some contain particulars."[8] (These "particular propositions" are now commonly called *singular.*) Many writers have had no difficulty treating these entities as propositions in the usual sense requiring truth value and other properties commonly attributed to propositions. They are especially likely to seem a plausible posit for hybrid cases describable only using both *de re* and *de dicto* constructions. A dance student might believe, *of* the instructor, *that* he is the world's most elegant dancer. The *de re* 'of' indicates the believer's having contact,

6. Speaks, op. cit., has already been quoted as apparently holding this view of content (as do many recent writers on perception). He also apparently endorses the supervenience view that "necessarily, any subjects which differ in their phenomenal properties also differ in their representational properties" (p. 21), but this plausible point leaves open the order of determination (if any).

7. Russell ([1912] 1959: 58). Acquaintance is a direct relation we have to our sense-data, to universals, and possibly to ourselves (46–52).

8. Bach (2010: 41).

perhaps ultimately perceptual, with the instructor, and the that-clause indicates something truth-valued.

An important connection between Russellian propositions and perception is readily captured by our terminology. Given property content as determined by the properties represented in a perception, it is obvious that the perceiver is in a position to believe (and is commonly disposed to believe) the object to be *F, G*, and so forth for the properties represented. Believing an object *to have* a property is equivalent to the minimal case of believing a Russellian proposition: though we refer to the proposition using a that-clause, the term for the perceived object is referential and non-conceptual. It is this object that figures in the Russellian proposition, not, as is usual when we attribute propositional beliefs, the object as conceived a particular way, say as the dance instructor. I could believe Juan to be doing the world's most elegant dancing without my having any inkling *that* he is the dance instructor. I would thus believe the same Russellian proposition believed by someone who does realize this. Our perceptions of the instructor, then, have the same Russellian propositional content.

Is it not, however, at best misleading to call something that "contains" a particular object—such as a tree one is viewing—a proposition, especially if one takes propositions to be abstract entities of a kind that can be "before the mind" when the believer is not in contact with any concrete entity?[9] To see the problem, consider propositions somewhat pretheoretically. Perhaps the most important properties of propositions, at least from the point of view of understanding their role in belief and communication, are these: 1. being bearers of truth value (they are usually considered its basic bearers); 2. being "objects"—contents, in a related terminology—of propositional attitudes, paradigmatically beliefs, but also judgments, expectations, doubts, fears, and other attitudes; 3. being terms of entailment relations; 4. being intersubjectively accessible, in the sense that two or more persons can consider, believe, affirm, etc., the same one; 5. being inferable from one or more entities of the same kind—roughly, being terms of (non-psychological) inferential relations such as evidential support;[10] 6. being expressible in principle by

9. Granted, sets are abstract, but a set of concrete objects (as opposed to a concept of such a set) is not abstract in the way propositions are conceived to be when they are taken to be about such abstracta as numbers and universals.

10. We can speak of one belief as inferentially based on another, but this does not undermine the view that it is a proposition that is inferred when, e.g., we conclude that *p* on the basis of premises for it. In any case, entailment and probabilification are the central cases of inferential cases in question here.

declarative sentences (at least in an infinitely rich language); 7. being intensional entities, in the sense that extensional equivalence is not sufficient for identity; 8. being finely individuated, in a sense implying that even necessary equivalence of propositions does not imply their identity; and 9. being at least the main basis of identity and individuation for *de dicto* beliefs and other propositional attitudes (a property related, in a complex way, to 2.).[11]

Which of these properties is plausibly attributed to Russellian propositions? Regarding truth value, if the copperbeach I am viewing is dense, then *that the copperbeach is dense* is plausibly called true. I can also believe this, as you can—if you can have the same proposition in mind. Can you have the same one in mind if you have no acquaintance with the tree? Here we can see that 'in', as used for having a proposition in mind, does not imply a spatial relation and allows for *indirect acquaintance.* You can have the tree in mind provided you have an appropriate connection with it—say by thinking of it as the one I have described to you, where you have a direct acquaintance with me and correctly presuppose that I am directly acquainted with the tree.

Suppose we accept the above points about how Russellian propositions can play some of the usual roles attributed to propositions. How are we to conceive Russellian propositions as terms of entailment relations? That this tree is dense entails that it has foliage. Does that entailment relation hold in all possible worlds? Since Russellian propositions contain contingent particulars, they do not exist in all possible worlds. The answer is presumably that the entailment relation holds in all possible worlds in which the propositions exist; hence there can be no world in which the first is true and the second false. If, however, propositions are abstract entities, there seems no good reason why they should not exist in any possible world, and it seems natural to think that ("pure") abstracta exist in all possible worlds if at all. Even apart from this, moreover, Russellian propositions would not be believable in worlds in which they do not exist. In such a world one could believe that if there are copperbeaches, they have dense foliage, since this is

11. More detailed characterizations of propositions are found in King, Soames, and Speaks (2014), in which each presents an account of propositions and a critical study of the others' account of them. This volume, as well as those cited by Crane (2013), also deal in several places with the special case of indexicals. Crane, e.g., says, "What is believed or hoped is *that something is the case* and *that something is the case* is a proposition . . . an object of thought" (p. 91).

(presumably) about universals, but could not have a belief that is about copperbeaches themselves. Relative to an existential understanding of 'about', this seems acceptable.

We can now see how further properties of propositions may be seen to belong to Russellian propositions. One might think that intersubjective accessibility cannot belong to them. But it can *for* those with an acquaintance with the relevant particular. As Russell might say, why *should* one have access to a proposition with a constituent one is in no way (even indirectly) acquainted with? Similarly, one can infer that the tree has foliage from the proposition that it is dense, provided one has the appropriate acquaintance. As to expressibility in a language, this is at least no more a problem for a Russellian conception of propositions than for any other conception of them: one must simply assume that the language in question *can* be used to say something about the relevant object(s). Given the usability in principle of an infinite language in any world, the expressibility condition seems fulfillable.

It is with intensionality that the difference between the Russellian conception of propositions and other conceptions is apparently greatest. The point is not that Russellian propositions are extensional entities. This is not so. Consider my "Russellian" belief that the copperbeach I am viewing is dense; although the position of 'the copperbeach' in a Russellian representation of this belief is extensional, that of 'dense' is not. Even 'having enough leaves to block sunlight' cannot be substituted without yielding a different Russellian proposition (since these predicates are not even necessarily equivalent—a spruce has no leaves but can be dense). Russellians can leave open, as can others, whether sameness of proposition requires, for singular propositions, synonymy of the relevant predicates or something weaker, say expressing the same property or a necessarily equivalent one, but it is not plausible to treat the predicative elements (what he called universals) extensionally.

In exploring the relation between perception and belief, then, I assume that the clearest way to approach the territory will be to use *de re* locutions to describe what some might think of as Russellian beliefs and *de dicto* locutions where we have in mind propositions of the sort that meet the nine conditions described above. Rather than say that the contents of perceptions are Russellian propositions, we can understand perceptual content in terms of properties represented in it and simply note that seeing *x as F* implies believing the Russellian proposition that *x* is *F* (at least for perceivers possessing concept of *F*) and leave open whether that is implied by simply seeing *x*. The next section provides some reason to doubt that we should accept that implication.

III. Perception and Belief: Cognitive and Conceptual Aspects

Many of us have heard such challenges as 'I don't believe you; show me'. These indicate the appositeness, in certain contexts, of "Seeing is believing." Indeed, if asked what we believe about the room we are in, we are likely to look around, as if our main beliefs about it will be visual or, at least, our visual beliefs are what is called for in the context. Normally we must "believe our eyes," which is why "I couldn't believe my eyes" often indicates astonishment, since we normally cannot help believing them in the kinds of contexts in question.

These and other common elements in everyday parlance can make it seem that, for *every* property clearly discernible in our visual field, we at least normally believe that something has that property: being green, tall, swaying, etc. The idea is that at least prominent visual contents of seeing produce corresponding beliefs.[12] Indeed, if we set out to determine what we believe while looking around us, then as objects come into view—a chair here, a window there, a moulding above—we may believe that they are around us, have certain colors, shapes, positions, and so forth for what is visually obvious. But there are many things we come to believe the moment we think of them that we need not have previously believed. The idea that contents of seeing entail corresponding beliefs is perhaps made more plausible (though it is not entailed) by a propositional view of perceptual content—one I have suggested is at best puzzling, particularly if seeing is not taken to entail noticing.

On my view, seeing a property may normally produce a disposition to believe that something has it (or at least to believe something *to have* it), but it need not produce a dispositional belief, much less an occurrent one, to this effect. It seems to be only under certain conditions that seeing entails (propositional) believing. Apparently, it is chiefly where what is seen has some significance for, or history with, the perceiver that seeing a property of the thing produces the corresponding property-ascriptive belief.[13] Granted, one could, on seeing an airplane

12. Fodor and Pylyshyn suggest something similar when they write, "Suppose that last Tuesday you saw a butterfly between your house and the one next door. Doing so adds a cluster (in fact quite a large cluster) of new beliefs . . . I saw a butterfly . . . there was a butterfly visible from my house yesterday . . . the total of my lifetime butterfly sightings has increased by one . . . and so on and on" (2015: 54).

13. For a case supporting this distinction see my 1994. For discussion of how a perceiver's history affects a kind of perceptual selectivity—a phenomenon distinct from cognitive penetration—see Orlandi (2014, e.g. 151–61).

in the sky, believe *it* to be moving westward, without believing a *proposition* expressing that fact; and doubtless such ascriptive beliefs are commonly formed where propositional counterparts of them are not. But why must seeing the plane in a way that licenses believing this proposition actually produce belief of it? If one is occupied with other matters and uninterested in what one sees in the sky, this seems neither necessary nor even likely (and these points may be generalized to other perceptual modes).

If we need not form beliefs concerning things we see that are of no interest to us, we may yet retain the raw materials that can yield propositional attitudes. One can see something, such as a small bird quickly crossing one's visual field while one is jogging, and later, when asked whether one saw what was moving overhead, truly say (initially) 'I have no idea'. On reflection, however, one may recall an image that enables one to ascribe certain properties to what one saw. Granted, this possibility is compatible with one's having tacitly formed the belief that what one saw was, say, a fast-moving speck. But neither seeing it nor visually recalling it in the initially indeterminate way illustrated, *entails* perceptual belief-formation as a condition of seeing the thing.

One might in such cases speak of *virtual belief.* If I see a bird flying overhead, I am *positioned* to believe it is flying overhead, even if I am concentrating on my footing and merely glimpse it. Similarly, we are positioned to believe many propositions self-evidently entailed by what we already believe if they come to our attention. But should we also think that every proposition *self-evidently* entailed by one that a person believes is virtually believed by that person? This would include disjunctions of the proposition with strange "far-fetched" propositions or obvious falsehoods. It would thus go too far even for cases in which the person can understand the entailed proposition. It is also possible that the thought of a proposition self-evidently entailed by something one believes might instead lead to doubting the already believed proposition and thereby to withholding it. Thinking of a consequence of something one believes can be like climbing an insufficiently

A contrasting view is proposed by Byrne (2018), who presents a nuanced case for holding that "Perception compels belief: the visual appearance of unequal lines is accompanied by the belief that the lines are unequal, absent (apparent) evidence to the contrary" (pp. 144–45) and goes on to say that for certain nonhuman perceivers "seeing is always believing" (p. 145).

supported ladder: the result may be not a wider view, but a collapse of the foundation.

The examples of perception given so far, together with my points regarding the functional dependence of phenomenal perceptual representations on the object perceived, should make it evident that I am suggesting a causal theory of perception on which to perceive something is, in outline, for it to produce or sustain, in the right way, an appropriate (even if highly inaccurate) phenomenal representation of it. Plainly, this theory goes with the view that perception is factive: there must be something to play the causal role in question. Commonly, that role is played reliably enough to enable us to have perceptual knowledge if we form perceptual beliefs appropriately corresponding to what we see. But the theory does not imply the view that seeing is believing or any other doxastic or propositional conception of perceptual content. The notion of content, as applied to perception, has various interpretations. If we are to preserve the intuitive idea that the content of something should be internal to it, then perceived objects are best not conceived as part of what constitutes perceptual content. This is not at all to downplay the external representational element in perception. But the representationality of perception is a matter of the properties the perceptual experience represents its object as having. These may also be represented even by hallucinatory sense-experience that is, in a certain way, qualitatively like the kind of perception embodying that type of sense-experience. This representational overlap is possible because of the power of phenomenal properties to provide a sense of what it is like to have the experience they partly constitute. In perceptual experience they are seemings, such as visual impressions of color and shape. This causal representational view also accommodates "inner perception" of elements, such as images, which are internal to the mind. That seems appropriate to the breadth of the general notion of perception; but my concern here is with ordinary sense-perception, especially vision. The most important point here, however, is that the causal character of the perceptual relation can be explained on the basis of the perceiver's receiving information about the object—information represented in the phenomenal character of the experience—without acquiring beliefs that propositionalize that information.

3

PERCEPTUAL LEVELS AND THEIR ACTION-THEORETIC COUNTERPARTS

We have seen four structurally basic cases of perception: simple, attributive (predicative), propositional, and aspectual kinds. We have also seen several kinds of content perception may be taken to have. But are there also levels, as in the domain of action? Is there, at least for simple seeing, a basic level? Might perception be parallel to action in this respect?

I. Perception and Action: The Structural Analogy

Perception is analogous to action in many respects,[1] but the structural side of the analogy has particular interest. Just as we do not do anything at all without doing something *basically*, i.e., other than *by* doing something else, and, in that limited sense, doing it "at will," we do not perceive anything at all other than by perceiving something basically, say by simply seeing its colors and shapes, as with visual perception of a tree. Now consider a counterpart case of action: my greeting you. I cannot do this without, for instance, raising my hand. I greet you *by* raising my hand. But for me, as for most people, that is a basic act: I do not do it by doing anything else. Someone else might be able to move the relevant muscles at will. I cannot: I can move them only by moving my hand. This shows a difference between a movement I make as an action and

1. A recent example of theorizing that focuses significantly on parallels between perception and action is E. Sosa (2015). His concern, however, is more with success conditions on each side and their similarity to one another than with the structural parallel I stress here.

Seeing, Knowing, and Doing. Robert Audi, Oxford University Press (2020). © Oxford University Press.
DOI: 10.1093/oso/9780197503508.001.0001

a movement of or in my body necessary for the action. Similarly, I see a rose by seeing its color and shape, but I do not see these by seeing anything else; and though my seeing is accomplished by events in my visual system, I cannot produce those except by bringing about seeing, say by looking, which is also basic for me.

There is no need, then, to deny that without a rose's conveying light to my visual system I do not (normally) see that rose. But *that* set of physical events is not my basic perception, any more than the relevant movement of my hand-raising muscles is my basic action of raising my hand. (I don't know how to move them except by raising my hand.) Moreover, much as my muscle movements underlying the action of raising my arm are not perceptual phenomena, neither the visual system's reception of the light nor my seeing the colors and shapes constitute my doing something. It must be stressed, however, that the structural parallels between action and perception do not undermine the ontological differences between them. For instance, actions but not perceptions are doings; perceptions but not actions are essentially (phenomenal) representations; and (in rough terms) actions are internally caused, whereas perceptions are externally caused. (Even inner perceptions doubtless have causes outside the "receptor system" that receives the relevant psychological information.)

Basic perceptions reveal something in the domain of *the perceptible*, something we can be perceptually aware of *by* (say) seeing. Many perceptible phenomena are not perceived basically, however, but only by perceiving something else—in the sense of something distinct from them even if intimately connected with them in the way that raising a hand can be intimately connected with greeting. We can grasp this point better by considering whether the kind of perceptibility in question is a matter of being, for us, "observable," where the object perceived is constituted roughly by something that, like the color of shrubbery, we can perceive basically, for instance "just see." The 'for us' reveals a species-relativity, but not the subjectivism implied by taking the 'for' to be doxastic, say entailing that what we can observe depends on what we can perceptually believe or know in the situation.

The relativity view here is that a given species or subspecies tends to have a characteristic basic level of perception—though individual members of a species may differ in the range of their basic perceptual capacities, just as we may differ in our repertoires of basic act-types: roughly, those we can instantiate at will. Some can, e.g., wiggle their ears at will and others cannot. The point here is not that the concept of perception requires positing an absolutely basic level across all perceiving species capable of perception. More generally, for any perceiving being and any time, there is a perceptually basic level for that perceiver at that time; but it does not follow, and I believe is not true, that there is some "ultimate" perceptual level that is basic for every perceiver at every time.

II. Constitutive Elements in the Visual Perception of Physical Objects

With the distinction between basic and non-basic perception in mind, let me sketch an analysis of some core elements in visual perception.

First, we never (directly) see all of an object such as a rose, an animal, or a building; we see only the part facing us. The most intuitive account of such seeing is that we see objects by virtue of seeing certain of their properties, such as (even if distortedly) the shape of their surface facing us. Compare performing an act, *A*, by realizing a subset of the act-properties *A*-ing objectively instantiates, as where I speak by forming words, though I also move my lips, produce vibrations in the air, and the like. Perception and action share a natural selectivity: the straightness of the tree trunk may be seen but is not something *by* which I see it, as causing vibrations may be something I do in speaking but is not a basis of my speaking.

Second, just as action need not arise from practical reasoning, no inference is required for perception: seeing the object is constituted by seeing the appropriate properties; it is not an inference, or dependent on our inferring, from propositions about the object, that it is (say) flat.[2] To be sure, if one reflects on what it is to see an object, such as a tree one is viewing, without seeing more than its facing surface, one may *then* infer that its rear looks like its front, and one may conclude that normally one does tacitly infer something like this. But that conclusion does not follow and on my view is not true.

Some qualifications are in order. Suppose that the ostensible—some might say visually presented—ellipticality that round dinner

2. It will be plain to those conversant with recent psychological literature that 'inference' is used quite differently therein. E.g. Clark explicates the "perception-as-inference" view of Richard Gregory, emphasizing "predictive processing" as "essentially a process of bottom-up feature detection" (2014, e.g. ch. 11, esp. 229–37. My position is neutral with respect to the nature and role of inference in this technical sense. For detailed discussion of how 'inference' is used in vision science, see Orlandi (2014, esp. 16–41).

plates, when viewed from an angle, appear to have is not a property those perceptible round objects ever have. Then, talk of seeing the properties of objects must sometimes be understood in terms of awareness of properties that, in some appropriate way, characterize or at least represent the object seen. At the phenomenal level, one sees the plate *as* elliptical. One has an elliptical presentation of it, we might say. There is of course a property of ellipticality, and we can understand how a phenomenally visual awareness of that property can, under the right conditions and in an oblique kind of way, represent to the viewer the shape of a round plate. Sensing elliptically, however (being "appeared to" ellipitically)—as is normal in viewing a round plate from a sharp angle—is plainly not a property of round plates, nor does it entail a sense-datum's representing them. It is a property of persons that they may easily have by virtue of being in some phenomenal (as opposed to intellective) way aware of the property of ellipticality. One would also be "objectively" aware of the roundness of the plate; this is consistent with one kind of seeing it *as* elliptical.

It might seem implausible that in having a perceptual experience we can be aware of a property when nothing we perceive has that property. But it is not as if there were nothing in the situation that instantiates a related property—indeed one that can be seen undistortedly by changing the conditions of observation. Given this familiar point, it seems clear that what the instantiation of a property causes in us in the way of aspectual perception (seeing as) is highly variable and need not yield a fully accurate representation of what causes that instantiation. Using the metaphor of a causal channel as opposed to a causal chain, we can see two points here. First, as many illusions show, not all the information that passes from the visible instantiation of a property (its instantiation by the perceived object) to the mind need be correct. Second, not all the information available concerning the instantiation need pass through at all. In some situations in which the shape of a coin is visually presented, that shape may not be accurately represented, and the thickness of the coin may not be perceptible at all.

What I have said leaves open that if one has *never* seen an elliptical object, one might never have the phenomenal property of visually experiencing elliptically (thus experiencing a phenomenal representation of ellipticality). But the possibility of hallucination apparently shows that sensory awareness of the property—phenomenal as distinct from perceptual awareness of it—does not entail simultaneous awareness of any object possessing it. Moreover, might not a perfect physical duplicate of a normal perceiver who has seen furry cats have the relevant phenomenal awareness upon initially seeing a furry cat, even with *no* prior acquaintance with fur or furriness? The capacity for such awareness apparently resides in our physical (or anyway replicable) constitution and does not depend on prior experience. We normally rise to an understanding of the abstract by experiencing it instantiated in the concrete; but there may be no necessity about this, nor should it be assumed that everything concrete is material.

I also leave open, then, what is needed to acquire a capacity to perceive (and conceive) physical properties, as well as how, cognitively, we correct for misleading appearances. Must we have drawn inferences about the relation between the elliptical appearance of round surfaces viewed from an angle, or is it enough that, in judging their shape, we "automatically" combine remembered tactile data (say, of the roundness of the plates) with visual data obtained from viewing the plates at a favored angle? Both are possible in creatures with different histories. My concern is to show that simple and attributive perception in themselves do not entail belief-formation and that inference is not required even at times when we "correct" for misleading appearances in such a way that we arrive at the same result we would reach if we were guided by making a sound inference.

III. Awareness of Events and Abstract Entities

The kind of awareness of properties so far considered—perceptual as opposed to intellective awareness—is phenomenal. But what we are aware of can be abstract, as where one simply reflects on the property of ellipticality. Intellective awareness, which such reflection entails, is not my concern here; but it is the conceptual kind that, on the epistemology I find most plausible, apparently underlies a priori knowledge.[3] Suppose, however, that we regard the objects of the most basic kind of perception as the sorts of physical properties by which we see spatiotemporal objects. Those objects themselves are plausibly taken to be seen by virtue of seeing their properties. How, then, can we maintain that perception is a causal relation to the object perceived? This is a problem if, as I think best, we do not take abstract entities, such as properties (unless perhaps they are conceived as tropes), to be terms in causal relations.

3. A sketch of the associated account of the a priori and references to alternative views is provided in my 2008a, and much further developed in chs. 8 and 9 of this volume.

An analogy should help. Imagine a mechanic's saying that a crack in my windshield was caused by a stone kicked up by another vehicle. This apparently means roughly that the event of the stone's hitting the glass cracked it, just as, in the action case, if someone said that *I* broke a glass, this would mean that something I did (an event) broke it. Among causes of perceptual experiences, what is the analogue of the hitting? A camera flash might cause a visual perception. But many perceptual causes (or causal sustainers) are not events. Consider ongoing impressions that sustain a perception, as where one looks at a seascape in a completely static gaze, and the seascape's continuing unchanged sustains (given the lighting conditions) one's ongoing vision. A natural account arises from analysis of event-causation and sustaining causation. My now seeing a seascape is causally (in a non-wayward way) sustained by the scene's having the observable property of being steadily illuminated. With momentary perceptions—such as seeing a camera's flash—the perceptual object's changing causes an event of, say, glimpsing its flash.

How should we describe the kinds of objects designated by the noun phrases naturally used in the relevant cases, for instance 'the camera's flashing' and 'the seascape's being sunlit'? These phrases can designate types or tokens. The event-type, flashing, is abstract and hence the wrong kind of thing to be a cause. But the event-token, say the camera's flashing now, is the right kind—what I call a *dependent particular.* It is a particular because it is a unique thing in time and, at least for physical events, space; it is dependent because there must be an object that instantiates the property of flashing (and, for at least event properties, *tokens* it). Ontologically, the object is more basic than the tokening: the flash depends on the camera, but not conversely.

If we take this view of events, including actions, then it is natural to hold that what causes our perceiving a substance is its instantiating a suitable property, normally an observable property, such as a color or shape property.[4] Unless the perception is strictly momentary, there will be both event causation and sustaining causation. Even for my seeing the camera steadily, however, there is an event of my *starting* to see it, followed by my continuing to see it. That state of continuing vision is sustained by the diachronic instantiations of the relevant camera properties; those instantiations' sustaining my seeing it is a (temporally

4. One might wonder how the causative property could fail to be observable; but the causative token need not be observable, as opposed to intimately connected with an observable property as, e.g., tokening light-ray reflection is intimately connected (but not identical) with coloration, which is observable.

extended) causal relation. An analogy would be lifting a briefcase and then holding it steady in one's hand: the upward thrust causes its rise, and the firm grip causally sustains its position above the floor.

To see an object, then, is to see some suitable subset of its properties,[5] which is a matter of an appropriate causal relation between its instantiating such properties and our phenomenal awareness of them. That awareness is an instantiation of certain phenomenal properties—a kind of representation of the visible properties in question. For the object to present itself is for it to cause, in an appropriate way, that kind of representation. This is of course a realist, representationalist theory of perception, but it seems as "direct" a realism as can account for the relevant data.

If the theory does not seem unqualifiedly a "direct" realism, this is not because it presupposes that "sense-data," which, even if mind-dependent, are objects in their own right, having such properties as color and shape, and intervening between the external object perceived and the mind. It does not presuppose sense-data. But in taking perception of physical objects to occur by perceiving their properties, the theory does take sensory experience to have "objects" in the way required by the phenomenal character of that experience, and to be capable of being, at the phenomenal level of what the experience "is like," qualitatively identical with ordinary perception.

What ontology is presupposed here? There are at least three possibilities: a sensory acquaintance with a visible property conceived as a universal, whether along Aristotelian lines (the first possibility) or on Platonic lines (the second possibility), and, thirdly, a sensory acquaintance with a trope, conceived as a particularized property such as the blackness of this particular print. Presumably the causal element in perception is, on the first two views, a matter of causation of the sensory experience by the object's instantiating the universal, where that experience is the perceiver's instantiating a phenomenal property. On the trope-theoretical view, the most natural interpretation would seem to be taking the trope itself to be a term in the relevant causal relation. A difference here is that whereas, on the Aristotelian and Platonic views, the perceiver's instantiating the sensory property is understood as a relation to the same property that the object instantiates, so that we can see the

5. The property might be relational: I can see a distant plane when I misperceive its color and shape but see its approximate location, and its relation to me produces a suitable phenomenal responsiveness to changes in it. I must here ignore these and other complications.

same property in different particulars, on the trope theory there are, for different objects of (e.g.) the same shape, different spatial tropes that bear some appropriate relation to each other.

The epistemology and phenomenology of perception I am developing may be adapted to any of these views, but the problem of empty hallucination is a challenge to all of them. What property or entity was Macbeth acquainted with if he perfectly hallucinated a dagger? If we take the Aristotelian view that the universals in question, such as the dagger's color and shape, must be instantiated, then must we posit a region of space to instantiate them? Such spatial realism is coherent, but so, it may be argued, is a mind in a world without space. For the trope-theoretical understanding of the case, it appears that some mental entity (perhaps a sense-datum) is the object of Macbeth's acquaintance. No such problem besets the Platonic understanding of universals, which allows for direct acquaintance with them. Presumably the Aristotelian view can also allow this provided there is some instantiation of the universal in question. All these views need a way to account for what causes the hallucination when there is no object (even a chunk of empty space) to do causal work, but this is not an ontological problem and may be solved by vision science.

Despite the high degree of metaphysical neutrality of my account of perception and hallucination, some might object that the theory represents perception as mediated by awareness of properties and thus as really indirect. I reject this: the properties are not intermediary concrete (though mind-dependent) objects, like sense-data, nor do they intervene between the object possessing them and the perceiver. In addition to positing properties, the only concrete objects the account posits are the perceiver and the thing perceived. The property instantiations are constituents in the perceptual relation itself and, ontologically, they are (in terms meant to be neutral between a trope-theoretic and a Platonic or Aristotelian account) built from universals and the perceptible particulars that instantiate them.

The points emerging above help to clarify the "representationality" of perception. This notion applies most clearly to seeing and touching, which can reveal primary qualities. We can normally draw, if only partially, what we see or, in many cases, what we touch. But for smell, taste, and even hearing we can do this only by correlating their deliverances with what is perceptible through sight and touch. To be sure, one can taste a sugar cube, which has primary qualities, and we hear pianos, which also have them; but gustatory and auditory sensations themselves are not of primary qualities. Shape and size have no taste or sound.

The experiential sound of middle C, the auditory experience that could occur in a qualitatively identical hallucination, is not a property of strings or soundboards, though a string may of course have the dispositional property of tending to yield that sound upon being plucked.

Given what has been said about perception of objects and the awareness of them that perception embodies, it should be apparent how we might sketch a parallel account of the awareness of abstract objects—*apprehension* of them. We have already seen that properties are perceptible—they are indeed that by which perceived objects present themselves to us. Abstract entities such as propositions, geometrical objects like squares, certain mathematical properties, and certain relations are not in the causal order, but that does not prevent our apprehending them. I take apprehension of abstracta to be a direct non-causal relation (and will say more about this in Chapter 9). It is phenomenally different from the causal relation that goes with perception, but note that with mere sense-experience, even the sensory awareness (as in hallucination) does not require an external physical object. This apparently shows that the object of a representational relation need not be physical. This is not the place to develop a full-scale theory of apprehension, but enough has been said to suggest how apprehension might be approached on the model of perception as understood here.[6]

IV. The Epistemological Significance of Perceptual Levels

Level distinctions can have many dimensions, and it is important to understand them without making some tempting epistemological mistakes. Consider seeing a piano by seeing the keyboard, legs, pedals, and distinctive shape. There is a kind of ontic dependence, since standing in the relation of seeing to the piano depends on standing in that relation to properties that, in an appropriate way, are indicative of it. There is also a kind of epistemic dependence, since (for one thing) if, on the basis of seeing them, one cannot know (or is not justified in believing), that the basic properties are present, one cannot visually know (or is not visually justified in believing), that there is a piano present.

This epistemic dependence is related to another: the conceptual dependence of perceptual belief, hence of perceptual knowledge as well, on an appropriate understanding of the concepts that figure essentially

6. I propose a more detailed account of apprehension in "Perceptualism in the Abstract Realm," in progress.

in the proposition believed or known. Dogs can perhaps believe a piano *to be* what a sound is coming from, but (unless they have a concept of a piano and of pitch) they cannot believe or know (the proposition) *that* a high-pitched sound is coming from the piano. Should we go further and conclude that perceptual belief that *p* requires not only having the concepts required for understanding this proposition but also concepts of every visible property *by* which one sees it? I think not. One can see contrasts in a painting without having a conception of all the contrast relations by which one sees them, say of the differing shapes, textures, and foreshortenings visible in it. Compare a non-basic action, such as amusing someone by producing a rare combination of split infinitives and misplaced modifiers. One need not have a conception of these for the act to depend on them in much the way seeing contrasts depends on seeing contrasting elements. This is not to deny that in some cases the dependence relation to lower-level elements implies a potential to develop concepts of them, but that is a different point.

There is also a psychological dependence in non-basic perception: the visual experience of a piano in the (normal) perceptual case imagined is causally and phenomenologically dependent on the visual experience of the relevant aspects of the piano that are basically seen. These dependencies raise a number of questions. Two in particular are both epistemologically important and of great interest here. One concerns whether perception is (intrinsically) "theory-laden," the other whether it is, at least in non-basic cases, inferential. These questions are highlighted by the structural analogy between perception and action. Just as theoretical sophistication and wide experience can enhance and otherwise influence one's capacity for action, they may affect one's ability to perceive phenomena and influence how we conceptualize what we see.

V. Is Perception Theory-Laden?

Given the account that has so far emerged, we can see several points about the popular idea that perception is theory-laden.[7] If the minimal

7. Especially since the work of N. R. Hanson, P. K. Feyerabend, and Thomas Kuhn dating at least from the 1950s there has been much reference to theory-ladenness but, in my view, too little analysis. This section—and in some ways Part One of this book—are intended to help fill this gap, but without an excursion into the lengthy literature on the topic and with an emphasis only on core elements of the issue.

case of holding a theory is having a belief or other cognitive attitude about something "unobservable," then we have seen reason to deny the strong view that perception entails holding a theory concerning its object. But this strong view is not plausible or commonly held. What many philosophers are at least inclined to hold is the weaker view that, for perceivers who have theories, perception is always influenced by at least one of them. What kind of influence might be in question?

Among the things one might mean by saying that perception is influenced by theory are that (1) what theory or theories one holds influences what properties or objects one perceives on at least certain occasions when one *is* perceiving things; (2) what theory or theories one holds may even affect what one *can* perceive; (3) given one's perceiving something, one must conceptualize it in a category supplied by a theory one holds or is influenced by; and (4) given one's perceiving something, what one perceives it *as* (if one does have an aspectual perception of it) is affected by a theory one holds or by which one is influenced. Call (1) the influence interpretation of the theory-ladenness view of perception, (2) the capacity interpretation, (3) the conceptual interpretation, and (4) the predicative interpretation. Proponents of the view that perception is theory-laden usually take it that perceiving something entails perceiving it *as* something or other and that the predication is influenced or determined by a theory. The fourth case, then, has at least two variants: in one, the perceiver *believes* the thing to have at least one "theoretical" property that it is perceptually taken to have (say, seen as having); in the other, it appears to the perceiver, in a phenomenal but not doxastic way, to have that property. Let us take (1) to (4) in turn.

An important preliminary point is that some of the plausibility of the theory-ladenness view of perception may derive from conflating theories with concepts or, perhaps, *having* a theory with having a certain kind of concept. Theories differ considerably from concepts, even if there are some concepts one simply would not have without having or at least understanding a theory. Some concepts, such as that of belief, moreover, are "theoretical" in the weak sense of (roughly) being non-observational and applicable (by human beings to other human beings) only on the basis of inferences from propositions about observables. If we can (perceptually) see that someone is angry, and if this entails believing that proposition, then our propositional perception, as embodying perceptual *belief*, is theory-laden in a weak sense. But although there are theories of anger, no particular one must be accepted or even understood as a condition for believing that someone is angry (unless it is needed for having the concept, as a folk-psychological theory might be). Nor, in any case, is believing that someone is angry required for seeing the person's anger. We can grant, then, that perceptual belief is conceptually laden even if we deny that perception itself is theory-laden. But what of (1) to (4)?

The Influence and Capacity Interpretations

The first theory-ladenness hypothesis concerns how holding a theory influences what one perceives (given a viewing or other evocation of perceptual experience). It is apparently causal and may well be true. The second hypothesis—claiming that one's theories may affect what one *can* perceive—may go significantly beyond causal theses but is also plausible. Both hypotheses need analysis and may or may not have profound philosophical implications.[8] To assess them would require exploring what kinds of objects are perceptible. Here, as is appropriate to the vagueness of 'see' and other perceptual terms, I am latitudinarian.

The topic of the range of perceptibility—e.g. the range of things one can see—can be treated only briefly in this book, but one point implicit already might be made explicit here: that apart from being guided by concepts or other theoretical elements, one might in fact be unable to have certain higher-order perceptions. One might not hear diminished chords differently than minor chords apart from learning elementary music theory, and one might see patterns on an x-ray differently owing to radiological training. Analogously, without development of a sense of justice—at least at the level of sensibility, but perhaps also at a kind of theoretical level—one might not see injustice in an unequal distribution of food to the equally needy; one might be able to see here only mere quantitative difference.[9]

8. Recent literature on cognitive penetration brings out some of what was said or implied in earlier literature on theory-ladenness. For much on how the former affects perception and justification of perceptual beliefs, see Siegel (2017b); and for some critical discussion of some contemporary views about the significance of such penetration, see Orlandi (2014); Tucker (2014); and Lyons (2016).

9. For Nicholas Sturgeon, "[Gilbert] Harman says, correctly, about moral 'observations': that they are all theory-laden, in that they can only be made by someone who already knows, or at least implicitly believes, a great deal about evaluative matters" (2006: 241–62, p. 253). Cf. "A physicist can't see *that* a proton is passing through a cloud chamber without already knowing a lot of physics" (p. 254, italics added). As the second quotation suggests, Sturgeon is not distinguishing simple from propositional perception here. The latter

As to how a theory one holds may otherwise influence one's perceptions, there are many possibilities, and it is a question for scientific inquiry how to characterize their nature and range. What is philosophically clear is that it is possible to have many perceptions without having a theory. Perception occurs in living things that are pretheoretical, presumably even preconceptual (or perhaps non-conceptual), and there is no reason to think that once we become theoretical beings all our perceptions *must* be influenced by some theory.

The influence and capacity interpretations of the theory-ladenness view are akin to the idea that perception is subject to cognitive penetration.[10] This notion has various interpretations. It differs importantly from that of seeing *as,* though it may be that every case of the former is one of the latter. If a grey imitation of a banana looks yellow to *S* (as reported in cognitive penetration experiments), this could be because *S* believes bananas to be yellow. The grey banana-shaped object will be seen as yellow, though that could also occur with no cognitive penetration. One case is yellow light cast over the object but no biasing antecedent belief; another is a kind of non-cognitive storage, in the visual system, of the often confirmed information that bananas are (generically) yellow.

On one interpretation, then, cognitive penetration influences what something is seen *as,* where "biased" seeing may or may not occur. On another, it leads to *seeing more,* which is a different notion. Experts may see more in a painting than novices or more kinds of leaf in a garden, but even the novice who sees all the kinds of leaf clearly may not see them as having the properties, such as being unhealthy, that the expert sees them as having. Where the expert sees more objects or ascribes more properties, this may be a matter of either better *attention* or greater *acuity.* In the former case, the novice might, with effort, see (in the basic sense) the same things (say colors and shapes) but not see them *as* what they are in the expert's mind. In the latter case, the novice does not and, without enhanced acuity, cannot see the same things, hence sees

requires conceptual capacity to understand the relevant proposition; given that point, for simple perception, roughly just observing something, I would account for Sturgeon's plausible points here partly by appeal to the influence interpretation.

10. There is much literature on cognitive penetration in both vision science and philosophy. In the latter category the works cited already by Siegel and Orlandi are instructive, and many of the papers in Matthen, op. cit., also contain detailed discussions. See also Stokes (2014, 2018).

less even at the basic level. That could explain failure to see the plants as, say, unhealthy.

The Conceptualist Version

The third, conceptualist version of the theory-ladenness view seems mistaken: perception as such (simple perception) does not entail conceptualization; and where it does embody conceptualization, what is required is conceptualization of some subset of the perceived properties, and that conceptualization need not be in categories supplied by a theory. The categories *might* of course belong to a theory and indeed to more than one, as do length and weight, at least under "theoretical" descriptions. In those cases there may be a question whether it is only certain technical descriptions that are peculiar to some particular theory. If so, one still need not know or accept that theory in order to perceive length or weight, and in any case some theories can be couched partly in non-theoretical language, as are some theories of the measurement of these properties.

Recall that even in lower animals, perception may be indicated by a responsiveness to perceptible information.[11] Even if some concepts may be plausibly attributed to them, their discriminative responsiveness, as with skillful hunting of prey, may be fine-grained without their having all the concepts required by the conceptual-ladenness view—unless, implausibly, we take discriminative behavior as by itself entailing concept-possession. Since discriminative behavior can result from mere conditioning, we need not so conceive such behavior in (at least) elementary cases. The relation between perception and action is again instructive. Perception guides much of our action, and when we act intentionally, beliefs and desires play a major role in determining what we do. They are conceptual in at least typical cases of this kind, but from the fact that when perception guides action jointly with such conceptual elements, the agent's response to it is conceptual, it does not follow that perception itself is conceptual.

The Predicative Interpretation

The fourth theory-ladenness view, the predicative interpretation, is, like the first, causal, and it may well hold for many cases of perception. We

11. For a theory of how perception may embody receiving information in the kind of non-propositional way I am illustrating, see Dretske (1981).

might first note that the fourth view might be plausibly considered implicit in the second: if perceiving something embodies conceptualizing it under a concept *C*, would one not see it as *C* (or as *C-ish*)? The answer is not clear. Conceptualization is more than minimally recognitional, and I distinguish minimally recognizing a perceived object (as mainly a matter of responding to a kind the perceived object is) from predicatively responding to it, which can embody seeing *as* but entails only taking the object to have a property. The former embodies a readiness to predicate some property that, for the subject, identifies the object as of a kind, but no actual attribution is entailed, as in the latter case. Minimal recognition is indeed possible for non-conceptualizing animals. Granted, even minimal recognition commonly activates a sense of familiarity, but this seems possible without conceptualization, as with many household pets, even if, in us, it entails a disposition to conceptualize the object recognized. This is in part why minimal recognition is open as to what property will figure in an attribution, whereas predicative responses are determinate regarding attribution, though they may be indeterminate toward what is plausibly considered a kind. Commonly, but not necessarily, the takings that constitute the attribution are doxastic. On a walk in a park, concentrating on fall colors, one may see picnic tables and parked bicycles and, even without focusing on them, minimally recognize them but make no attribution to them. Compare that with seeing a dog at twilight in the woods. Here, if caution is a factor, one might see it as a dog as opposed to a wolf, where there is some canine attribution.

As this case suggests, seeing *as* is implicitly contrastive, at least in many cases. However, for indefinitely many properties *F*, *G*, etc., we can perceive some object *as* being *F* or as being *G*, and so on, without also *believing* it to have the property in question. Its presenting to us some kind of appearance of having a property does not entail our believing it to have that property, even if we have concepts needed for forming that belief. Some of these properties may be theoretical, some not; some, but not others, we may know the object to have. Aspectual seeing, then, may but need not be doxastic, especially where the predication it embodies is not based on holding a theory. Contrary to the predicative interpretation, however, perception, as with simple seeing, need not be aspectual.

Thus, even if the conceptual version of the theory-ladenness view is taken to entail the predicative interpretation, they are not equivalent. The latter allows for predications influenced by a theory one holds, but also provides for predications not drawn from a theory. We have seen that (3), the conceptual version, is not true under the first, doxastic, interpretation; and (3) is also too strong under the second, theoretical-ascription reading *if* the range of 'theoretical' is not so broad as to encompass the merely conceptual. In that case, the thesis would be consistent with my account of perception.

Much conceptual work must be done to clarify various theory-ladenness views, and much philosophical and psychological reflection is needed to appraise them. What is said here is meant to show that this book is largely neutral with respect to the more plausible philosophical and (empirical) psychological views in this indefinite range.

VI. The Importance of "Background Beliefs" and Perceptual Levels

The idea that perception is theory-laden is readily connected with the view that it is inferential, though neither position entails the other. Let us consider the inferentialist view as applied where it is most plausible: to cases of non-basic perception. Here I presuppose a conception of inference that is based on a commitment to preserving its relation to reasoning and adequate to both everyday discourse and much mainstream epistemological parlance. So conceived, inference is roughly a passage of thought from one or more propositions (the "premise set") to another proposition on the basis of (or at least causally assisted by) a sense of some support relation between the former and the latter.[12] This captures many conceptually important elements in the concept of inference, among them that it admits of validity and invalidity; that it may be intentionally undertaken but may also simply occur non-intentionally on considering certain sets of propositions; that it is episodic and not dispositional; and that it is an instance of reasoning, or at least corresponds, in content and some causal properties, to reasoning. The view implies that a person's inferring something entails some conscious event, even if momentary—though not a consciousness or belief *that* the event is occurring.[13]

In previous work I have taken the perception of emotion, much like perception of intentional action, to illustrate how perception is possible

12. This conception is developed and defended in my 2006, esp. ch. 8.

13. This allows for the formation, without inference, of *inferential belief*, as where *S* believes *p* non-inferentially (say from wishful thinking), learns that *q*, which is an excellent premise for *p*, and comes to believe *p* on the basis of *q in the way* S *would have, given a normal formation of the belief that p by inferring it from q.* Such cases would illustrate believing *for a reason* without instantiating believing *on the basis of reasoning* (which is a kind of inference).

when its object is perceived not by seeing its properties in the way we do in seeing physical objects, nor with the aid of inference, but by seeing or otherwise perceiving properties—often visible properties—reliably related to it.[14] Imagine a context in which I see a motorcyclist ride carelessly over my treasured flowerbed. Think of the angry outburst that might be a response to this sight. Here perception of my anger seems possible for an observer of the scene as a non-inferential response to such highly reliable indicators of it as the outburst accompanied by pointing and shouting. We might speculate that from an evolutionary perspective the "function" of perception is to enable us to navigate the world safely and skillfully, and playing that role as well as it does seems to require higher-order perception or is in any case more efficient given such perception in place of the corresponding inference.[15] In any event, it seems essential for fully understanding perception that we see how it *can* reliably guide such navigation. Fulfilling that function leaves open many ways in which information needed for navigating the world can reach the mind and guide the agent.

A further concern of some philosophers is how much we represent, and can thereby know, perceptually. Natural kind properties, such as *being water* or *being a spruce tree*, present one kind of challenge, and certainly emotion properties and moral ones might seem to be such that one can perceive them only given a tacitly inferential role played by "background beliefs." Does one not need to learn what a spruce looks like in order to see one *as such*, as opposed to, say, seeing it as a conical arboreal plant?

At least four points are needed here. First, there is no question that the brain must process information in order for us to perceive such psychological phenomena as anger or such natural objects as spruces. The brain presumably does more here than when we simply have the basic color, shape, movement, and sound perceptions we would share with dogs. But this point does not entail that seeing anger requires forming a belief that the person in question is angry; nor does it entail that, in the many cases where such a sight does yield this belief, the belief is inferential. Even if a belief is formed only given a large amount of (non-doxastic) perceptual information or much brain activity or both, it

14. In, e.g., my 2012, chs. 2 and 3.

15. For a view of perception that has some similarities to mine but is more "practically" oriented and provides a conception of the navigation metaphor, see Bengson (2016). He conceives perception as "fundamentally practical" in the sense that it renders perceivers "*poised* for action."

does not follow that it is inferential. Second, granting that "background beliefs" may be essential for *possessing* at least certain of the emotion or natural kind concepts that a person may need as a condition for *having* the emotion-perceptions in question, it does not follow that either an emotion-perception or a belief it elicits need be "causally grounded in," or—especially—*justificationally* based on, such beliefs. I doubt both claims.[16]

The third point here is that my account of perception accommodates the point that the beliefs one holds can "causally affect" what experiences one has, as well as what one *notices* in the sense that implies making a kind of discrimination. The fourth point is that although, in some way, perception, including certain instances of emotional or moral perception, can be in part *conceptually* constituted, this does not entail that perception is specifically "theory-laden" if that term implies either that it *inferentially* depends on some belief or conception or that perception is necessarily distorted (or even biased) by or as a result of a theory accepted by the perceiver.

VII. Aspectual Perception, Inference, and Recognition

Aspectual perception, the main case for which I use 'seeing *as*', needs special comment. In some cases in which one sees a thing as *F*, this represents an inference of a kind. If one sees an infant as microcephalic, this may lead to seeing it as a victim of the Zika virus that afflicted the mother. The latter attribution, which is theoretical in content—and might be considered a "theory-laden" perception, might be *based on* the former, in an epistemic sense closely analogous to the sense in which one belief may be based on another when the latter expresses one's evidence for the former. We might speak here of a quasi-inferential relation between aspectual perceptions. It would be *cognitive basing*, but not the doxastic kind commonly called "belief basing." Perhaps some of the motivation for considering perception itself inferential arises from conflating inferentiality with mere cognitive basing.

16. This is not to deny that perceptual knowledge, including recognitionally knowing by sight that the person before one is Sally, can depend on one's having other knowledge. But the kind of dependence in question does not imply that the relevant perceptual knowledge is inferential, nor is that equivalent to being "immediate." For a notion of immediate knowledge that illustrates this point and shows how, e.g., knowing the fruits before one to be avocados can be epistemically dependent, see McGrath (2017).

One might also arrive at an aspectual perception by a kind of subsumption of the case under the generalization—possibly one that constitutes the accepted content of a background belief—that (at the time in question) microcephaly is usually due to Zika. Recognizing a place as where one once dined might also seem inferential, if it is based on seeing a familiar pattern of colored glass in a ground-floor window. There is, as it were, an evidential passage of thought from the (phenomenal) visual content to recognition. Associational bases of aspectual seeing may also seem to make it inferential. But as common as aspectual perception is—indeed, a case can be made that seeing *as* and its counterparts for the other senses are among the norms for sense perception in human beings—we cannot parley the pervasiveness of cognitive basis relations in aspectual perception into implying that simple perception, or even *every* case of aspectual perception, is intrinsically inferential.

It is important to see that my view is not that perceptual beliefs are non-inferential because they cannot be in some way *produced or sustained* by other beliefs, such as background beliefs, or by some episode of inference. Nor do I hold that perceptual beliefs must be *uninfluenced* by other beliefs. These are all causal possibilities. My point is epistemic: perceptual beliefs, whether *de dicto* or *de re*, are neither inferentially nor justificationally *based* on other beliefs and hence their *justification* does not rest on that of other beliefs.[17] This is important for understanding their normative status. Perceptual beliefs, like basic actions, are in a sense ground-level.

There is no need to deny that in practice we cannot always tell whether a belief is perceptual or inferential. Suppose I believe that if people look away from me in answering a delicate question, they are lying. If, when someone does this, I instantly come to believe the person is lying, is that because of a momentary unselfconscious subsumption

17. This point does not entail that perceptual justification is indefeasible, or even that it is not *negatively* dependent, in the way defeasibility implies, on the perceiver's beliefs. This point is explained in chs. 8 and 9 of my *Epistemology* (2010). In Part One of Siegel (2017b) she proposes a view on which perception itself may be rational or irrational, as well as a view on which it may be inferential. It may be apparent why I do not hold these views or take the justification of (*de dicto*) perceptual beliefs to depend on whether the underlying perception is cognitively penetrated; but, by making more use than she does of a partial account of aspectual perception (especially seeing *as*) I can explain many of the data she notes.

(hence inferential), or does my belief result from a non-basic perception? Much depends on whether the generalization is internalized in the special sense that one acquires a sensitivity to the particular fact as part of a pattern. Recognizing a pattern and forming a belief that *p* on that basis, say, believing that Don is angry because he behaves angrily—not because one *believes* Don behaves angrily—is different from coming to believe that *p* by (separately) grasping a fact that is part of the pattern, subsuming the fact under a generalization, and thereby forming the belief that he is angry. The perceptual belief is *recognitional*, whereas the inferential one, as premise-based, is *conclusory*. But this difference may sometimes be phenomenologically undetectable. Such recognitional beliefs are a kind of response to a pattern, not to a truth-valued thought or occurrent belief.[18]

It is also essential to see here that a belief, and especially a perceptual one, need not arise by inference from premises just because one *has* premises for it among one's beliefs. When we do infer a proposition or engage in reasoning that leads to our inferring something from one or more premises, the inference takes us mentally along a path from what is represented by one or more psychological elements to what is represented by another such element.[19] It is true that we can traverse

18. Here Fodor and Pylyshyn (2015) make several points helpful in understanding the perceptual phenomena in question with recognition and related perceptual responses. Ch. 4, e.g., explains how "representations of (at least some) properties of indexed objects are stored in the object file corresponding to that object" (p. 95).

19. This metaphorical statement does not entail that inference (in the process sense) is propositional and roughly equivalent to 'reasoning': a kind of mental tokening of an argument. A detailed statement of my broadly propositional view of inference is provided in chs. 5, 7, and 8 of *Practical Reasoning and Ethical Decision* (2006). Some philosophers and psychologists use 'inference' more broadly. See, e.g., Clark (2014) and Green (2010): "The inferences I speak of here will not in general consist of the derivation of one proposition from a set of others . . . they will more commonly take the form of a positioning of an object in egocentric space, an attribution of absolute and relative trajectories, and so forth" (p. 49). On this view, inferences need not be drawn, or figure in consciousness as reasoning does, or be valid or invalid, or voluntary, if indeed they constitute *doings* at all. I am not arguing that perception cannot involve inference in a broad technical sense. Arguably, perception—as where one "estimates" size and shape of a distant object or "updates" one's sense of the speed of a flying object by visual cues—is Bayesian, in the sense that (among other things) "The perceptual system estimates environmental conditions . . ." For detailed discussion of the Bayesian element in perception, see Rescorla

such a path without noticing it, but the mind also has its shortcuts. The territory may be familiar; our destination may be in plain view; and through the power of the imagination or some other informationally sensitive capacity we can sometimes go directly to places we would ordinarily have to reach by many steps. Perception is often like imagination in this and, without bypassing consciousness entirely, it can take us from information acquired directly by vision to a belief that might, under studied conditions—or less favorable conditions—also have been reached by inference.

One source, then, of a tendency to posit inferences underlying the formation of perceptual belief is assimilating information processing that does not require inference to propositional processing that does. Another source of the tendency to posit inferences in perception is the resistance to foundationalism of one kind or another. On any plausible conception of a foundation, an inferential belief is not foundational, whereas perceptions and perceptual beliefs may be.

We have noted a sense in which some perceptions are basic for the perceiver and others are based on them. Perceptions are like actions in that some are, for a given perceiver at a given time, basic and other perceptions are not. In neither case does the relation in question—seeing *x* by seeing *y* and, in the domain of action, doing one thing by doing another—entail inference. In neither case, moreover, does this structural point imply that there must be an absolute as opposed to a species-relative, basic level. The perceptual basis relation in question is epistemically significant but does not entail inference. Recognizing this allows, however, for our concepts and theories both to influence perception and to figure in perceptual beliefs. But we have seen no reason to think that perception itself embodies inference or is necessarily theory-laden in a sense implying potential bias by a theory or even dependence on theoretical concepts. Nor have we seen reason to believe that perceptual beliefs are inferential or cannot constitute a kind of basic non-inferential knowledge. It is true that our theories can influence what we perceive, particularly where the effect is to lead us to see something *as* a theory we hold says or implies it is, but much as action constitutes a direct way in which, however complicated the causal underpinnings,

(2017). He shows how Bayesian information-processing in perceptual systems is intelligible without endorsing Helmholtz's "constructivism," on which perception embodies unconscious inferences.

we intervene in the world, perception constitutes a direct way in which, however long and complicated the causal conditions for it, the world intervenes in the mind. There remains much to be discovered about how perception yields justification and whether it does so in the same way as it yields knowledge. Exploring those possibilities is the task of the next chapter.

4

PERCEPTION AS A SOURCE OF KNOWLEDGE AND JUSTIFICATION

If propositional knowing entails believing, as I assume here, and if, as I have argued, perception as such (simple perception) does not entail belief-formation, then perception as such does not entail knowledge. Still, our perceptions in fact yield a great deal of knowledge and provide a basis for far more of it than we normally acquire from it. Imagine hiking in a forest. We may see many pine cones but, concentrating on birdsongs, need not form beliefs about them. We are nonetheless in a position to know much about any of them that lie squarely in our visual field. Seeing is not believing, but it does position us to believe and know a great deal. Nature is doxastically economical but informationally generous.

I. Perceptual Knowledge

As I enter the forest I may see, and believe, that it is dense, that I will be walking among trees, and that I may slip on a pine cone. These beliefs may affect how a pine cone appears to me, but that does not entail believing something specifically about it, as opposed to guiding my path by a sense of obstacles to be avoided. The concepts of action and perception are so related that, even if (physical) action must in general be guided by perception (including kinesthetic perception), and even if intentional action requires a guiding belief, the question of what beliefs, and how many, can guide what behavior, and in what ways, is left open. It is a matter for psychological investigation. Perhaps, in order to walk in the forest for some distance on "automatic pilot,"

Seeing, Knowing, and Doing. Robert Audi, Oxford University Press (2020). © Oxford University Press.
DOI: 10.1093/oso/9780197503508.001.0001

I need only want to walk there and believe I must watch where I step. These elements may trigger an ambulatory vigilance of a mainly non-doxastic kind. The assessment we might make of this matter after thorough psychological investigation may constrain the range of plausible philosophical views, but the position taken here leaves much latitude for accommodating new information from either philosophical reflection or empirical investigation.

One thing cases like the forest walk show is that the property-responsiveness of perception—which is central for its entailing our discriminative responsiveness to objects we perceive—is not just cognitive but also behavioral, and that it can be so even if there is no doxastic ascription, even through attributive belief-formation, of the properties to which we respond. Is any kind of conceptual property-ascription required, as opposed to a kind of elemental discrimination of these properties? Why isn't discriminative responsiveness to certain properties enough to guide many kinds of intentional action, somewhat as, in the animal kingdom, it presumably guides even highly skillful goal-directed action? In answering this, we may seem forced to choose between lowering our conceptual standards for explaining perceptually guided intentional action to include animals and locating our similarity to animals at a preconceptual level. This is not an unavoidable choice. It is possible to do justice to both sets of demands, though a preference for simplicity may at times seem to favor minimizing conceptual requirements for the perceptual guidance of action. Part Three will consider this problem in some detail. The related question that is our main concern here is how, in broad terms, perceptual belief must be based on sense-perception if it is to constitute knowledge.

In approaching this question, I am taking perceptual knowledge to be knowledge based on perception. A paradigm of such knowledge is a true perceptual belief that *p* which is an element in seeing that *p* (I assume here that such true, propositional, visual beliefs constitute knowledge). English does not provide fully parallel idioms of the forms of 'hearing that *p*', 'touching that *p*', 'smelling that *p*', or 'tasting that *p*', but there are instances of each of these that semantically parallel 'seeing that *p*' where it expresses visual knowledge. 'Feeling (tactually) that *p*' is particularly akin to 'seeing that *p*'. We may speak of feeling that the surface is smooth, or feeling it to be smooth, or feeling it as velvety; and one might speak of tasting that there is too much garlic in the salad, hearing that a crow is cawing, and smelling that the grass is freshly cut. These are all marginally idiomatic cases in which, if we heard the locution in a normal use of English, we would know what the idea is and what kind of knowledge is implied. The general question, then, is how the sensory beliefs in question must be related to perception to count as perceptual beliefs.

Here it is fruitful to proceed on the plausible view that knowledge is reliably grounded true belief, where (at least in the case of empirical knowledge) this implies an *appropriately* reliable causal connection between the fact that *p* and the belief that *p*. Again, we should focus on the discriminative responsiveness that is crucial for perception to occur at all and essential in accounting for the reliability of the process or relation causally responsible for the genesis or sustenance of the perceptual belief.[1] In describing how this responsiveness is crucial for perceptual knowledge, I will often speak as if the knowledge in question is propositional, but my intention is to clarify attributive (objectual) knowledge as well and indeed to treat it as more basic.

Some cases of justification do not exhibit this discriminative responsiveness. Consider lotteries. Suppose I hold one ticket in a fair lottery which has a million tickets and will have just one winner (say me). Before the winning ticket is announced, it has no property perceptible to me that distinguishes it from the losers, and my (normal) belief that my ticket will lose is not perceptual. The counterpart point holds for the other tickets. In perceptual cases, by contrast, discriminative responsiveness is present, as indeed may hold even with knowledge of one's future acts based on one's now intending them (we are typically conscious of, e.g., the difference between intending and merely wanting to do something). A possible explanation of the difference is that there is nothing we are aware of in considering any ticket we hold that would cause it to win or to lose (or would yield a law connecting its character with winning or losing), whereas, in the case of the plane, we can readily imagine how something in the circumstances we observe does cause the plane to appear to us and would cause an observer positioned just as we are to see a plane like the one we see.

One might think that high probability of loss is the crucial element blocking knowledge that one will lose. But on reflection, this is not obvious. Suppose that a sudden cloudiness could be, but almost certainly is not, distorting one's image of the plane one is looking at and sees, where the distortion would prevent one's knowing the plane is there. Even when there is some probability of such distortion, if it is as low as that of winning the lottery with a single ticket, one can still see the plane

1. For important points concerning the kinds of responsiveness in question, see Goldman (1976) and Dretske (1981).

and thereby know it is there, whereas one does not know that one will lose the lottery. We can also know we will raise our arms even though there is a chance of sudden prevention that is no more improbable than winning the lottery.

One might think that the lottery case is essentially the same as the much discussed barn case, in which one sees a barn but cannot thereby know that it is one because one is lucky to have sighted a barn rather than barn facades all about that one would have mistakenly taken for (facing surfaces of) barns had one's glance fallen on one of them.[2] Here my view may open up another perspective. I grant that there is a kind of randomness in both cases: one might as well—indeed, might much more likely, have seen a façade, as one might as well have held a winning ticket. But there is also an important difference. Whereas a close inspection of one's ticket, all the other tickets, and even the fairness of the lottery would not yield knowledge that one's ticket will lose, in the barn case a closer inspection—on a perceptual basis—would suffice for knowledge, at least where it yields enough information about the composition of the visible surface. One kind of difference, then, is between having too little of the right kind of evidence—the visual—and the wrong kind altogether. If this difference is as important as it seems, we can treat the barn case as one of unfavorable conditions accidentally occurring, rather than as one that, in the nature of the situation, as with the lottery, could not provide for the relevant discrimination.[3]

2. Detailed discussion of this case is provided by Goldman (1976). (Goldman has attributed this case to Carl Ginet.)

3. This is not to imply that there *cannot* be, in both cases, a complicated description of the exact circumstances of belief formation such that, given that description and the laws of nature, the probability of the ticket's losing and also that of the structure's being a genuine barn is 1. This is consistent with the kind of causation that figures in the concept of perception being different in the two cases. For instance, in the barn case we can readily conceive of a sharper perceptual capacity that changes the verdict, whereas in the lottery case our conception of the kind of process needed to yield knowledge is of a different kind and seems both more complicated and inferential rather than perceptual. It should be noted that denial of knowledge in the barn case need not be based on the point that one might easily have had a *different* and false belief; it may (more plausibly) be based on the point that this fact calls attention to the situationally inadequate grounds one has for *this* belief. Skeptics may say that such grounds are *never* adequate; contextualists and others would hold (as I am inclined to here), that in "ordinary" cases they are.

II. The Hierarchical Character of Perception

So far, I have talked as if propositional knowledge is what is in question, for instance as if what one would believe in the facade countryside is that that structure is a barn. But of course one might believe instead that that red building is a barn, or that that rust-colored wooden shack is a barn. But must there be *any* propositional belief here? Isn't the basic issue whether the perceiver knows the object seen *to be* a barn, regardless of how it is otherwise conceptualized (consistently with being a barn)? To be sure, if we ask *what* the person knows, the answer is typically expected to take the form of 'that *p*'; and in communicating knowledge to others one might use a propositional expression, such as 'That ramshackle structure is a barn'. But if there is nothing *S* sees (or otherwise perceives) to be a barn, then there is no such proposition *S* knows either. If there is no *F* that *S* sees, then *S* has no *de re* (visual) knowledge of an *F*. This does not hold if there is something *S* sees and some barnlike property *S* sees it to have. Perceptual knowledge of this attributive kind can occur on occasions on which no corresponding proposition is perceptually known to *S*.

Part of the point is this: if there is no barn *S* simply sees, then there is nothing *S* sees *to be* a barn either. The idea I am suggesting is that *de dicto* perceptual knowledge is at the top of a hierarchy whose base is simple perception. In simple perception of ordinary physical objects, seeing certain visible properties of them is perceptually basic. Seeing an object is indeed *constituted* by such seeing, when that object's instantiating the visible properties appropriately causes—we could say *discriminatively causes*—the visual experience in question. Seeing the barn to have a certain set of properties is at the next level (or anyway a higher level). On the basis of this objectual seeing, the perceiver is in a position to form a propositional belief, and that may express knowledge.

A special property of the perceptual hierarchy is a kind of determinacy from the top down paired with a kind of indeterminacy from the bottom up. If I (visually) know that the tree is green, I see it to be green—which is attributive perception—and of course I see it, which is simple perception. Moreover, I see it, at least in part, *by* seeing its green color. Thus, propositional perceptual knowledge entails corresponding cases of attributive perception, including attributive belief; and, for each property in the set of properties the object is perceived to have, attributive perception also entails simple perception of that property. If you see a tree to be green, you see the green that is its color. But, if we view the matter looking upward, I can see the object (say, at night and even non-delineationally) without seeing it to be green; seeing it is indeterminate with respect to seeing it to be anything in particular, though it commonly yields such attributive seeing. Secondly, I can see it to be green without forming a propositional belief that it is green—I might form no propositional belief at all or form the false belief that the *house* is green, that the *tent* is green, and so forth for indefinitely many referential notions. Attributive perception, though it entails dispositions to form propositional perceptual beliefs, is in this way indeterminate with respect to propositional perception.

Suppose, however, that I do see that the tree is green—a case of propositional perceptual belief. Must it also be a case of knowledge? Suppose I am convinced by credible friends that I have been often deceived by bleached trees in green light and, though this is false, I justifiedly believe it. Then it might seem plausible to say both that I see that the tree I am viewing is green and that it is not the case that I know this. The belief that it is green does not represent knowledge, one may think, because it is "epistemically defeated" by the illusions I justifiedly believe I have been having and may know are possible. But the term 'epistemic defeat' is both vague and technical and may designate a defeat of justification as well as a defeat of knowledge. I prefer to allow that the case could be one of knowledge without justification—provided it is true that *S sees* that the tree is green as opposed to just visually believing this. This helps to explain why, in such a case, although suspending judgment would be preferable from the limited point of view of justification, the (visual) belief that the tree is green is a highly reliable guide to action in just the way knowledge normally is. The knowledge can be well-grounded in evidence and thus, as a cognitive representation, a good guide to action, even if the would-be justifiers are defeated or *S* is cut off from them altogether.

This case is supported by pragmatic considerations. There are times when we are unwilling to say we know but *do* know, as where our confidence level is low or we suspect a trick. Seeing that *p* might entail knowing that *p* even if there are cases of visual knowledge such that a conscientious possessor of it would neither self-ascribe knowledge that *p* nor unqualifiedly assert *p*. The case of the green tree seems of this kind. There is no need to resolve this matter here. The notion of knowledge is not without some vagueness, and the existence of a borderline case of this kind (if it is one) would not constitute a significant objection to my account.

Whether we are referring to propositional or to attributive belief, it should be apparent that (as argued already) perceptual knowledge need not be considered theory-laden as opposed to conceptual—though one can use 'theory' so widely as to include conceptualization. This is not to deny that perceptual knowledge may embody concepts, such as anger, that are theoretical in *some* sense, even if what is seen is perceptible, as anger commonly is. We may also grant defeasibility by theoretical considerations, as with the case in which I am deceived into believing a green tree to be bleached and really white. But that is a vulnerability, not a "ladenness" or a positive dependence.

III. Perceptual Justification: External and Internal Dimensions

Suppose seeing that *p* does entail knowing that *p*. It does not self-evidently follow that it entails being justified in believing that *p*. Recall the possible case in which I know that *p* but justifiedly believe, on massive credible testimony, that I have been hallucinating the kinds of things *p* concerns. The strong connection between perceiving and believing in such cases—where *p* is perceptually quite evident and brought to mind—might sustain the belief despite my having justification for believing that I should not believe *p*, where this higher-order justification is of a kind that defeats my prima facie justification for believing that *p*. Can we not be properly puzzled at some of the beliefs we hold, sometimes from grounds for doubt that undermine our justification for holding the beliefs? This conclusion seems inescapable. It need not, however, result in skepticism about the possibility of perceptual knowledge. Indeed, it makes room for the possibility that nature may reveal and bring home truths to us even where, at a "higher" level, we have a good reason to doubt those very truths.

Here is it essential to see that the possibility of perceptual knowledge without *overall* justification does not entail that perception does not always provide *prima facie* justification—roughly, a justificatory ground that, apart from the kinds of defeaters we have indicated, yields overall justification. If we see *x*, say by seeing its *F*-ness, for instance its being a red, woody-looking, windowed, barnlike side wall, and if we have the needed concepts, we are *prima facie* justified in believing there is a barn there. We are normally not criticizable for actually believing this, *unless* considerations arise that weigh more heavily against the belief than our grounds for it weigh in favor of it. Note, moreover, that the *force* of even these defeating considerations depends on perception, for instance on someone's pointing out that we have found through touch that our visual experiences are untrustworthy.

A major question that now arises is whether it is perception as such that yields perceptual justification or whether the embodied sense-experience is what does. One reasonable answer is that what is properly called *perceptual* justification must derive from perception. I accept this for precise uses of 'perceptual', but the term is used more widely. This may be because what we commonly conceive as the kind of justification that comes from perception—the kind crucial for intellectual responsibility and, implicitly, for the ethics of belief—is based on sense-experience of a kind possible without perception. Moreover, if there were no *sense-based justification*, surely there would be no perceptual justification. (I here presuppose an internalist view of justification, though some externalist views about justification might accommodate the point.) Perception is plausibly considered a basic source of justification, it seems, because it constitutively manifests a basic—apparently non-derivative—source of justification.

This last paragraph is controversial. Reliabilists about justification would tend to deny that sense-experience is the basic justificatory element in perception, though they need not deny that sense-experience, as normally arising in genuine perception is reliably connected with the relevant facts in much the way perception is. I cannot here argue in detail for the internalist view of justification (though it will receive further support in Chapter 6), but it does seem well supported by some of the cases I have described. Moreover, there is surely no reason to deny the possibility of combining an externalist, reliabilist conception of knowledge with an internalist conception of justification.[4] One reason this has not been common in epistemology, I suggest, is that *normally*, basic sources of justification for belief—perceptual, memorial, and a priori, for instance—so connect with knowledge that typically (some would say 'normally') when a *true* belief is robustly justified on the basis of one of these, it constitutes knowledge. It must be kept in mind, however, that the notion of justification has other homes, as in relation to action and non-truth-valued attitudes, and that knowledge can, as I have argued, occur without justification.

Not all reliabilist views of knowledge entail a reliabilist view of justification. For one thing, the possibility of knowledge without justification

4. Timothy Williamson has expressed doubts about this in his 2007a. My initial reply is in the same volume (my 2007b), and some points made there are developed further in this chapter.

does not in the least affect the case for reliabilism about knowledge. The kinds of examples supporting this possibility are all cases in which reliable grounding of the relevant beliefs is plain. One possibility, then, is a case for perception yielding knowledge without the experiential elements that ground justification. Blindsight would be such a case, *if* (or where) it is genuinely seeing yet is not accompanied by any experiential element to which the perceiver has access *and* is a potential ground of justification. In my view, perception is experiential in a way that precludes this—indeed, I think it is precluded by taking perception even to be representational, provided that is understood phenomenologically and not simply cognitively, i.e., in terms of yielding beliefs or other truth-valued attitudes. On my view, if you perceive something, there is something it is like, experientially, to stand in that relation to it; the relation is representational; and its representational character is both accessible to introspection or reflection and so connected with what you perceive that, if you have the concepts needed for justified beliefs whose content matches the representation, then you have justification for holding those beliefs.

IV. The Perceptibility of Normative Properties

One test of a theory of perception is how well it does justice to all the contexts in which perceptual language is properly used (at least nonmetaphorically). With this in mind, we might ask how well the theory of perception and perceptual knowledge just sketched can accommodate perception in the normative realm. Here I take moral perception as representative.[5] There is no need to consider moral perception an exact analogue of physical perception, at least of perceiving everyday visible objects seen in normal light. Moreover, if moral properties, such as wrongness, are perceptible, they are (e.g.) seen *by* seeing other properties. The relevant analogy, then, would be to seeing physical properties, say that of being a lilac tree, *by* seeing color and shape properties. Furthermore, for moral perception, as for other kinds of higher-level perception, at least low-level conceptuality is required. To

5. That it is representative is shown in my *Moral Perception* (2013a). For informative recent discussion of higher-order perception, see the collected essays in Bergqvist and Cowan (2018). My 2018a, contained in that collection develops the theory of *Moral Perception* and meets some objections. Further discussion of *Moral Perception* relevant to this book is provided by other contributors, including Milona (2018) and Vayrynen (2018).

see wrongdoing, I must see some evidence of it and must understand that element *as* indicating wrongdoing. This goes beyond sensory representation in a way that is broadly conceptual.

Given these points, consider whether you can see *A* wrong *B* by, for example, witnessing *A*'s slapping *B*. Arguably, what is observable is such things as *A*'s slap. You see the action of face-slapping—indeed, you might count *A*'s slap as among the "observable facts"—because you see and hear the action (in a context in which you can tell that the trigger is, say, an unsuppressed sneeze). Granted, even if you can see the basis of the wrong, here the slapping, your seeing the wrong depends on your understanding the significance of the discrepancy between this action and a mere sneeze as triggering a slap. Similarly, you must also understand the significance of the color and shape of lilac leaves to know that it is a lilac you see. The fact that perception of a kind of thing (as such) requires some understanding of what that kind is does not entail that a specimen of the kind cannot be perceived to be such.

If we are to speak of perceiving a higher-order property such as wrongness, the natural kind properties of biological species, and correspondingly, of acquiring perceptual knowledge, *by* perceiving other properties (though non-inferentially), we should observe the distinction made earlier between basic and non-basic perception. Perception of the shape and color properties even of faces is more basic than perception of the property of being—as we might put it—Jane-faced. I might believe a person is Jane because of "how she looks," but this belief is normally a response to her *being* Jane-faced rather than to *believing* that she looks like Jane, as where that likeness-belief provides a premise for inference. The relation of the base properties to moral properties is at least as intimate as that of facially constitutive properties to that of having the face in question, and, to take a quite different case, more intimate than that of anger-expressive properties to being angry. There is no good reason not to speak of moral perception if we can speak of facial perception and perception of anger.

It might occur to someone reflecting on these cases to object that I have ignored a disanalogy. Whereas faces and lilacs are visible, anger, being psychological and a kind of "underlying" condition, is not. Perception of anger, then, differs from that of many natural kinds in being "cross-categorial" or in any case embodying great disparity: emotions are categorially different from their behavioral manifestations and the disparity between emotions as experientially inward and those external manifestations is great. But note this. Although being a lilac is a biological property and the colors and shapes by which we recognize lilacs are not biological, we can still see lilacs and know perceptually that they are lilacs. Moreover, the phenomenology of seeing a face as such versus seeing the colors and shapes by which we recognize it is quite distinctive, even if the property of being (say) "Jane-faced" is also visual. We can grant major differences in kinds of perception without giving up the idea that perception may occur not only in the physical realm but also in the psychological and normative realms.

Perceptual justification for attributing higher-order properties is, in some of the ways brought out here, non-basic. In both examples, if we do not have good grounds for believing that the base properties are present—say the red-faced look and screams of the angry person or the face-slapping by the unjust one—then we do not have good grounds for ascribing an emotion or moral property on the basis of them. This kind of dependence is a kind we have seen in the case of higher-order perception of natural kinds. It is not unique to emotional, moral, or other normative ascriptions, and it holds for both knowledge and justification. If we lack grounds for believing Jack is flushed and screaming as he hears of his son's wrecking the car, we also lack good grounds for believing, on that basis, that he is angry. But notice this difference: although his having these properties is excellent evidence that he is angry, it does not entail that proposition, whereas *A*'s slapping *B* does entail that *A* is (prima facie) wronging *B*. In the first case, the grounding relation is empirical and contingent; in the second, it is (as I argued in *The Good in the Right* [2004]) a priori (i.e., a priori true) and necessary. Moreover, in the first case, we perceive a fact by what *it determines*; in the second, by what *determines it*; but in both the perceptual knowledge is reliably grounded by virtue of a causal relation.

My conclusion, then, is not that moral cognitions, such as moral judgments, cannot constitute perceptual knowledge but that they are epistemically, though not inferentially, dependent on non-moral elements. If we know *perceptually* that a sadist wronged his victim by burning the latter's hand with a cigarette, we know this non-inferentially, on the basis of our adequate perceptual grounds. The need for this basis manifests an epistemic dependence, but not an inferential dependence—a kind of premise-dependence: the grounds are perceptual, not propositional. On this score, the case is like knowing perceptually that a bird is a hawk: one knows this not by inference from ornithological facts but by a characteristic shape and flight pattern. In both cases our justification is also perceptual: we see the burning and, as with facial recognition, believe on that visual basis and non-inferentially, that he wronged the victim. Our justification for this perceptual belief is as strong as we would have for believing this non-perceptually, on the basis of premises ascribing the property whose instantiation we have directly witnessed. The belief can constitute perceptual knowledge because of the way it is based on a phenomenal responsiveness to the set of properties that ground the moral property. That responsiveness, in turn, is causally grounded in perception of certain of the natural properties on which the moral property is consequential.[6]

The position on perceptual moral knowledge defended here is an application of the *phenomenological reliabilism* explicated in this and the previous chapters. I take this view to yield an understanding of perception in general, and it can also account for the possibility of intersubjectively accessible grounds for a wide range of moral judgments. It also explains how moral knowledge, like knowledge of other higher-level properties, can meet strong reliabilist constraints.

Perception, and certainly seeing as a paradigm, is experiential, causal, and representational. As embodying a discriminative response to the object perceived, perception empowers agential perceivers to navigate their world; it provides indefinitely rich information about its objects; and it enables conceptually equipped perceivers to acquire knowledge and justification regarding normative and other higher-order propositions. But in its simplest forms, perception is neither doxastic nor even conceptual. Seeing does not by itself entail believing. Seeing *that* something is so does entail believing that it is so and indeed knowing that it is. This holds even for intellective seeing. Illusion may of course beset perceivers; we may, for instance, see something, thus visually perceiving it, but see it as having a property it does not have. We may also be deluded by sense-experiences that constitute hallucinations: here we have experiences *as of* seeing, but do not see. Similar points hold for the non-visual senses. Still, some possible hallucinations have a likeness to seeing close enough to justify certain visual beliefs that hallucinations produce.

Perceptual knowledge, then, requires more than does the counterpart sensory justification for the same proposition or property

6. Aesthetic perception is significantly similar to moral perception but there are important differences. For an informative appraisal of the possibility of aesthetic perception, see Logue (2018) and Lopes (2018). My case for the existence of moral perception does not depend on the possibility of counterpart aesthetic perceptions, but I am inclined to countenance them.

attribution; *knowledge* must be reliably grounded in facts. But neither perception nor sense-experience entails cognition. Perception provides a basis for more knowledge, and the latter for more justification, than we acquire or need. Perception is an abundant source of both knowledge and justification, and it is essential in providing premises for inferences whose content goes far beyond its deliverances. It is not, however, an inferential process, nor is perceptual knowledge inferential. Perception, in its simplest forms, is a non-doxastic source of beliefs and other cognitions, and it gives us knowledge and justification regarding myriad elements in our experience of the world.

5

REASONS, PERCEPTUAL GROUNDS, AND NORMATIVE EXPLANATION

Chapters 1 to 4 present the main lines of an account of perception, a conception of its phenomenological element, and its role in yielding knowledge and justification. Both knowledge and justification are commonly considered normative, and, in the case of justification, uncontroversially so.[1] But so far we have not explored a normative concept that might be considered more basic than that of justification, indeed perhaps encompassing the grounds of justification. Is the (or some) concept of a reason the most basic of normative concepts, as on the "fundamentalist" factivity view? There are many kinds of reasons, but this chapter concerns normative reasons, the distinction between those and normative grounds, and the relation of both to perception as a basis of justification and knowledge. Reasons are commonly taken to be facts. This chapter indicates what appears to be a non-factive way to ascribe theoretical reasons—reasons for belief.

I. The Diversity of Reasons for Belief

The discourse in which reasons figure is multidimensional. One might think that given how often our beliefs and knowledge depend on

1. In my terminology, knowledge is normative *in upshot*, as pain is, because they a priori entail a normative proposition, say that there is objective evidence for the relevant proposition or that there is objective reason to relieve the pain. But this capacity for grounding normativity does not entail normativity *in conceptual constitution*.

Seeing, Knowing, and Doing. Robert Audi, Oxford University Press (2020). © Oxford University Press.
DOI: 10.1093/oso/9780197503508.001.0001

perception, perceptions might themselves be a kind of reason. Many philosophers would countenance, as answering such questions as 'What is your reason for believing he came home?', 'I heard his voice', where the reason is identified with the content of a perceptual report. If perceptions themselves are not reasons, we need to understand why. Reasons discourse indicates not only a diversity in kinds of reasons there are but also several distinct yet related notions of reasons. I want both to sketch these notions and to consider whether there is an illuminating way in which they can be unified. I begin with some common kinds of reasons.[2]

Normative reasons for belief I take to be reasons (in the sense of objective grounds) there *are* to believe something, for instance to believe that global warming continues. Some normative reasons *to believe* (a proposition) are reasons for any normal human being to believe: they are in that sense universal, and they weigh in favor of the rationality of the belief in question. Other normative reasons, however, are *person-relative:* reasons there are *for* a specific person. For me, but not for others, there is reason to believe my itch is from a tick bite.

Normative reasons are often contrasted with *motivational reasons.* To be sure, talk of being motivated to believe something may invite an assumption of doxastic voluntarism, but it need not. Believing that someone has donated to Oxfam may motivate you to believe that the person will donate to a refugee relief fund you intend to propose, but this does not imply that you can voluntarily believe the latter. To avoid such misleading interpretations, we might better speak here of *inclining reasons for belief.* These, like motivational reasons for action, are *possessed reasons*: reasons *S has* to believe (or do) something, such as my reason to write a check, a reason I have because I promised to support a cause. Reasons we have can also be theoretical and, whether theoretical or practical, can and often do explain actions. If my reason to believe that you will write a check to Oxfam at least partly explains why I believe asking you for a donation is promising, it is in some way explanatory and not just inclining. But possessed reasons are potentially explanatory even if the agent never acts on them or forms a belief on the basis of them. Their explanatory power is potential both because *S* may not

2. Here I draw on an account of reasons for belief given in my 1986b. My treatment of reasons in this book refines the earlier one but also stresses that beliefs expressing reasons can be *de re,* e.g. believing an entailment *to hold* between *p* and *q,* as well as *de dicto,* as where *S* believes *that p* entails *q.* In my 1986a, I treat the practical case of reasons for action quite similarly.

act or form a belief on the basis of them and because they may be had (possessed) only in an "implicit" way: they may be had when only potentially conscious, as where the reason is a proposition one would believe only by putting together facts that one possesses, but has never interconnected.

Many possessed reasons belong to the third main category just indicated: that of *explanatory reasons for belief*. These are reasons *why* someone believes *p*, say why I believe that one should avoid wasting electricity. But a reason why I believe need not be inclinational (motivational, in broad terms). Something very different, including depression or brain manipulation, might explain why I believe something, such as that I am disliked, without being motivational and without constituting a reason I have for that proposition. We might, then, call such merely causal elements reasons *why a belief occurs*, rather than *reasons for believing*, but they are still reasons why a proposition is believed. The typical cases of explanatory reasons for belief, however, are not just causal grounds of it, but motivating.

Explanatory inclining reasons for belief (counterparts of motivating reasons for action) are a complex kind ('inclining' is compatible with being either partially or fully causally sufficient and with being either actually or potentially so). To introduce another locution, explanatory reasons for belief are normally *reasons for which* we believe something, and they thereby ground a possible reasons-explanation of our believing it. They are, then, explanatory, possessed, and, when a reason for which one believes genuinely counts in favor of the proposition or action in question, also normative. A reason for which someone believes *p* need not be a good reason, though good reasons we have to believe something are reasons for which in principle one can believe it. A normative reason, however—one there *is* to believe *p* (or to *A*)—need not incline one to believe (or, in the behavioral case, motivate one to act), but it is at least possibly motivating.[3]

II. Reasons as Distinguished from Grounds

From much epistemological literature, particularly in writings discussing skepticism, one might get the impression that any rational belief is based on a reason. This idea is natural if one takes it that, for any rational belief, one ought to be able to say something in answer to the

3. This view is defended at length by Lord (2015).

skeptical question, intended as a request for a justificatory basis, 'Why do you believe *p*?' A satisfactory answer will typically take the form of stating a reason in the sense of a supporting consideration, for instance, that I *see* that *p*, which is a reason there *is* for me to believe it. Still, there are many cases of belief in which grounds for belief are not properly considered reasons for it—even if in much philosophical discussion of reasons, 'reason' is used to encompass grounds. An example will bring out the difference.

Think again of perceptual belief. Suppose I see smoke billowing from a distant hillside. I will immediately believe something is burning there. My ground, epistemic as well as causal, for believing this is *my seeing smoke*. Suppose, however, I am talking by telephone to a friend far away who has conflicting information and asks my reason for believing something is burning on that hillside. I will not say 'My seeing smoke'. I will likely answer by affirming a proposition, such as the proposition that I see smoke from it. This that-clause does express a reason for my belief, but my smoke-belief is itself grounded in my seeing the smoke; and the belief is not the ground—at least not the *original* ground—of my believing that there is fire. There I believed *on a visual ground*, not a propositional one, and when I gave a reason for believing there is fire, my reason was not the ground itself but an affirmation of the presence of that ground. We may certainly say that my visual perception of smoke is the reason, and explains, *why* I believe that. My seeing smoke may also explain *how I know this proposition*. But not every reason *why* someone holds a belief is a normative ground or indeed a ground at all, as brain manipulation illustrates; and seeing smoke—the perception itself—would not normally be called a reason I have for my belief, as opposed to a (explaining) reason why I have it.

A supporting point here is that normative reasons (both theoretical and practical) are always and naturally expressible in that-clauses, which have truth-valued contents, whereas grounds, such as sense-experiences and memory impressions, need not be so expressible but can still justify truth-valued attitudes.[4] My reason for believing that there is a fire beyond on the distant hill *is* that there is smoke billowing from it; it is identical with that proposition and is what I state to my friend on the phone. My visual experience of smoke is not a proposition, though

4. That reasons are propositionally expressible is a view clearly held by Scanlon (though he does not to my knowledge distinguish them from grounds): "The things that reasons are, as I have said, the same kinds of things that can be contents of beliefs—propositions, one might say" (1998: 57).

it corresponds to one and may be in a sense described or at least reported by it. As a ground, however, my experience can justify my reason-expressing belief, and it does this by conferral rather than transmission. It does not admit of being justified or unjustified and thus has no justification to transmit.

The difference between justification by conferral and justification by transmission is important. Grounds do not invite the regress or circle encountered if one supposes that propositional attitudes are justified only by elements of the same truth-valued kind. That is partly why the distinction between grounds and reasons is important. A reason one has for believing *p* admits of a why-question answerable by citing a belief supporting that reason. A ground for believing *p*, such as a visual experience, is a reality that can justify beliefs in a basic way—by conferral—that does not admit of the kind of inferential support a reason provides for a belief held on the basis of it.[5]

For propositional specifications of reasons, the practical case is strongly parallel to the theoretical case. Take belief as representative of truth-valued propositional attitudes. In the practical case there are, as in the "theoretical" case of belief, reasons *to*, reasons *for which*, and parallels for the doxastic cases: we may simply substitute, for 'to believe *p*', 'to *A*', or '*A*-s', where '*A*' represents an act-type. But there is a difference: where belief is in question, we have a disanalogy to the infinitive case. Although we can intelligibly say, e.g., that (1) *S* believes *p to please* the teacher, which is parallel to (2) '*S A*-s to please the teacher', (1) is not equivalent to (3) 'The reason for which *S* believes *p* is to please the teacher', which is the counterpart of the practical ascription (4) 'The reason for which *S A*-s is to realize *G*'. The latter ascribes a possessed reason; the parallel belief-ascription (3) seems to express only an explanatory reason rather than a reason *S* has to believe *p*. Formulation (3) is roughly equivalent to (4) 'The reason *why S* believes *p* is to please the teacher'. The best explanation of the disanalogy seems to be that practical goals, such as pleasing someone, do not serve as reasons, or as bases of reasons, *to believe*. They may, of course, yield reasons to *cause*

5. Wilfrid Sellars is widely known for arguing (e.g. in 1956) that justification *requires* a basis in something that admits of it, as with the propositions constituting reasons for belief of the kind in question. I have discussed this issue in detail in my 2001, citing Sellars and others (often proponents of epistemological coherentism) holding the same view.

oneself to believe, but those are practical reasons and quite different, as evidenced by the way they are properly evaluated.[6]

Suppose these considerations are sound and the linguistic analogues of infinitival specifications of reasons to act—such as 'believes it to please the teacher'—indicate only reasons *why* and not reasons *to* of a normative kind. Might there not still be a close theoretical analogue of infinitival specifications of reasons to act? Suppose we start with the question 'Why do you believe *p*?', where this is a request for a normative basis of belief. This is answerable by some locution of the form of 'on the basis of *x*', where *x* is not a proposition but something experiential such as seeing smoke rising from the hillside, seeing the flames in plain sight, hearing a sour note, and my sense of uneven rhythm. Granted, one *can* put 'the fact that' with any of these to yield a phrase, such as 'the fact that I see smoke rising from the hillside', which designates the occurrence of the experience. But *it is because of the experience that there is such a fact to cite*; neither the fact nor, especially, the counterpart reason-expressing proposition (say, that smoke is rising from the spot) yields the experience or is epistemically more basic than the experience. A similar point holds for answers to 'Why do you believe *p*?' that begin with 'Because *q*', where *q* is a proposition reporting the perception or other kind of experience, as with 'Because I remember seeing . . .' The fact that a basis of belief may be propositionally specified does not entail that, unless so specified, it fails to explain or justify the belief for which it is a basis, or does so less well than citing a reason for which the belief is held, if indeed it is held for a reason.

Generalizing, we might say roughly this: if a reason for which *S* believes *p* is that *q*, the proposition that *q* in some way indicates an experiential or cognitive basis, *x*, say a propositional perception or a belief, for *S*'s believing that *q* (this allows, as we should, that a basis on which *S* believes *p* can be another belief, whether that is justificatory, as it may or may not be, or only explanatory, as it will be). Moreover, where *x* is a basis on which *S* believes *p*, there is a proposition *q* that does or can express a reason for which *S* believes *p*.

This view leaves open whether, in the normative order, grounds are more basic than reasons, but they apparently are. For one thing, one might believe *p* on a basis such that one cannot understand a propositional formulation of it, as where a child, on the basis of hearing a dynamically unbalanced and rushed violin passage, believes the violin passage sounds bad, but cannot, without instruction, understand

6. I have argued for this in detail in ch. 3 of my 2001a and other works.

a propositional expression of that basis. A further point is that even where such understanding is possible, the basis of belief need not proceed *through* a basis-expressing belief. This second point explains one reason why a belief based on an experience need not be inferential—thus typically based on another belief—even if it epistemically depends on something else such that it *could* be inferential should that other element be propositionally accessible to the perceiver in the right way. Believing *p* on a ground, such as hearing screechy violin playing, does not entail believing *p* inferentially on a premise asserting the presence of that ground.

III. Reasons and Grounds for Belief: The Practical Analogy

The contrast here between reasons and grounds in relation to beliefs parallels a difference not widely addressed and often not noticed. Reasons for action (say *A*-ing) admit not just of propositional expression—e.g. *that A*-ing will bring about *G* (some goal), but also infinitival expression—*to* bring about *G*. This propositional expressibility of practical reasons must not be allowed to mask something significant but easily missed. A good case can be made for thinking that the propositional expression of the reason is in a sense less basic than the infinitival one. Note first that the practical attitudes and, correspondingly, the contents of infinitives, are not truth-valued, and that propositions, which are the contents of reasons expressed by that-clauses, are truth-valued. One point, then, is that reasons for action, propositionally expressed, can be appraised in a way that does not apply to them as expressed infinitivally. The that-clause may be true or false, whereas the infinitive clause is not truth-valued and need not express an actual state of affairs even when the counterpart that-clause is true. My reason to *A* might be that it will help Gail, but even when this is true, it does not follow that I *A* or that I help Gail.

A more important contrast may be this. That *A*-ing will bring about *G*—say, will reduce pain—apparently counts as a (normative) reason to *A*, *in virtue of* the desirability of *G*. The desirability may itself be instrumental, but the case of most interest here is the one in which *G* has non-instrumental value: normally, value "in itself." On this dependency view, that *A*-ing will bring about *G* is not intrinsically normative but owes its normative authority—roughly, its supporting the rationality of acting on it—to a normative property of the relevant state of affairs or act-type, *G* (*G* may be an act-type, e.g. pleasing a friend). By contrast, the normative authority of bringing about *G*, say reducing pain, seems to be intrinsic to it and basic (or at least more basic, normatively, than that of the proposition that an action will reduce pain). *To reduce pain*—which is equivalent in such contexts to *reducing pain*—is desirable in itself in a sense implying that there is reason for *any* action that contributes to this. Reducing pain, like yielding pleasure, is what might be called a constitutive aim of practical reason.

Is there a parallel in the theoretical case? If we may again use the metaphor of constitutive aim, we might say that for theoretical reason, a constitutive aim is truly representing the world of experience, internal as well as external. True propositions do this, but as we have seen in examining perception, they do it by expressing what experience does or may reveal. My experience is now dominated by the green and copper tones in my view. That representational basis explains why I can say, in answering 'What is your reason for believing that there are multicolored leaves before you?', 'My visual experience clearly indicates them'. That visual experience is indeed closer to the facts to be truly represented than is the report of them, and if the experience is perceptual and fully veridical, its occurrence entails those facts. Similarly, the goal of reducing pain is closer to the desirable state of affairs—which is the content of the motivating goal—than is the proposition that taking aspirin will yield it. That proposition expresses only an instrumental connection to pain, whereas the reduction of pain—expressed by the infinitival expression of the reason, is good. The instrumental connection might be of no interest to the agent if reducing pain were not good. The analogy to the theoretical case is partly this: much as grounds of reasons for actions indicate the desirability of the actions the reasons support, grounds of reasons for beliefs indicate the believability of the propositions those reasons support.

IV. Reasons as Explanations

We have now seen considerable diversity in types of reasons for belief and action and in the corresponding locutions used in ascribing them. Is there a way to unify this territory? I suggest that there is—though not without appealing to a notion whose complexity presents a challenge to philosophical analysis. I refer to the notion of explanation. Take first (external) normative reasons. If *R* is a reason (for anyone) to believe *p* (or to *A*), then the proposition that *R* explains (at least in part) why anyone *should* (other things being equal) believe *p* (or *A*). This is a kind of normative explanation; but it is clearly an intelligible kind of explanation that should be countenanced in its own right, and it is appropriate that reasons should be paired with explanations. From here, it is a short step to seeing that reasons there are *for S* in particular to believe *p* or to *A* can be represented as considerations that explain why *S* (possibly in contrast to other agents) *should* believe *p* or should *A*.[7]

Inclining reasons to believe *p*, those *S* has to believe *p* (or for believing *p*—the more natural expression where *S does* believe *p* for such a reason), present a different problem. For we do not believe (or) act on all the reasons we have. This holds for normative reasons as well as inclining ones. We thus need to appeal to hypothetical explanation here. For *S* to have, at *t*, a reason, *R*, to believe *p* (at roughly that time) entails *R*'s explaining, at least in part, or being capable of so explaining *S*'s believing *p* at *t*. If the reason is in a certain way minor, it may be capable *only* of partially explaining why *S* believes *p*. But the kind of explanation it can ground is not different; this is confirmed by the possibility that where *R* can only partially explain why *S* believes *p*, there is in principle some combination of equally strong reasons supporting the same belief or action that can fully explain it.

Granted, there is a substantive assumption here: that having even a minor reason to *A* has this degree of at least potential explanatory power. That, however, is confirmed by (1) the apparently self-evident proposition that a reason one has to believe *p* (or to *A*) may have a psychological strength such that it can serve as one *for which* (at least in part) one believes *p* (or *A*-s) and by (2) the self-evident proposition that if *R* is in fact a reason for which *S* believes *p*, then there is a way in which *R* at least partly explains *S*'s believing it. It is easiest to see this in the case of action. Minimally, *A*-ing can be explained by appeal either to *S*'s *believing* the instrumental proposition *R* expresses or to *S*'s *wanting* to bring about the goal specified by *R*. Notice, however, that a purported belief-explanation of *S*'s *A*-ing may be defeated by noting that *S* in no sense wanted to bring about *G*. Similarly, a purported desire-explanation of *S*'s *A*-ing may also be defeated by knowledge that *S* did not believe (or in any way take it) that *A*-ing would (or, e.g., might) realize *G*. In this way, such single-barreled explanations may be considered in a way

7. This kind of explanation is discussed informatively by John Broome in, e.g., *Rationality through Reasoning* (2013). I should add that if *R* is expressed infinitively, e.g. as 'to cure my headache' as in the aspirin case, the explaining reason might be this: that taking it will cure my headache.

elliptical. The point is quite consistent, however, with the explanatory unification of reasons I have proposed.[8]

The propositional, often belief-ascribing, specification of reasons raises an important question for the case in which *R*—say *that taking this pill will relieve my headache*—is false. If reasons as expressed in that-clauses are taken to be factive, this case will be rejected in favor of something like the view that *S* acted only for an apparent reason. I have argued against this factivity view at length elsewhere[9] and will here simply indicate some reasons to regard it as too narrow.

One point that disconfirms the factivity view is evident when we consider the sense in which a reason may be provided by *reasoning*. Here the theoretical case is easier to describe. Suppose that, as is common, I formed my belief that *p* on the basis of reasoning from *q*. I will then find it especially strange to think that I believe *p* for no reason. Believing on the basis of reasoning seems to be a main basis for explaining what it *is* for beliefs and actions to be reason-based. My reasoning might even be valid, hence formally good. In one terminology, if my premises are false, the trouble with my reasoning (hence my inferential ground for *p*) is external; it is with the *inputs* to the reasoning. This defect does not preclude my conclusion's being both drawn from plausible premises I justifiedly believe and held for a reason.

Furthermore, on the factivity view, if I am asked for my reason for believing *p*, and I sincerely say that my reason is that *q*, I can be corrected—told that *q* is not my reason—(1) without being thought either insincere or wrong about why I believe *p* and (2) on the ground that *q* is false. But this would be a mistaken way to correct self-ascriptions of explaining reasons for believing (which may also be normative). We normally presuppose that others (apart from self-deception and other special cases) are correct when they sincerely offer their reasons for believing or doing something, and we do not properly take the falsehood of a proposition offered as a reason to falsify this presupposition of self-knowledge. Suppose a credible person tells me *q* is false. Assuming that I now doubt that *q* but do not immediately cease to believe *q*, I will still *not* now doubt that *q* is the reason for which I have believed *p*. I will

8. Davidson (1963) presumably noted this and spoke of "primary" reasons for actions as combinations of desires and instrumental beliefs. He was thinking of what I call *reason states* (intentional attitudes that express reasons), and he had in mind a "full" statement of the intentional elements that underlie intentional action.

9. In my 2007a, which treats the issue in more detail than is possible here.

instead think that perhaps I *ought* not to have believed *p*, and perhaps should now no longer believe *p* if I have no basis for it other than *q*. I may also come to cease believing *p*.

A second point about critical discourse may now be seen. If the factivity view is correct, not only may I be told that I was mistaken in taking *R* to be a reason; I should see that I was also mistaken in thinking that I believed *p* for a reason *at all* (unless I had another one). What is the best alternative account? Recall the case of believing, on the basis of seeing smoke, that there is a distant fire. Here it looked to me as if smoke billowed from the hillside. Now suppose I had hallucinated but had an exactly similar visual experience. I would then still have said that my reason for believing that there is fire is that I see smoke. But I do not see it. The factivity theorist will likely say here that I believed for an *apparent* reason: that it looked to me as if there was smoke on the hillside. This proposition is true, but what I believed, given my very clear visual impression of smoke, is that there *was* smoke on the hillside. Now I *did* have a ground for believing there was fire: my visual experience. But grounds can yield reasons that justify without yielding knowledge, much as justified true premises in an argument can yield a justified true belief that does not constitute knowledge. Rejecting the factivity view does not force us to claim that, if the hallucination happened to coincide with a fire on the hillside, *S* would *know* there is one. Distinguishing grounds for believing from reasons for believing, and taking reasons to be ground-dependent in the ways illustrated, enables us both to do justice to reasons discourse and to avoid taking justifiedly and truly believing to constitute knowing.

The practical case perhaps more clearly illustrates the narrowness of the factivity view. If I say my reason for taking an aspirin is that it will relieve my headache and I am wrong, the factivity view invites saying that I acted for an apparent reason, say that it seemed to me that it would relieve me. If, however, we say this and retain, as we should, the idea that explanatory reasons are often expressed by beliefs connecting the action explained with *S*'s goal, then we seem forced to conclude that I acted on a (propositional) reason I did not believe—that taking the pill would *apparently* relieve my headache. This is not something I believed, at least in the common case in which I am quite sure of the pill.

If one doubts there is a real difference here, consider how, in a court of law, it would matter whether one had a cautious, qualified belief that the accused apparently drove a blue car, which might well be true, or the false belief that the accused drove one. So, applying this to the aspirin case, we have a dilemma: either I acted on a proposition I did not believe or I am mistaken in thinking that adducing my instrumental belief about the pill as a means to relief genuinely explains my taking it.

To hold that propositions constituting reasons for belief (or for action) need not be true is not to deny an important pragmatic point about reasons discourse. Perhaps in second- and third-person *ascriptions* of reasons for belief or action, whether of (a) reasons for anyone at all to believe *p* or to *A*, or (b) reasons for a specific person to believe *p* or to *A*, or (c) reasons *for which* a particular person *does* believe *p* or perform *A*, *a (defeasible) presupposition of truth predominates.* Hence, if we think *p* false, we normally do not cite it as someone's reason for believing that *q*, or for *A*-ing, unless we cancel the truth presupposition, e.g. saying 'that—as he claims—*p*'. Take the question, 'What reason does Sally have for supporting Jonathan?' We usually would not say 'that he is the best candidate' if we disbelieve this—though we might cite the corresponding reason state, saying that she *believes* he is the best candidate, or use 'as she sees it', or in some other way distance ourselves from the usual presupposition of truth.

One might think that the factivity view must be presupposed by the idea that the notion of explanation unifies the diverse kinds of reasons. This is especially likely to be claimed in the light of the case in which 'reason' is clearly factive: that of reasons *why S* believes *p* (or *A*-s). I grant that in this case 'explanation why', like 'reason why' used in the same way, is factive. But note three things. (These hold for belief as well as action, but for brevity I consider just the latter.) First, a reason why *S A*-s need not be one *for* which *S A*-s. Second, where a reason does embody falsehood, as with false belief that a pill will relieve a headache, there *is* a counterpart fact—that *S believes* it will—that does explain the action, in the context of the presupposed want for the relevant goal. The third point is quite different. We speak of inference to the best explanation where clearly we are using 'explanation' to refer to statements not presupposed to be true (since there are jointly inconsistent explanatory statements in question).[10] I leave open whether this shows that we do not presuppose that genuine explanations are factive or whether (as I think more plausible) we are referring to hypothetical

10. It may be that in the case of abductive explanation we speak of the best explanation *of* the relevant phenomenon, rather than of explanation *why* it occurred. But in hypothetical cases I do not see this as undermining anything said in the text.

explanations—statements that, if true, are genuine explanations. Either alternative will sustain the view that the notion of explanation provides a way to unify the diverse kinds of reasons we must countenance.

V. Normative Reasons and Their Grounds

It should be apparent that the structural view of reasons so far sketched is neutral with respect to the question of what sorts of considerations constitute reasons. But as indicated in my examples, we may hold a (generic) *perceptual principle*:

> If, at *t*, a proposition, *p*, sensorily seems true to *S*, then, at *t*, there is a reason for *S* to believe *p*.[11]

The sense-experience itself is a *ground* for believing *p* and guarantees that there is a reason to believe it—namely, *that* the experience is occurring at *t*. I am taking it as obvious that (assuming there are normative reasons at all) sense-impressions—a kind of "evidence of the senses"—are among their grounds. On the practical side, it may be even clearer that reducing pain is a reason for *A*-ing when *A*-ing will achieve this than that yielding pleasure plays the same role; but I believe that it does.

Given how diverse sense-experiences are, we may expect a sense-experiential theory of reasons for perceptual belief to be highly pluralistic. This goes with the point that there are many kinds of experiential grounds and reasons, even for a given sense such as vision.[12] A parallel

11. This leaves open how good a reason there is. That depends on many conditions, including the vividness and steadiness of the seeming. For John Morrison, there is such a thing as "perceptual confidence": "According to perceptual confidence, experiences are belief-like in yet another way: they can assign more or less confidence" (2016). If 'assign' is understood, as seems most plausible here, to mean roughly 'imply', this seems appropriate—provided there is a perceptual belief or disposition to form a belief, to which confidence may be attributed. But I see no reason to take experiences themselves to be bearers of confidence, as opposed to properties that yield confidence in, e.g., persons and their judgments. I agree with Morrison, however, that differences in perceptual experience, say in clarity, patterns, or fineness of grain, both justify different degrees of confidence in corresponding propositions and facilitate knowing them.

12. For an indication of the breadth and plausibility of hedonism, see Moore's (1912) and Crisp (2006).

point holds for intellective (say intuitional) experiences (which will be addressed in Part Two). I have already illustrated how sense experience can normatively ground beliefs. We should now pursue further the question how these experiences might constitute grounds of reasons.

In supposing that there are grounds for reasons, we need not deny that there is a sense in which reasons themselves may be grounds. Propositional grounds, however, by contrast with what seems normal for experiential ones, can be grounded, rather as premises can be premised. This is easiest to see in the theoretical case. You might believe *p* on the ground that *q*, which entails or otherwise supports *p*. In this case, you believe *p* for the reason that *q*. Where grounds for belief are reasons, they are normally expressed by that-clauses. For cases of belief in which grounds for belief are not properly considered reasons for it, think of perceptual belief. As noted earlier, if I see flames rising from a distant hillside, I will immediately believe that something is burning there, and my ground for the belief, both normative and psychological, would be *my seeing flames*. Grounds provide a basis for beliefs, and accordingly for reasons, that affirm the presence of those grounds; but the ability of grounds to justify beliefs does not depend on our forming the beliefs in question.

In the light of these points, it is natural to take non-propositional grounds to have a kind of priority over reasons or propositional grounds. It appears that the reason-giving force of my reason for believing that there is fire is my visual experience of flames. Without that experience I could claim to have a reason to believe there is a fire, but I would not (unless from another source) have a (perceptual) normative reason. To put the main point here in terms of earlier chapters, it seems to be in virtue of the representational qualities of my experience—such as the visually presented colors and shapes of flames—that I have my reason to believe there is fire before me. The qualities in the abstract explain the normative force of the reason in the abstract; the qualities of my actual experience explain why there is normative reason *for me* to believe there is a fire.

If reasons can be grounded, and if, in particular instances, reasons derive their normative power from the qualities of relevant experiences, does this support the reducibility of reasons to experiential considerations of the kind in question? I do not claim this, nor take grounding to be a reducibility relation.[13] My view is simply that normative reasons for

13. The literature on grounding is now extensive, but the view that it is not a reducibility relation is widely held and plausible. For a defense see P. Audi (2012).

believing have their status as genuinely supporting belief in virtue of some experience on which they are in some way based. For knowledge of the world, it is perceptual experience that is central.

Reasons come in many forms, and our vocabulary for describing them is rich and sometimes elusive. There are, for instance, reasons *to* believe, *for* believing, *for which* one believes, and *why* one believes; and, in both practical and theoretical cases—for example in behavioral and doxastic instances—there are internal reasons we have and external reasons we do not have, such as reasons to believe a road is dangerous. We have normative reasons for beliefs, as well as for acts, in virtue of certain experiential states. These states are above all the kind that ground the rationality of believing the propositions in question or the desirability of the relevant acts; and reasons are themselves apparently normatively grounded in certain experiential elements. These elements include, on the evidential, theoretical side, sensory events and states, and, on the practical side, hedonic elements. Reasons for belief are unified by their explanatory scope and power. Such normative reasons are grounded in experiential elements, including perceptions as a central kind, that have a major role in explaining both why we have the normative reasons we do and why we believe or do as we do in responding to those reasons. These points conclude a sketch of reasons and their grounds in experience, especially perceptual experience but also experiences such as pleasurable and painful ones, that provide grounds of value: of the good and the bad and of much else. It is only a sketch, but the basic lines yield a structure that can substantially guide our efforts to fill out the details.

6

THE AUTONOMY OF JUSTIFICATION

Any serious reader of Descartes's *Meditations* (1641) is likely to have the sense that it is possible to have experiences in which one seems to see an external object but does not. Descartes used vivid dreams as one way to get this across, but contemporaries may prefer the idea of a brain in a vat: one receiving just the kind of stimuli that our brains normally receive in perception. The Cartesian legacy here—centered on the apparent possibility of hallucinatory experiences qualitatively just like perceptual ones—is powerful. On my view, even apart from the possibility Descartes argued for—that a person could exist without a body—it is possible in principle to have a hallucination that, qualitatively, is exactly like that of seeing a clock on the wall. This experience could justify believing that there is, for instance, a clock on the wall. If so, then sense-experience, even unaccompanied by the perception in which it is normally embodied, is apparently what yields the kind of justification we are considering.

I. Epistemological Internalism

The conception of justification that best accommodates this perspective is internalism. On my version, what justifies believing p is something accessible to the believer by introspection or reflection, and I take at least three kinds of thing to be internally accessible: occurrent mental phenomena such as the sensory impression of typeface before me, dispositional mental phenomena such as beliefs, and certain abstracta, such as concepts and propositions. Abstract objects include both simple cases like the concept of a square and complex concepts such

Seeing, Knowing, and Doing. Robert Audi, Oxford University Press (2020). © Oxford University Press.
DOI: 10.1093/oso/9780197503508.001.0001

as that of a person. So far, the view developed in this book is strongly experientialist, but the internalist element in my theory of perception needs further explanation.[1]

The starting point for our purposes is the idea that, as argued in Chapter 1, perception is experiential and has sense-experience of some kind as an element. The latter condition seems both appropriate to the nature of perception and supportive of internalism about justification. For perceptual knowledge, moreover, there is reason (setting aside general skepticism) to think that sense-experience, which carries the representational element in perception, will reflect facts. Certainly this best explains why, guided by our sense-experience, we so often succeed in navigating the world.

If, however, justification is possible without knowledge, as it evidently is, justification has a kind of autonomy relative to knowledge and even truth. It is, after all, under the control, as it were, of internal phenomena and is possible when it neither yields knowledge in beliefs based on it nor captures any truth in its content. Autonomy, however, does not imply that justification is isolated from facts. Justification is also intimately connected with truth in important ways. What, then, is its connection with knowledge? Justification (in the form of justifiedly believing) is in one way very similar to knowledge and in another way quite different from it—here I abstract from the difference concerning the truth of the proposition in question. Justification is similar to knowledge in being generated (at the foundational level) by experiential sources—indeed the same ones we commonly conceive as yielding knowledge, such as sense-experience in the case of perception and memory impressions as regards the past. Justification differs greatly from knowledge, however, in being essentially dependent on experiential grounds and, related to this, connected with critical practices in a way that knowledge is not. Let me address these points.

II. Does Knowledge Entail Justification?

Regarding knowledge in contrast to justification, consider how natural it is to speak of machines as knowing. A driverless car is naturally said

1. Internalists may or may not hold some form of the privileged access view, which, in a strong form found in Hume ([1739] 1888, pt. 4, sec. 2), entails that we can neither be ignorant of nor mistaken in self-ascribing certain of our mental states, such as an appearance of red before us. For extensive discussion see, William P. Alston (1971) and my 1974.

to know that another car is getting too close, a computer to know when its battery is low, and a good thermostat to know when to raise the heat. I am not claiming that a non-experiencing thing literally has knowledge, especially self-knowledge, though we can use 'knows' for certain self-reporting machines and need have no sense of being metaphorical. It is far more difficult to imagine a natural use of 'justified' for machines. Imagine a short circuit that causes a driverless car to beep to signal a nearby vehicle when the signal indicates that, but where there is no vehicle near. The beeping obeys the controlling switch. Is the beep "justified" since it obeys the switch it is supposed to obey, or is the car justified in beeping? This seems doubtful. Clearly the car is malfunctioning. Is it, then, *un*justified? Here neither the car nor the sensors are naturally called unjustified.

It also seems wrong to say of properly working sensors that they are "justified" in sending signals to the switch that controls beeping. We understand this only analogically: they "judge" as we would from our visual representations of nearby vehicles. If they err, we fix the car; we don't criticize them or use terms presupposing normative responsibility. Being justified or unjustified implies a liability to a kind of criticism not appropriate to machines—at least not to all the kinds naturally said to know this or that.

Might persons be like at least some machines in being capable of knowledge without justification? On my view, "mechanical" knowledge is possible without justification even for persons who are capable of justification or for other beings who have experience and mentality. A crucial indication of this is an ability to respond to certain stimuli by forming—without an experiential basis—beliefs that surely constitute knowledge. Consider the *idiot savant* (a person some psychologists have called a "lightning calculator"). Imagine that neither a sense of a good track record, nor even a sense of intuitive plausibility, underlies or even accompanies the immediately formed belief that, say, the product of 54 and 942 is 50,868. (Nor, I think, would an intuitive sense of truth in this kind of case be a likely suitable ground for genuine knowledge, but that is not the point.) If this is an instance of many and varied correct calculations, then, given a flawless track record, we are likely to say the person knows.

This arithmetic example is meant to add realism to my case, but given that the matter concerns conceptual possibility, we can be more speculative. Might it not be possible for an omnipotent God or some appropriately powerful potential creator of persons to give us knowledge of many kinds of things by sheer implantation of beliefs having an appropriately reliable connection to the facts underlying their truth? Even brain manipulation by scientists of the future could give us beliefs that one would unhesitatingly call knowledge. Imagine *blindsight upgraded*: suddenly—perhaps through an implanted x-ray diagnostic program—I find I have detailed beliefs about repairing a mower I look at: I believe that the gas line is plugged by sludge, that flushing will clear it, and so forth for a number of propositions leading to repair. I might go right to work, puzzled that I never read or even thought my way to the propositions. I tell you why I am going to do the things in question, and I succeed in the repair. If, puzzled as I describe the facts, you ask normative questions such as how I know, or what reasons I have, I will have to say something like "I just know these are the things to do." If I succeed repeatedly in such cases, we will likely to regard this knowledge claim as confirmed. This does not entail the possibility of finding something that *justifies* me in holding the beliefs that constitute the implanted knowledge.

Granted, when we believe some proposition *p* and can think of no evidence, it may be natural to have it come to seem that *p* if we consider *p* and *retain* our belief. Believing a proposition sometimes tends to make that proposition seem true on consideration—though of course considering it can also lead to relinquishing it. If, however, *p* is not implausible, this need not be likely. Such *belief-based* seeming, unlike perceptual, memorial, and intuitive seeming, is not necessarily justificatory.[2] A plausible explanation of this point is that a merely belief-based seeming is not *ground-based*, as is the kind that confers prima facie justification. Sensory grounds are the kinds we have been examining, but they are not the only kind, and intuitive grounds will be explored in Part Two.

We should also grant that when a person demonstrates know-how of a kind that seems to presuppose propositional knowledge (as in the repair case proposed), we may be more disposed to attribute justification. But this may be because the success that confirms know-how, such as repairing the mower, carries evidence of knowing the propositions that typically would be known by possessors of that know-how. It is not because the knower antecedently had justification for them. (The controversial view that know-how is equivalent to propositional knowledge—which, though I am not presupposing it here, would support my case—will be examined in Chapter 10).

2. This is explained in my 2013b, which argues for the special normative power of sensory, memorial, introspective, and intuitive grounds.

Justification is necessarily experiential in the ways we have seen, as where it rests on sense-experience supporting *p* or understanding the content of *p* (the understanding can be dispositional, but, as Chapter 8 will explain, its justificatory power in that case rests on its ability to yield an experience of understanding upon appropriate consideration of its object). I do not claim that the sources of justification are a priori fixed in number or function. This is not required by the point that the concept of justification is to be explicated by conceptually central connections to experience. It is, e.g., central to the concept of justified belief that clear, steadfast sensory impressions of the kind we have in normal perceptions yield prima facie justification for beliefs to which they are appropriate. If I have a clear, steadfast impression of arboreal green, then I have prima facie justification for believing that there is green before me. I may also know this, but—and here again we can see a major difference between justification and knowledge—I could fail to know it because I am hallucinating, whereas such a possibility need not affect my justification. I could also know it *without* any sense-experience or other ordinary route to belief formation. If an omnipotent God had designed my cognitive system so that it responds reliably to the relevant light rays, I might know that there is green before me even if I am utterly unable to become aware of why I believe there is. My belief would not be perceptual; but, as even the possibility of knowledge from testimony shows, knowledge of a perceptible phenomenon need not be perceptual knowledge.

There is a related contrast between knowledge and justification. Whereas false belief need not be criticizable for not constituting knowledge, unjustified belief is by its nature criticizable, and its possessor is at least prima facie criticizable for holding it. This point depends on distinguishing a belief's simply not being justified and its being unjustified. A tiny child just forming beliefs may have many that are not justified; but, much as it is improper to call a perfectly ordinary unremarkable tree insensitive because it is not the case that it is sensitive, it is improper to call a tiny child's belief that its pet cat is reading the book it is sniffing *un*justified because it is *not* justified.

More positively, it appears that 'justified' and 'unjustified' (and, I think, the concepts they express) apply to creatures only when their level of conceptual development makes them eligible for a certain kind of criticism and they can be in some way held responsible for being justified in certain beliefs. This does not apply to 'know' and its cognates, as illustrated not only by the case of certain machines but also by that of tiny children. Related to this, in the domain of belief, an important contrast with *S*'s knowing that p is *S*'s ignorance of *p* (or having no inkling that *p*), and a second important contrast is with mistakenly believing *p*. In neither case need there be any liability to criticism.

If, as I have maintained, justification is autonomous with respect to knowledge—neither being dependent on it nor being a constituent in it—should we not also hold that knowledge is autonomous relative to justification? We certainly may, but in epistemology the notion of knowledge has tended to be dominant, often with a suggestion that the importance of justification is in contributing to knowledge and serving as a necessary element in it. I can accept a version of the contributory view, but I believe that justification is immensely important in its own right. The rest of this chapter will clarify this view.

III. The Practice-Relativity of Justification

How does the internalist view of justification sketched here square with the traditional view that knowledge and justification are intimately related? One might think that the way to reconcile these two views is to frame an externalist conception of knowledge *and* justification and thereby preserve the frequently affirmed thesis that knowledge entails justification. It is true that the commonest cases of knowledge are constituted by justified true beliefs, but is it really plausible to say that *S* is justified in cases in which *S* has reliably grounded belief that (as in the lightning calculator case) intuitively seems an instance of knowledge but (1) is not based on or even accompanied by any apparently evidential experience; (2) cannot be justified by *S* by appeal to any other accessible element, such as a track record; and (3) partly for this reason, *S* may be puzzled at having? We have seen cases of several kinds that indicate that we could have ample grounds to ascribe knowledge where one cannot plausibly ascribe justification. This is not only a possible case of knowledge without justification, but one in which *S* (having no memory of the good track record we know of) would likely not even claim justification.

An at least partial explanation of this point is a major contrast between the concepts of justification and knowledge in what might be called their dialectical function. The concept of justification is *practice-relative* in a way the concept of knowledge is not.[3] There is a practice

3. The relativity here is a matter of what I take to be a universal practice of justifying beliefs, especially by appeal to sense-experience. I am not speaking of conceptions of justification that anchor it in such frameworks as might be

of justifying beliefs, and the universal coin that purchases success in this process is adducing experiential, internally accessible elements. These are elements the subject is aware of or can, by introspection or reflection, become aware of. By contrast, there is no practice of knowledge. There is a practice of *showing* that one knows, but this is a matter, not necessarily of showing one is justified but of showing that the basis of one's belief suffices (at least probabilistically) for the truth of the proposition in question (or, in the case of objectual knowledge, for the relevant property attribution). Behaviorally, one could show that one knows by, e.g., answering arithmetic questions and doing such associated things as getting through mazes. These need not count toward justification.

It is true that in *citing* determinants of beliefs that counts as knowledge without justification, as an *idiot savant* like the one portrayed above might (in principle) do after the fact, one would be justifying the relevant belief.[4] But this supports only the weaker view that there is an intimate connection between knowledge and justification—that the grounds of justification support attributing knowledge. I accept this but it does not support the thesis that knowledge entails justification. We can stand on grounds we have no way to see are sustaining us.

Here is a related case. Imagine that I find I know how far away certain birds are though I don't see or hear them. On being told that brain manipulation enabled me to know the distances by a "decoding" of the sound waves reaching me from birdsongs, but without any awareness of the sounds themselves, I might be able, by learning the mechanisms involved, to provide ordinary evidence inductively supporting the distance beliefs in question. I had knowledge without justification; but when I discovered how I knew, I could *give* justification. In giving it I cite evidences of kinds I would have gotten in the usual accessible ways involving a correlation of sound waves and distances, visual impressions of birds, and so forth.

constituted by mystical experience. The kind of practice relativity appropriate to those is explored, in ways partly inspired by Reid and Wittgenstein, by Alston (1990).

4. The elements cited would have to be described in enough detail to make their implying justification clear. In the case of the idiot savant, e.g., it would not suffice to justify believing that 54 x 942 = 50,868 by saying that believing this is determined by a neural process; one would need to add something like 'a process that, like a calculating machine, reliably generates correct answers to such problems'.

Seeing the autonomy of the concept of justification relative to that of knowledge is particularly difficult because our main ways of showing that someone knows (given a supposition of truth) is to adduce justifiers. Indeed, we cannot even properly explain what it is to know without citing the kind of phenomena I have taken as intrinsically justificatory. That is certainly not sufficient for such conceptual explanation of knowledge, since the presence of justification does not entail truth, which is necessary for knowledge, or even imply truth with high objective probability (as may be indicated by relative frequencies). For justification, such probability is not even necessary. Justification can come from hallucination-based beliefs and is possible even in a Cartesian demon world.

Parallel cases in which knowledge is possible without justification can be constructed not only for arithmetic cases, but also for direct knowledge of the past without memory justification, for knowledge of the future without inductive grounds or other accessible grounds, and, in my view, for testimony-based knowledge—which may have a priori as well as empirical propositions as its objects. This point, and indeed the case against taking knowledge to entail justification, depends on conceiving justification internalistically but is neutral with respect to whether the content of the justified beliefs in question is internal or external in a semantic sense. That issue is not my concern here.[5]

IV. An Integrated View of Justification and Knowledge

Why, however, does justification go so well with knowledge? In part, though we do not conceive knowledge as entailing justification, we do conceive it as constituted by the kind of belief whose existence may be properly argued for, though not entailed, by citing the constitutive basic sources of justification, such as sense-experience and memory impressions. Showing that a person justifiedly believes *p*, however, is different from showing that the person knows that *p*. The former (at least for empirical propositions) constitutes adducing support for *p* in

5. Critical discussion of my view that we can integrate an externalist view of knowledge with an internalist view of justification is provided in Williamson (2007a). My response in that volume, *Rationality and the Good*, edited by Timmons, Greco, and Mele (2007), supplements what is said above and also indicates how my view squares with a plausible account of the internal-external distinction in relation to content. See esp. pp. 230–241.

a way that presupposes or entails the belief's being based on the relevant justifying elements and does not entail that *p* be true. Showing that someone knows that *p*, as we have seen in various examples, constitutes showing that the belief that *p* is properly fact-based (appropriately grounded and true). It is a process not of knowing—there is no such process—but of showing that the conditions for knowing are satisfied. But there is a process of justifying, and success in this process can show that the target belief is justified with or without entailing, or even providing objectively good evidence for, its truth. Hallucinatory experiences that the person cannot discover may suffice.

The internalist thesis that the raw materials of the process of justifying a belief are accessible to the believer goes with the idea that in principle, if we justifiedly believe *p*, we can normally exhibit our justification by adducing some adequate ground we have—an ability normally guaranteed by the accessibility of internal grounds. Justifiedness is the kind of property whose possession is based on the sorts of accessible elements appropriate for the process of showing and thereby exhibiting that property. I call this the *process-property integration thesis.*[6] There is no analogue for the property (or relation) of knowing.

A unifying idea here—one that indicates how knowledge and justification are both "epistemic"—is that truth is in a sense the critical norm for both. The same truth-conducive factors, such as sense-experiences, are constitutive of the norms governing both. Positively, the kind of accessible elements that yield justification for believing *p*, such as sense-impressions of color and shape, also support claims to know that *p*. On the negative side, attributions of either knowledge or justification must be withdrawn upon presenting the attributor with good overall evidence against *p*. Perceptual evidence is an important case, but a proposition's entailing a contradiction is always counterevidence regarding it. An attribution of justification, however, must be withdrawn only if the counterevidence is of the kind that yields justification to begin with. The actual falsity of *p* does not entail that believing it is not justified, whereas an attribution of knowledge is falsified (though not necessarily rendered unjustified) by the falsehood of *p* or indeed by the presence of conditions that, even if inaccessible to *S*, make *S*'s believing p more

6. I first explicated this view in my 1988. I should add that showing that *S* not only *has* justification for *p* but *justifiedly believes p* requires showing that *S* believes *p on a* justifying basis. This point parallels the difference between *S*'s merely having an adequate reason for *p* and its being a reason *for which S* believes *p*.

likely than not to be mistaken in the relevant circumstances. The barn case illustrates the latter point. The counterpart claim does not hold for justification.

The case of memory has special relevance here. Consider recalling a perception. In principle, such recall could provide images of everything one perceived on the remembered occasion. This would give one access to representations—with degrees of vividness depending on memorial acuity—of everything one saw (or otherwise perceived). These representations, such as visual images, are both internally accessible and fitted to be cited in a process of justifying a belief. If they are also veridical, then, by citing appropriate properties they represent, *S* can (normally) show knowledge as well as justification. But even if they are not veridical, in adducing them *S* may still both show justification and, accordingly, creditably aim at truth.

One might speculate that in the course of evolution we have been selected for cognitive and indeed doxastic receptivity to facts and for a disposition to guide our behavior using conceptual categories that reinforce this receptivity and facilitate communication built on them. (Theistic as well as naturalistic attempts to explain this coincidence are possible). There might be a chain: from perception to discrimination to conceptualization to focusing on—and appealing to—indicators of truth. This chain runs from perceptually encountered fact to representation of fact or (when we fail) of apparent fact. Knowledge is the more primitive case, and in having it we are more similar to higher animals than we are in having justification. Having that seems to come with communication and critical practices. The ability simply to know is more primitive than the ability to go through a process of adducing the grounds on which we know.

V. The Disjunctivist Challenge

There is a way in which a conception of the very content of perceptual experience can appear to undermine the internalist approach to justification and, so far as its grounds are the same as those of justification, knowledge. As brought out in Chapter 2, the content of perceptual experience has been widely taken to be propositional, at least in the sense that it is constituted by Russellian propositions. This view goes well with the idea that reasons are factive, though it is not entailed by that view and does not entail it. Many important beliefs are perceptually justified, and (as noted in Chapter 3) it is natural to answer some requests for justification by saying such things as 'I see it', where this expresses a proposition that may be considered a reason for believing *p*, e.g. that there is a fire in the distance. If one thought that all justified beliefs are justified by reasons and that the reasons justifying perceptual beliefs are facts expressible by propositions capturing part of the content of perceptual experience, it would seem natural to think that sense-experience, which occurs in hallucinations, cannot justify in the same way as reasons and is not the crucial element in the justification of perceptual beliefs.

This "propositionalist" factivity approach to understanding justification and knowledge may partly explain the appeal of disjunctivism, which characteristically denies that there is a "common factor" between perception of an object and a perfect hallucination of it.[7] Consider a case in which, like Macbeth, one has a visual experience qualitatively identical with that of seeing a dagger. The argument might go as follows.

(1) Seeing a dagger is factive: its content, propositionally conceived, includes a proposition (presumably a Russellian one) which, as content of a veridical experience of seeing a dagger, entails (the fact) that there is a dagger before one.

(2) This perceptual content is *external*, and the belief embedded in seeing that there is a dagger before one has a similar external content. But

(3) A hallucination does not have external content (assuming that, as with Macbeth, it is not factive). Hence,

(4) A hallucination does not have the same perceptual content as the qualitatively corresponding perceptual experience (though it can seem to have it). Thus,

7. For general discussion of disjunctivism see Fish (2010), esp. ch. 6; and for a detailed defense of a version of the view see Pritchard (2012). On a theory of perception consonant with mine on the issue, see Johnston (2011). That volume contains much else pertinent to this book, including further crucial discussion of disjunctivism by Nida-Rumelin (2011). Burge's verdict is peremptory: Regarding disjunctivism as "the view that no explanatory kind of perceptual state is common between veridical perceptual states and perceptual illusions," he says, "Naïve realist and other philosophical views of perception that maintain disjunctivism are incompatible with scientific knowledge" (2010: 392–93).

(5) Identity of perceptual content is not a common factor in perceptions of something and qualitatively identical hallucinations of it.

Epistemologists have long thought, however, both that the two kinds of experiences can be intrinsically alike, and that it is plausible to take this to indicate identity in a kind of content—the kind that goes with accurately describing what one "visualizes," as we might put it. (This is a kind of property content, in the terminology of Chapter 2.) Even if we do not take people to be infallible about the content of their experience, we may consider them generally reliable regarding what they are sensorily acquainted with, say what colors they are visually experiencing.

On my view, what is shared between ordinary perceptions and their counterpart hallucinations is plausibly called property content; and if there are visual beliefs that ascribe visible properties to something on the qualitatively identical grounds such content provides, we can explain their difference in terms of the distinction between *de re* beliefs in the perceptual case and (non-Russellian) *de dicto* beliefs in the hallucinatory case. This leaves us with the need to explicate the kind of proposition that is the object of the latter beliefs, but that is a problem we face in any event.[8]

VI. The Elusive Notion of the Content of Perceptual Belief

Let me sketch a possible conception of the content of propositional (*de dicto*) perceptual beliefs. It is agreed on all sides that Macbeth did not believe any physical dagger *to be* before him (or believe, *of* some physical dagger, that it is before him). Let us also assume that we need not posit a sense-datum dagger to provide an object to which he attributes a property. He does, however, have a kind of conception of a dagger, at least in terms of visible properties. His sense-experience guarantees this if only by clearly embodying acquaintance with the properties that, by some causal process whose exact nature is not a philosophical question, give phenomenal content to his experience. (These are not phenomenal

8. I do not deny that one *could* devise a way of taking *de dicto* belief to encompass *de re* belief, as Chisholm did in "Knowledge and Belief: De Dicto and De Re" (1975). But he is able to do this only by employing the notion of a haecceity, and I see no reason to take the success of his reduction (if it does succeed) to undermine my results. If *that* kind of reduction succeeds, my points can be re-formulated in terms of different kinds of *de dicto* cases.

properties, though one may be acquainted with those as well.) He may, then believe (e.g.) *that* the dagger in his visual field is golden.

I cannot here provide a theory of how the singular term 'the dagger' is to be analyzed here (a major task), but my point is that in the veridical case Macbeth might have the *same de dicto belief* as in the hallucinational counterpart in which he also believes a proposition he might express by saying he believes the dagger (which he presupposes is physical) *to be* golden. The underlying point is that his experience is the same in both cases. Despite the difference in his relation to the physical world in the two instances, he can have the same *de dicto* belief in both. This is not to downplay the importance of the difference in the causal relations he bears to the physical world in the two cases; but what makes possible his having the same *de dicto* belief in both is the experience he has in each. This view is supported by the point that, on discovering he was hallucinating, Macbeth would naturally think his belief that there was a dagger before him was false, not that he didn't really believe that there was one before him.

We can also imagine a case in which (1) I hallucinate a dagger that seems ten feet before me, when in fact there is a bare wall two feet closer to me which would hide it if it were suspended where it appears to me to be, and (2) from the other side of the wall, you actually see an exactly similar dagger displayed in the same light, at the same height, in the same position in your visual field, etc. Here it is quite plausible to say that you see the (or a) dagger I only hallucinate—or see one just like the one I hallucinate. Saying this is even more natural if, in the same circumstances, my hallucination is induced by a machine designed to give me an experience as of seeing the very dagger you actually see.

If we keep in mind the naturalness of taking the content of something to be *in* it, we can also see the plausibility of saying that the content—as opposed to the object—of my experience is the same as that of yours. This is plausible, anyway, for experiential content, the kind one can be aware of and, under good conditions, describe. Granted, there is a *kind* of experience Macbeth cannot have in both cases: the relational kind that is usual when we experience the behavior of external objects. This point is illustrated by the difference between one's experiencing a rainbow, which you and I can equally well see, and one's experiencing pain, which is not external. But the kind of experience that figures in the *de dicto* visual belief is the same in both the hallucinatory and veridical dagger cases just described. What differs is how that belief leads to engaging the world—in the relational case, to (say) gripping the dagger and in the other to reaching emptyhandedly in the relevant direction and realizing there is no dagger there. My assumption here is that we are comparing qualitatively identical cases in both of which the *properties* Macbeth is in some way acquainted with are the same, but in the one case they are instantiated in his environment and in the other not. (How one can be acquainted with properties not instantiated in a concrete object will be considered in Chapter 9). Descent from the conceptual level to the physical level will be satisfying in one case in a way it is not in the other. What of ascent from the physical level to the conceptual?

Here it is helpful to think of intuitive induction. When children learn that 2 + 2 = 4 by combining pairs of objects and counting the foursome created, they are not generalizing in the way one would in doing enumerative induction. That naturally works with physical things and their properties, such as balls rolled down an inclined plane in measuring acceleration. Intuitive induction is not a process of, say, finding more and more evidence for a generalization, which then appears more and more probable. Indeed, could one not by intuitive induction learn general, even a priori, truths given the same sense-experiences, without the experiences' even being veridical? That some general truths are in principle learnable without enumerative induction and even without physical evidence is a possibility internalists take seriously.

Experience, when sufficiently discriminative, provides a ladder to properties—to seeing them, for instance, or, in abstract matters like pure arithmetic, to apprehending them. Our nature is such that descending is also possible for us and sometimes automatic. A main reason for this is apparently that we perceive things *by* perceiving their properties (in the sense that the object's instantiating that property causes, in a special way, our experiencing the property), and given this causal connection we have a kind of downward pathway "back" to the object. We are, as it were, designed to find what is (perceptually) causing our sensory experience, e.g. the object seen. The properties by which we see it indicate how to get to it in the sensory realm.

VII. Perception and Singular Reference

The extent to which our actions and even our thinking are governed by *de dicto* beliefs is easily exaggerated, particularly in relation to perceptual belief. *De re* belief enables us to think and act in highly sophisticated ways. We can avoid slipping on a mossy stone by believing the stone *to be* slippery even if we do not conceptualize it in the way required to believe *that* it is mossy or a stone or anything in particular.[9] An important point here is that when we form a genuinely *de dicto* perceptual belief, there is a way to secure singular reference to the perceived object by the causal path that yields the perceptual experience in the first place. This raises a major theoretical question. Is the idea here that if one perceptually believes in a normal case *that* the dagger before one is steel-grey, one believes an abstract "Fregean" proposition constituted by the concept of a dagger predicatively linked to being steel-grey and is simply *able* to locate the physical dagger corresponding to this predication? This question calls for explanation.

First, in speaking of perception as hierarchical, I have maintained that in perceptually knowing, say seeing, that *x* is *F*, one knows *x* to be *F*, where that requires having a causal connection to it. The same holds for true perceptual beliefs that *x* is *F* (where they are the normal kind constituting perceptual knowledge). This suggests that in perceptually believing, say believing on the basis of visual experience, that the dagger before us is steel-grey, we in some way have in mind the dagger we believe to be steel-grey. Typically that is so, and our pervasive use of that-clauses in ascribing beliefs must not be allowed to obscure the point. Note that 'I believed that Myrna was her twin sister', which is a natural remark given the easy idiomatic use of that-clauses in belief ascriptions, does not express the impossible proposition that Myrna is her twin sister but the point that I believed Myrna to be her twin sister. I do not think, however, that all *de dicto* ascriptions of propositional perceptual beliefs must be ways of expressing *de re* beliefs. What may commonly hold in such cases is that the concept we exercise in forming propositional perceptual beliefs (and affirmations) is *applied referentially*, on the basis of perception. The referential application is enabled by the causal connection between the perceived object and the belief; the conceptuality of the belief is carried by the way in which, in the context of affirmation or, more broadly, of belief possession, we conceive the object that we believe to have the predicated property.

Nothing said here, then, implies that we do not have beliefs *about* physical objects we perceive or that our propositional perceptual beliefs do not have an essential connection to what they are about. But we have

9. If we attribute slipperiness, we may be in a position to believe that that slippery thing is slippery, but we need not have any such belief for our perceptual experience to have property content appropriate to guide behavior. I say 'may be in a position' because it does not follow from the ability to attribute a *perceptible* property *F* to an object that one can conceptualize *F*-ness in the way required for believing *that* the *F* is (say) *G*.

seen that what a (propositional) perceptual belief (or affirmation) is "about" can be a matter of causal connection to the object perceived as well as a matter of the abstract content provided at the level of concepts (or properties understood as abstract elements). Macbeth's belief was about an apparent dagger—not in the sense that there is a mental or non-physical object of the belief, but in the sense that its content was determined by properties in his sensory field and his concepts related to those. Here, however, lacking an actual perception to provide a downward pathway from his conception of a dagger to an actual one, he could not exercise that concept referentially. By contrast, my belief about the color of the print I see now—my belief that the print is black—is referentially and not just semantically, about the entities with those properties, and its content is acquired by an exercise of a concept (that of being black) referentially connected to the properties of the print that have causally led to my seeing them. I see them to be black, and, if on the basis of that perception I form the *de dicto* perceptual belief that they are black, I have ascended the ladder from simple perception to conceptualization.

There is far more to be said about how justification and knowledge are alike and how they differ. But our reflections have indicated no reason to doubt that in life as we know it sense-experience is crucial for both. Justification is characteristically produced in our ordinary perceptual experience, but sensory justification is also possible without an external cause. In that case, the justifying elements remain accessible to the subject and in principle adducible in a process of justifying an ascription, to an ostensibly perceived object, of properties present to the senses. Knowledge is not practice-relative in the same way. Perceptual knowledge can in fact arise where justificatory processes are not possible for the knower; it is also external in requiring an actual causal connection to what the knowledge is about or to something that, like an intention to raise one's hand, causally determines the truth of its propositional object. This external causal grounding may yield a reliable route to truth without yielding, as it normally does, internally accessible grounds of justification. These grounds, of course, may justify false beliefs. Justification, then, is autonomous in a certain way relative to knowledge, as the latter is autonomous in a certain way relative to the former; but the grounds of justification that give it a distinctive character are also essential in human knowledge, particularly in everyday perceptual knowledge, and in much of life we may rationally hope that, at least in major matters, knowledge and justified belief coincide.

PART TWO

PERCEPTION AND THE A PRIORI

7

PERCEPTION, INTUITION, AND APPREHENSION

This book is about perception, knowledge, and action. It is not a comprehensive treatment of even one of these vast topics but is meant to clarify each in relation to the others and, particularly, to indicate how our basic knowledge arises in experience. Some of that basic knowledge is perceptual, but some is also intuitive. There are various reasons to treat perception and intuition together. They have important similarities and instructive differences. Both are experiential, non-inferential, and evidential. But perception is a relation to something physical, and intuition is characteristically not. There are intuitions *of*—roughly, regarding—certain abstract elements, for instance entailment in logic or unity in poetry. But intuitions need not take this form. Nor need they arise from a relation to anything physical. The concern of this chapter is not only to describe some similarities and differences between perception and intuition, but also to take account of certain major similarities in framing a conception of how epistemology should accommodate both perception and intuition in providing as unified a theory of knowledge and justification as we may reasonably seek. In particular, I will be developing an account of a priori justification and knowledge in which intuition plays a role and perceptual justification and perceptual knowledge provide models for understanding their a priori counterparts.

I. Perception and Intuition

Perception may engender intuitive experience. Seeing a painting can give rise to a general intuition that dark colors with unsmiling figures

Seeing, Knowing, and Doing. Robert Audi, Oxford University Press (2020). © Oxford University Press.
DOI: 10.1093/oso/9780197503508.001.0001

hidden among them tend to be gloomy. Conversely, intuition may give rise to a perceptual experience, perhaps one influenced by a general intuitive sense regarding the kind of thing in one's perceptual field. Hearing an aria, for instance, may evoke an intuition that the kind of rhythm one hears is cheerful and thereby lead to seeing the singer as happy. Intuitions may of course be particular as well as general. From reading a certain poem, one might have a singular intuition that it should be read aloud in a particular way, and this in turn might lead one to listen carefully to a reading and to hear intonations one would have missed. Intuitive cognition can enhance perceptual acuity.

The question of how perception and intuition are related is complicated by the not uncommon cases in which 'intuition' is loosely used for certain instances of perception, as where you have an intuition of disapproval on the part of a friend who is intently listening to a plan or of anger in a person you are speaking with. Such intuiting is like simple perception in having no truth-valued object, but it could evoke an intuition *that* one's friend is disproving, which is truth-valued. This could be a case of intuitively seeing that the person is angry and thereby non-inferentially taking it that the person is angry, in the way one intuitively takes it that, for instance, the language of a poem is artificial. This taking could be a case of the proposition's seeming true, with or without your actually believing it. The taking, a kind of construal, could also yield belief. In either case, however, that of an intuitive perception or that of a similar perception without an intuitive element, the sense-experience is essential to the perception.

For a non-perceptual intuition, by contrast, as where one is just vividly imagining the aria, perception is not an essential accompaniment and may play no role. Even if you hear it in your mind's ear, you are not actually hearing it. If, in some cases in which perception is an occasion for the formation of an intuition, we can speak of perceiving that *p*, say that the kind of rhythm one hears is cheerful, as a kind of intuition that *p*, this is no reason to doubt that perception and intuition are conceptually independent and often operate separately.

One difference between perception in general and intuition in general, then, is in domain. In the primary cases of intuition, it operates in the abstract realm whereas ordinary perception is confined to the spatiotemporal. This is understandable in a sense that seems neutral with respect to Platonism regarding abstracta. Consider hypothetical cases, as where we imagine a punishment of a first-time juvenile user of marijuana and have the intuition that it is too severe. The intuition is about something at once particular (the offender) and abstract (severity).

But one could take the raw materials to be images that affect cognition much as perceptions embodying sensory counterparts of the images might, and by this strategy one might attempt to avoid positing Platonic entities.

II. Structural Parallels between Intuitional and Perceptional Discourse

Discussion of intuition must take account of the discourse in which the concept is appealed to. Here the relevant literature includes ethics as well as epistemology and metaphysics. It is in ethics, however, that, at least since Sidgwick, many moral philosophers have called themselves intuitionists. Intuitionism, as understood here, includes them but is also (in part) the view that intuitions have evidential weight. Let us consider varieties of intuition and the extent to which these may be unified.

In the tradition of ethical intuitionism, which includes a major epistemological element, we find at least six cases of intuition. All the main ethical cases to be described here have epistemological parallels.

Cognitive intuitions—intuitions *that p*—have propositions as objects and are in that sense propositional. Many epistemologists have the intuition that our visual beliefs could be justified even if we were victims of a Cartesian demon. Many of them also believe this, but cognitivity does not entail belief; and though intuitions have been widely conceived as beliefs, I am not here taking them to be essentially doxastic.

Intuitiveness is a property of propositions relative to a person, though we may speak of propositions as intuitive simpliciter where we think anyone (in an implicitly indicated group) would find them intuitive. For me, the Cartesian claim about justification is intuitive. This is in part to say that it is plausible "in its own right"—taken in itself, apart from premises for it, it appears true. It evokes the sense of non-inferential credibility. I can think of premises to support it, but I find it credible on the basis of what it says independently of what something else says *for* it.

A third case, then, is related to the first two. Propositions, when they are considered intuitive or regarded as intuitively known, may be called *intuitions.* You might, for instance, call *p* a widely shared intuition; and, in building a philosophical account of, say, reasons, we might speak of what intuitions—roughly, what intuitive truths—we should preserve or what intuitions we should try to explain.[1]

1. Moore goes so far as to say that in calling propositions intuitions, he means "*merely* to assert that they are incapable of proof" (1903: x).

Objectual intuition, the fourth case, is akin to simple perception. It is a kind of non-propositional intellectual perception: a direct apprehension of either a concept, such as that of entailment, or of a property or relation, such as the property of justifiedness or the relation of entailment. When *occurrent,* these direct apprehensions ('apprehension' is a preferable term for them) are, significantly akin to sensory perceptions: as with perceptions, their object is in some way present in or (more accurately) to consciousness. The same cognitive content is, however, dispositionally instantiable. If I now have, occurrently, an intuition of the fittingness of believing *p* to evidence you present for it, I need not cease to have the intuition when the matter recedes into memory. The intuition may readily resurface when the topic arises later. Intuitions, like memories, may be had in more than one way: those occurrently in mind are like money in the hand; those possessed only dispositionally are more like money in the bank.

A fifth case is indicated where writers on intuition view it as a kind of non-inferential judgment: a sort of intellectual verdict on a proposition or situation.[2] In ethics, certain moral judgments—*judgmental intuitions*—are often so viewed, as where, on considering an accusation against a friend, one thinks, 'That is unfair'. Judgmental intuitions seem to entail (or indeed to be equivalent to) a kind of assent: the sort of affirmational response normally taken to underlie sincere judgments as made in oral affirmation. They are counterparts of occurrent propositional perceptions, such as seeing that someone is angry. A judgment that is held dispositionally, say after being made and then retained, might be considered a doxastic intuition.

These five cases are connected with a sixth: just as we have perceptual "faculties" such as vision, we have intellectual faculties, including intuition—reason, in one sense of that wide-ranging term. The faculty of intuition is a kind of apprehensional capacity: a non-inferential capacity through which we know what we intuitively do know. It is appropriately called 'non-inferential' because of the way it responds to content in context: above all, to the appearance of truth in propositions considered in their own terms rather than as supported by premises. Intuition is

2. Identification of intuition with judgment fits some of Ross's references to "convictions" and is explicit in some citations below, e.g. from ch. 2 of Ross (1930). Echoing a widely held view, Sinnott-Armstrong, Young, and Cushman say: "When we refer to *moral intuitions,* we shall mean strong, stable, immediate moral beliefs" (2010: 246). Further pertinent discussion is provided in Stratton-Lake (2002) and Huemer (2005).

like perception in the directness of its cognitive deliverances, yet it does not require unresponsiveness to premises. We may welcome the discovery of propositions that support an intuition, and it may become stronger in the light of them or indeed rise to a certainty. Some people might be said to go by intuition in controversial or delicate questions; others might be said to mistrust intuition, even in their own case. In different circumstances, intuitions may come rarely, may be inhibited, and may not come fast, any more than an aesthetic response to a complex painting need come at first look. Some people are unintuitive compared with others, as some may be impercipient compared with others.

Consider what earlier I called a perceptual principle, to the effect that if *p* sensorily seems true to *S*, then there is a reason for *S* to believe *p*. A practical analogue might be a promissory principle: If one promises to *A*, one has a prima facie obligation to *A*. W. D. Ross and most other intuitionists would likely say, using the six locutions just described, that it is through our intuitive capacity that we can see the truth of the principle; that when the principle is considered with adequate understanding, it is intuitive; that one has an intuition of the obligation-making power of the relation, promising; that one may have an intuition whose content is this principle; that the principle itself is *an* intuition (a kind of intuitive datum); and that judgmental intuitions may have such principles as their propositional contents.

Intuitions as cognitive attitudes—propositional as opposed to objectual intuitions—need special attention. Ross and many other philosophers have spoken of intuitions mainly as a kind of belief, e.g. as convictions.[3] His view here manifests a doxastic (belief-entailing) conception. Moreover, it remains common for philosophers and others to report their intuitions about hypothetical cases with a clear implication that they believe the propositions in question.

In recent work in epistemology, by contrast, intuitions are often treated as intellectual seemings—roughly, instances of a phenomenal, attentional sense of the truth of the proposition in question. This sense reflects, though it does not entail, the proposition's being intuitive: having a truth-appearance of a kind analogous to but distinct from

3. For Ross, "the moral convictions of thoughtful and well-educated people are the data of ethics, just as sense-perceptions are the data of a natural science. Just as some of the latter have to be rejected as illusory, so have some of the former; but as the latter are rejected only when they conflict with other more accurate sense-perceptions, the former are rejected only when they conflict with convictions which stand better the test of reflection" (1930: 41).

a sensory appearance, such as one experiences with perceptions of colors and shapes.[4] These seemings—call them *episodic intuitions*—are often taken to entail inclinations to believe, but they are not beliefs and, like visual impressions whose accuracy one doubts, do not entail forming beliefs.

Seemings that *p* are propositional in content but, unlike beliefs, they are essentially occurrent phenomena. They require conscious space in the way occurrent beliefs do, but even when vivid need not yield belief. They may indeed be resisted, for instance where one wants not to believe the proposition, say that a friend's poem is superficial. Here one might have a propositional seeming arising from an objectual intuition, say an aesthetic intuition of superficiality. Whether or not we call the aesthetic intuition a "seeming," the relation between the appearance of superficiality and the intuition that the poem is superficial is akin to the relation between simply seeing something and seeing *that* it has a property.

III. Intuitions as Evidential Cognitions: Two Intuitionist Traditions

Ethical intuitionists have paid too little attention to the phenomenology of intuitions, and intuitionistic epistemologists have tended to focus on the episodic, phenomenal conception of intuition with little appreciation of the doxastic conception. But in neither tradition is there any rejection of the potential role of intuitions as conceived in the other. How the two conceptions are related needs explanation. A central question here is whether, although intuitive seemings do not entail believing their propositional objects, doxastic intuitions nonetheless depend on

4. See, e.g., Bealer (1998: 207) and Goldman and Pust (1998: 179–97). Of the common modal equivalence approach used by Gettier and others to show, by appeal to intuitions, that knowledge is not equivalent to justified true belief, Goldman and Pust say "Intuitions are mental occurrences . . . with contents about objects in modal space" (p. 184). But cf. Gopnik and Schwitzgebel: "We will call any judgment . . . an *intuition* just in case it is not made on the basis of some explicit reasoning process that a person can consciously observe" (1998: 77). Similarly, Williamson remarks that "so-called intuitions are merely judgments (or dispositions to judgment)" (2007: 3). Whether judgmental intuitions entail belief is not settled in the context, but normally what one judges is so one also believes.

intuitive seemings.[5] Answering this should help us to explain a difference between moral philosophers and epistemologists in their main conceptions of intuition—or at least their main appeals to it.

There is some basis for considering the doxastic notion of an intuition to be historical, in the sense that it entails a connection to the past, say an intuitional experience with the same content. In avowing a doxastic (previously dispositional) intuition that *p*, say that one should keep promises, we normally presuppose that it has an appropriate connection with an episodic intuition. But imagine a perfect psychological duplicate of me. My duplicate, at the very moment of creation, has the same beliefs and doxastic intuitions that I have, at least given plausible assumptions about the supervenience of the mental on the physical. I thus leave open whether doxastic intuitions *must* trace back to or be based on episodic ones, "intuitive seemings." They characteristically do. Perhaps, for the typical cases of intuition and certainly for many, we may conceive episodic intuitions as the basic kind. A unified account of intuition centered on episodic cases might, in rough outline, go as follows.

Doxastic intuitions are related to episodic intuitions in both a forward-looking and a backward-looking or downward-looking way. Doxastic intuitions embody a disposition to have episodic intuitions with the same content (a forward-looking property) and normally have a basis in them, whether contemporaneous or historical. If one believes *p* at *t* on the basis of its seeming to one that *p* at *t*, this is "downward-looking" rather than backward-looking. Both cases apparently exhibit the same dependence of the doxastic on the episodic.

Intuitiveness in a proposition, *p*, is a truth-appearance of the kind manifested in an episodic intuition that *p*: broadly, the proposition's evoking a sense of non-inferential credibility. The sense of intuitiveness commonly takes dispositional forms. Much of what is intuitive for us at a time is not then in our consciousness; but its being intuitive is a matter of how we experience its seeming when (in normal conditions) we entertain it. There is of course a many-sided relativity here: what is intuitive for one person need not be so for another, and what you find intuitive at one time you may not find so later.

5. It is possible to have an intellectual impression of something non-propositional, such as an inclusion relation between two categories; there is no need to discuss those cases separately. They may, like perceptions of physical objects, generate inclinations to believe particularly for propositions supported by perception. But, like propositional intuitive seemings, they do not entail believing the propositions in question.

Objectual intuition, when occurrent, is an apprehensional consciousness of the concept, property, or other object with a focus that makes possible episodic intuitions about one or more aspects of it; and, when dispositional, objectual intuition is related to the episodic case essentially as dispositional propositional intuitions are related to their episodic counterparts. An intuition of entailment, e.g.—roughly, an intuitive conception of it—might be dispositional except on such occasions as considering it in a given instance, say in an argument one is given, or in focusing on what entailment is, as when asked this by a student.

Judgmental intuition may be conceived as (in the primary case) an assenting cognitive response to an expression of episodic intuition. Since judgments can be held as well as made, there is a dispositional case here too. If, confronted with a prospect of action, one has a judgmental intuition that it would be wrong and retains this cognition in memory, one would then *hold* the judgmental intuition in question.

The "faculty" of intuition is the rational capacity whose central exercise manifests itself in the formation of episodic intuitions of the kinds just described and also in the retention of an appropriate range of dispositional cognitions having the same propositional or other objects.[6] It is (in ways Chapter 8 will describe) crucial for understanding a priori propositions. This faculty can be biased in some, virtually absent in others, and, in still others, very acute or often active, or both.

This fivefold account partly explains why, at least in non-philosophers, self-ascription of intuitions typically indicates belief. We *tend* to believe what we find intuitive and ordinarily do not report intuitions to others unless they represent at least weak beliefs. It may also be true that in most contexts of self-ascription, as in making a case for some point, doxastic intuitions more readily yield premises or considerations we would like others to share. The account also partly explains the point, implicit in the concept of having a doxastic intuition that *p*, that if one *considers p*, one tends to find *p* intuitive. Think of a typical case in which the basis of a doxastic intuition that *p* is a previous episodic intuition that *p*. Then it is expectable that, upon comprehendingly considering

6. One might call it a non-inferential capacity, as I have in earlier work with the idea that it is not centrally realized in drawing inferences; but it must not be thought that the capacity to draw inferences is not also an element in our "reason" or that conditionals corresponding to inferences may not be "intuitive"—they commonly are, and we tend to draw inferences more readily when such conditionals are intuitive for us.

p—unless under defeating conditions that eliminate its appearance of truth—one will again have an episodic intuition that *p*.

Brief as it is, this phenomenological sketch suggests an explanation of the difference, at least in emphasis, in the way moral philosophers, especially ethical intuitionists, and epistemologists have tended to view intuition. Moral philosophers regard their main normative principles as justifiable and, if not as intuitions in the sense in which certain propositions are so called, at least as fully consonant with intuitive judgments subsumable under the principles, say about specific promises or about cases that, like an accident victim bleeding on the sidewalk, patently call for beneficence. Moreover, even non-intuitionist moral philosophers have considered intuition to be sometimes needed to determine what one should do in difficult moral situations. Here, too, it is natural to take the deliverances of one's intuitive rational capacity to be doxastic, as they commonly are.

By contrast, at least since Descartes, epistemologists have been deeply concerned with skepticism and perennially preoccupied with the regress of justification. Consider this: beliefs admit of justification, and if intuitions are beliefs ("convictions," e.g.), then, particularly if they are fallible, they admit of justification and may need it. Suppose, however, one takes intuitions with self-evident objects to be unprovable and, like Ross and other moral philosophers, considers singular intuitions to be admissible as "data" in ethics, and in that way foundational. One may then see no need to justify these cognitions.[7] But suppose that, like many epistemologists, we want to stop the regress of justification. We will then seek, even for perceptual beliefs of a kind moral philosophers typically see no need to justify, grounds for justification that can *confer* it. These—unlike reasons construed propositionally—do not admit of justification, hence cannot be attacked as lacking it. Intuitional experiences can play this role.

Episodic intuitions, then, can serve as data at the ground level—or *some* ground level. Some grounds are harder than others, some higher, offering wider perspective, some richer, providing better fruits. We need not take justificatory grounds to be infallible or indefeasible supports for belief, but such grounds do confer prima facie

7. This view is central in phenomenal conservatism as defended, in somewhat different versions, by Chisholm in his *Theory of Knowledge* (1977) and other works of his and by Huemer (2005) and others in, e.g. Tucker (2013), which contains a defense of the more nuanced internalist view I am partially presenting here.

justification on beliefs based on them. Doxastic intuitions, moreover, as non-inferential cognitions, may rest directly on such grounds. That non-inferential basis does not guarantee truth, but it does eliminate defeat of the kind due to inferential dependence on a false premise or invalid reasoning.

It should be stressed that in neither intuitionist tradition is there a basis for a not uncommon stereotype of intuitions as "gut responses." Perhaps this stereotype gains some traction from the thought that intuitions are like perceptions, or indeed are intellectual perceptions. Suppose they are. Perceptions can come slowly, as where one is just awakening or a shadow beclouding one's line of sight is receding. Where we are speaking of propositional perceptions, which are analogous to propositional intuitions, there may certainly be something akin to intuitive reflection, say attentive focusing, that can be needed before propositional perceptual beliefs are formed. Consider viewing a landscape painting. It might take focusing and even reflecting before seeing (and thus believing) that it shows an owl on a long branch amidst thick foliage, rather than a bird-shaped clump of leaf and twig. In neither case need inferences be drawn. There remains one difference, however: intuitive seemings are responses to what is before the mind (even if that comes from perception); perceptual seemings are responses to what is present to the senses. An intuitive seeming may often generate a belief with the same content, much as a perceptual seeming may, but where there is no need to form a belief or to make a judgment, and especially where one's attention shifts after a seeming arises, either kind of seeming may remain just that.

IV. Intuitions as Apprehensions

Intuitive seemings may have a phenomenology that is vivid and often inclines *S* to believe the proposition in question. Like perceptual propositional seemings, they are also non-inferential. Still another similarity is indicated by the naturalness of speaking of seeing in both cases—with the eye of the mind, as it were, as well as with the physical eye. Given these similarities, one can see how we might view intuitions as a kind of perception. Indeed, if we may speak of intuitive apprehension and take (physical) seeing as our perceptual paradigm, we find the same range of locutions. Take entailment as an object of intuition. We may have an intuition *of it* as a relation connecting propositions. We may intuit *that* *p* entails *q*, find *p* intuitive, or intuitively take entailment *to hold* between *p* and *q*. For all this, it seems clear that, in the most characteristic cases, intuition is intellective and perception sensory, and that there are corresponding phenomenal differences.

Consider a philosophical intuition, say that believing is not a process. This proposition seems clearly true, and there is something it is like to consider it with the intuitive sense of its truth. But this is not what it is like to have a sensory impression that green leaves are before me. This allows for similarities. Perhaps I could not have this sensory impression of green without ever seeing a green thing; and perhaps my intuition about believing requires my having in consciousness a concept or property (hence some object). It is plausible to take such general and philosophical propositions to have as constituents (even if not their only constituents) the concepts they are in some sense about. Perhaps some kind of objectual intuition is a basis of a propositional intuition much as simple perception is a basis of propositional perception. We may, for instance, say of poor logic students that they have trouble "getting" (apprehending) the concept of validity or have too few or misguided intuitions about specific entailments (the latter is an analogue of perceptual illusions wherein there is contact with the object perceived but a false impression about it); and we may say of good students in ethics that they readily apprehend fittingness relations. Here the analogy is to objectual perception, but the object is abstract.

One may grant a major phenomenological difference between intuition and perception but still take the two to coincide in special cases. Perhaps perceptual data can converge on the same proposition. Still, seeing that *p* entails believing *p* but does not entail either that the belief is intuitive or that there is any intuitive seeming that *p*. It may be that when we say such things as that we intuited someone's nervousness, we are indicating that we are manifesting a faculty of non-inferential discernment and through it see that the person is nervous. Consider too the analogy between intuitive apprehension and moral perception. Just as one can see the injustice of a deed or of (an instance of) goodness in a person, one may apprehend the concept of injustice or the concept of personal goodness. Indeed, might the perceptions of the properties be a normal route—perhaps the only ordinary route—to apprehension of the corresponding concepts?

In other work I have suggested, as a plausible hypothesis meriting empirical investigation, an epistemological developmentalism. This is the view that from a conceptual and epistemological point of view, there is a progression, apparently corresponding to normal human development, in which the first stage is sensory acquaintance (normally of a perceptual kind) with properties and an ability to discriminate some from others; the second is conceptualization of the properties in question, a stage that makes it possible to apprehend them; and the third is framing propositions in which the concepts figure—*exercising* the concepts, we might say—as where one forms a belief that, for instance, slapping other people is wrong.[8] (This view will be extended in Chapter 9.)

If perception is a normal route to apprehension, and if apprehension of concepts and properties is similar to perception in being a phenomenally discriminative response to something experienced, then perception and apprehension should be expected to have structural similarities. We have seen parallels in the locutions appropriate to each. They also agree in matters of factivity, types of content, and directness. In their propositional forms, for instance—at least for the general cases of 'perceives that' and 'apprehends that' (uncommon though these may be), they are characteristically factive. Both, moreover, may have propositional or objectual contents; and both are non-inferential—neither premise-based nor based on some other element that admits of justification.[9]

Perception provides an occasion for the formation of intuitions—both as seemings and, in some cases, as intuitional beliefs. Perception is also both structurally parallel to intuition and experientially representational in a way that enables conferral of justification. Each has the parallel forms indicated by the several locutions we have considered. Moreover, both perception and intuition are non-inferential; both, in the forms in which they do not embody beliefs, yield inclinations to believe. Granting that intuitive seemings seem the wrong kinds of elements to be premise-based, we can make sense of one seeming's being based on another in a quasi-inferential way, as where a person seems to me anxious on the basis of seeming to me preoccupied with possible failures in a plan we are making. This is analogous to seeing something by seeing properties of it, as in the case of seeing trees by seeing colors and shapes. Such terminological latitude is compatible with the most important point about (occurrent) intuitions in relation to inference: that, like certain perceptions, they are direct responses to something one considers or

8. For detailed illustrations of this developmentalism, see my 2008b.

9. One exception is self-directed cognitions with elements in one's own mind, assuming we count these as objects as intuitions or perceptions: these may have objects admitting of justification. One might "perceive" one's own beliefs or "intuit" that one wants something one had forsworn.

otherwise experiences; they are not indirect intellectual responses to a premise. Both are experiential; and, as experiential, non-inferential, and phenomenally representational, they can confer justification. This ascription of directness to intuitions goes well with the paradigmatic status of intuitions whose objects are luminously self-evident axioms. That role of intuitions in a priori justification and knowledge will be considered in some detail in the next chapter.

8

TOWARD A THEORY OF THE A PRIORI

Logic and pure mathematics are domains in which we find clear cases of the a priori. Even where a priori propositions are expressed in everyday terms—as where someone says that if Jill is taller than Jack, then Jack is shorter than Jill—and agreed to be a priori, many philosophers will be inclined to hold that they are a kind of logical truth. One thing that all clear or at least uncontroversial cases of the a priori appear to have in common is being either self-evident or at least self-evidently entailed by something self-evident. This gives self-evidence high importance in understanding the a priori. On my view, it is in fact the basic case of the a priori, in the sense that the other cases are adequately understandable only in relation to it.[1] Being self-evident is widely taken to be a status that marks propositions as capable of being known and justifiedly believed on the basis of understanding them. This chapter explicates and defends a version of that view.

1. This is argued in my 1999b and *Epistemology*, third edition (2010). A basic idea is that what is self-evidently entailed by a self-evident proposition is (broadly) a priori. Given this, provability on the basis of self-evident entailments may also be accorded a priori status—being *ultimately* a priori, in my terminology. The significance of the distinction between the broadly and the ultimately a priori depends on the point that, unlike entailment itself, self-evident entailment is not transitive. For related recent work on the a priori, some of which treats self-evidence in particular, see Boghossian and Peacocke (2000) and Casullo and Thurow (2013).

Seeing, Knowing, and Doing. Robert Audi, Oxford University Press (2020). © Oxford University Press.
DOI: 10.1093/oso/9780197503508.001.0001

I. The Concept of Self-Evidence

In speaking of the self-evident, I presuppose the approximate correctness of this account:

> *Self-evidence*: Self-evident propositions are truths meeting two conditions: (1) an adequate understanding of them is a ground for justification for believing them (which does not entail that anyone who adequately understands them *does* believe them); and (2) believing them on the basis of adequately understanding them entails knowing them.[2]

In explicating this account, I have made various points to clarify adequate understanding—*comprehensional adequacy*—but much remains to be said about it. This is the kind of understanding that can enable philosophical analysis, but that description yields a desideratum rather than a definition.

Skepticism about the clarity of the concept of self-evidence is not uncommon. If the self-evident is viewed as "self-justifying," such skepticism is understandable. I make no use of that notion and consider the relation of justification irreflexive. The propositions most plausibly thought to merit the term 'self-justifying' seem understandable in terms of grounds of justification accessible through attentively considering them. With this in mind, I think of self-evident propositions as those evident in themselves. Their *being evident* need not be evident, but their *truth* is evident "in" them and so need not be seen externally, e.g. via premises. This point is important for my aim of reducing the motivation for skepticism about the existence and significance of certain kinds of self-evident propositions.

A further source of skepticism about self-evidence is suggested by the question how anything can be self-evident, at least non-trivially, given that the philosophically most interesting cases of presumptively self-evident propositions are subject to disagreements between rational persons who seem to understand those propositions. Chapter 9 will address this issue; here my main concern is to clarify the right kind of understanding, the kind philosophers need for explicating self-evident propositions and that anyone needs for believing self-evident propositions on a basis that entails justification for believing them and

2. This account derives from my work in the early 1980s but first published in some detail only later in the 1988 (first) edition of *Epistemology*, then in my 1996 and in "Self-Evidence" (1999), which expanded my earlier treatments. I take a *ground* for justification for p to be such that, in virtue of having that ground, one has that justification.

enables one to know them. Call this *self-evidential justification*, i.e., the kind of justification one has for believing a self-evident proposition in virtue of adequately understanding it.[3] We should also acknowledge the possibility of *indirect* justification for self-evident propositions, e.g. on the basis of a proof or testimony. Self-evidential justification, then, is not equivalent to justification for believing a self-evident proposition. It is not, moreover, a kind of justification different from all others. It has in common with intuitive justification—justification grounded in intuition—dependence on understanding *p*.

It is natural here to wonder how, in relation to the self-evident, understanding is connected with intuition. A preliminary point is that although both 'understanding' and 'intuition' have dispositional and occurrent uses, philosophers most commonly speak of understanding in reference to dispositional cases of it and (in epistemology, at least) of intuition in relation to episodic (hence occurrent) cases of that. Much of what we understand, including numerous propositions, we do not have in mind, whereas I have an occurrent understanding of that very point as I consider it. Similarly, I have, dispositionally, many intuitions in memory, including the intuition that having justification for a proposition is possible when it is not before the mind.

With these points in view, we should ask what kind of understanding of self-evident propositions is adequate in the relevant sense: such that, in virtue of having it, we are justified in believing the proposition.[4]

3. It must be granted that the relevant kind of understanding may genetically depend on experience, but this role does not imply evidential dependence on experience (at least perceptual or introspective experience) for self-evidential justification. For an attempt to show that presumptive self-evidential justification depends on experience in a way that undermines the distinction between the a priori—viewed as not *evidentially* depending on experience—and the a posteriori, see Williamson, e.g. his 2007b. For a critique of Williamson's case see Thurow, "Understanding to the Rescue," in preparation.

4. This is cautiously expressed because I want to leave open both that there can be something else (surely related to understanding) in virtue of which self-evidential justification might occur, and that the relevant grounding relation might be transitive, so that if adequate understanding in a certain kind of case is possessed in virtue of a further element, then self-evidential justification might in that case also be possessed in virtue of that element. Consider one way in which understanding and intuition might be related. In the kind of case in question, understanding *p* (where *p* is self-evident) might be grounded in seeing how *p* is true, and intuition that *p* grounded in occurrently understanding *p*. Then the intellectual seeing in question would also ground the intuition. In any

Suppose *p* is self-evident and that I consider it with the relevant kind of understanding. Then in considering it I am occurrently justified in believing it and, as a rational person, will *tend* to believe it, even if I do not believe it. Where the understanding is occurrent, in a sense entailing that one has *p* in mind in a kind of direct way, it also tends to produce an intuition, but it need not. It often will not where I do not believe *p* (or even disbelieve *p*) or (as will be illustrated shortly) even where I do believe it. Intuition that *p*, then, does not invariably ground or even accompany self-evidential justification.

This is not to deny an intimate relation between occurrent justification and intuition. At least when occurrent, intuition can yield occurrent justification. Moreover, occurrent understanding of a self-evident proposition—as with considering it in a way that yields seeing how it is true—tends to yield intuition with that proposition as content. I take occurrently *understanding* a proposition to be analogous to perceiving a structured object, and I regard occurrently *intuiting* a proposition as a cognitive (though not necessarily doxastic) attitude toward it and as requiring occurrently understanding it. A cognitive attitude of any kind entails some degree of understanding of its propositional object, much as perceptual belief entails some perceptual basis, even if rather faint. Cognitive intuition that *p*, moreover, may be a basis for believing a self-evident proposition whether or not it is a basis of self-evidential justification for believing it. It can achieve the latter, normative status only if it embodies adequate understanding.

II. Understanding as Central for Knowledge of the Self-Evident

The notion of understanding a proposition is important in its own right, but if the proposed account of self-evidence is sound, it is also important that we have an informative account of understanding self-evident propositions and indeed of adequacy of such understanding. I have in mind adequacy at the level of good comprehension, the kind of comprehension appropriate both to having a clear sense of the truth of *p* and to that sense being sufficiently stable to tend to survive reflection on *p*. ('Comprehension' is a near synonym of 'understanding' so I make no pretense that it provides more than limited explicative help here.) We could speak of *full* understanding, but I leave open the possibility of

case, it would seem that occurrent intuition can yield self-evidential justification for *p* only if it is itself grounded in an adequate understanding of *p*.

comprehensional adequacy that, even if it cannot have certain defects, is expandable.

A good account of adequate understanding does not necessarily include an account of the basis relation that holds between an adequate understanding and a belief of *p*, a relation such that, if *p* is self-evident, then, in virtue of being based on that understanding, the belief constitutes knowledge. I take this basis relation to be a (non-deviant) causal sustaining relation and to differ from the inferential relation characteristic of one belief's being based on another, as is usual with premise-based beliefs. A belief that is self-evidentially justified at a given time is non-inferential at that time. (This does not imply that inference has no role in understanding self-evident propositions or that they cannot also be known inferentially.) It will help us to consider some types of self-evidence and explore how understanding figures in those.

It is natural to begin with "definitional" cases that meet a very high standard—synonymy of definiens with definiendum. (Some might take real definition to be more relevant, but I cannot pursue that possibility.) Thus, if 'triangle' is definable as synonymous with 'three-sided plane figure' then the proposition we express by 'All triangles are three-sided' is self-evident. The same kind of case can be made for the proposition that all vixens are female and for similar analytic propositions.[5]

On the proposed account of self-evidence, we must countenance some cases that appear synthetic, say the proposition that nothing is round and square. The syntheticity of this has been challenged, but I do not believe the proposition can be shown to be either analytic or empirical. If *roundness* were analyzable as, say, being conceptually equivalent to a conjunction of negatively described shapes, such as being non-oval, non-polygonal, etc., one of which is being non-square, the proposition

5. There has long been controversy over the clarity of the notion of the analytic. I have in mind the kinds of propositions plausibly thought to meet the Kantian condition of having their subject's 'containing' their predicate (though these are not the only cases). Take, e.g., <Knowledge is appropriately grounded true belief>, where *knowledge* is the subject and *being a belief* is predicated of it. Quine characterized the idea semantically (though non-endorsingly) as one of a proposition reducible to a logical truth by putting synonym for synonyms. Thus, if 'vixen' is synonymous with 'female fox,' 'All vixens are female' reduces to 'All female foxes are female,' which is a substitution instance of 'All that is *F* and *G* is *G*.' This both expresses a formal truth and illustrates Kantian containment.

would be analytic. But even if an equivalence is obtainable in this way, such conjunctive accounts fail as analyses.

Normative propositions are a different case. Intuitionists in ethics and in epistemology have argued for the self-evidence of some of these. Ross thought it self-evident that if one promises to do something, one has a "prima facie duty" to do it.[6] Like Moore, Prichard, and many earlier philosophers, Ross took the self-evident to be unprovable, though not in need of proof, and he represented the self-evidence of the everyday moral principles he formulated as like that of a mathematical axiom or a form of inference.[7]

Self-evident formal truths must also be considered. If, with the unprovability claim in mind, one considers logical truths, one can readily evaluate that claim. It is self-evident that <it is not the case that *p and not-p*> but this seems unprovable if provability implies the existence of premises "epistemically prior" to what they prove. By contrast, consider the proposition that if *p* entails *q*, and *q* entails *r*, and *r* entails *s*, and *s* is false, then *p* is false. This is clearly provable in some standard systems. For some provable self-evident propositions, there are epistemically prior premises. Granted, even apparently rock-solid formal propositions can be questioned, but they are sufficiently credible to be useful in both everyday reflection and standard modern logic, and I presuppose their self-evidence and, at least in some such cases, their provability.

The account of self-evidence is not relativized to persons, but at least since Aquinas we have had a distinction between self-evidence simpliciter and self-evidence *for* a person. It should be clear how, on my account, there can be propositions plausibly called self-evident *for* one person but not for another, i.e., they exhibit

> *Relativized self-evidence*: *p* is self-evident *for S* if and only if (1) *p* is self-evident simpliciter, and (2) *S* adequately understands *p*.

Consider the proposition that first cousins share a pair of grandparents. There are people who, at least for a time, do not see this as true. This is commonly because, on first consideration, some people do not adequately understand it. For many of these, however, it would be wrong to say that they do not understand it at all. Some might understand it even at a high enough level to enable immediate correct translation into a language they know equally well. Call the minimal case of such

6. See Ross's *The Right and the Good* (1930: 29).

7. Ross called the moral principles he considered self-evident, "self-evident just as a mathematical axiom, or a rule of inference, is evident" (1930: 29).

translational understanding *mere semantic comprehension.* Relativization can bear on all three kinds of case (and likely others): adequately understanding, mere semantic comprehension, and the cases lying between these.

Within the category of self-evidence for a person, we may distinguish between mediate and (in a temporal sense) *immediate* self-evidence. The idea is roughly this:

> *Immediate self-evidence*: *p* is immediately self-evident for *S* at *t* if and only if, upon considering *p* in the light of adequate understanding of *p* at *t*, it is self-evident for *S* at *t*.

We can then say that a proposition mediately self-evident for *S* is one that is not immediately self-evident for *S* but is self-evident and such that normally, upon reflection—possibly requiring reasoning, but without dependence on a premise for *p* or on new information from an external source such as testimony or reading—*S* will adequately understand it. Much will be said about adequacy of understanding and, by implication, about possible routes to it through reflection on *p*. The main reason for introducing the notions of relativized and mediate self-evidence for some person is to indicate how to understand a distinction made by Aquinas[8] and, especially, how to resist the common idea that what is self-evident is also obvious.

III. Understanding and Imagination

We have seen that reflection on a proposition may be required for adequately understanding it. What constitutes understanding may be clarified by connecting and comparing it with a related notion, that of imagination. Imagination may sometimes seem required for adequate understanding. Consider the proposition that *it is possible for a man to be both father and grandfather of the same person.* To see the truth of this, most people must consider the relations of grandparenting and parenting. Those who do must avoid being misled by the normally applicable proposition that parents do not beget children with their own children. Once we realize this is contingent, we can see that if a man begets a child by his daughter, he is both its father (by virtue of that fact)

8. I refer to his distinction between what is self-evident for us and what is self-evident for God (which would be anything I call self-evident). For an instructive study that clarifies his views on this and related matters, see Cory (2018).

and grandfather (through being father of the child's mother). This possibility is easily obscured by the normal no-incest presupposition, and there may be some luck involved in someone's realizing the truth in question—call it *the incestuous proposition.*

Whether or not luck sometimes figures in coming to understand a self-evident proposition, it need not. The deeper question is whether imagination is required. I do not mean imagination of the minimal sort needed to image (or somehow characterize) an instance of a concept of a simple kind, but rather the sort that tends to indicate some creativity. Doubtless a person of imagination may see how the incestuous proposition is true more readily than one lacking imagination. But I am supposing that imagination is not normally needed for seeing what, apart from a readily discernible false assumption, is clearly possible given one's concepts.[9]

These considerations suggest that the kind of understanding essential for justification for believing a self-evident proposition is achievable without exercising imagination, at least in the sense in which that activity implies something not entailed by an exercise of intellect. But the distinction between the "faculties" of intellect and imagination is not sharp, and my view does not require denying that in some cases, achieving understanding may manifest some degree of imagination. I take the rough "sufficiency of intellect" view just suggested to be plausible for the clear cases of comprehensional adequacy regarding self-evident propositions. The view cannot be established apart from an account of imagination, but perhaps what has been said will suffice here.

One point on which the incestuous proposition is instructive is this: what is discovered using one's imagination can be a matter of luck—of an epistemologically significant kind. This is the non-defeating kind such that, even if one believes something only by good luck—as where, on considering the incestuous proposition, one happens to remember Sophocles' *Oedipus Rex* (which describes this kind of incest)—the belief may still constitute knowledge.

A second point pertinent here is this: where one believes a self-evident proposition only by an exercise of imagination that does not manifest one's adequate understanding of the proposition, one may not have self-evidential justification for the belief. Again our example is instructive. Suppose one came to see that p is true by accidentally learning of an instance reported (with no description) in a medical

9. A similar case would be the proposition that first cousins can share two pairs of grandparents. This seems knowable by an adequate exercise of intellect.

journal. Given this medical testimony one might imagine an elderly man and baby, with the former being both grandfather and father of the latter, but without "putting two and two together" and thereby seeing *how* this can occur. This broadly testimonial route to belief or knowledge apparently need not expand one's antecedent understanding of *p*. The belief may manifest simply taking what is actual to be possible, something consistent with merely seeing *that p* is true and not *how*. This point does not imply that exercising imagination does not require intellect or that it cannot enable one to see more than one otherwise would—it often does. Possession of imagination *is* required for certain kinds of understanding, say of poetry or even philosophical metaphors. But the self-evident is a kind of truth accessible to the intellect. Some propositions accessible only to the intellect *and* the imagination working together may be provable and a priori, but that is a different point.

It should be granted that adequacy of understanding does require something that may imply some degree of imagination: a grasp of generality. Understanding of a proposition is not implied just by familiarity with an instance of a property or relation that figures in it, say (for fatherhood) of a particular man's being father of a particular child, where one understands this biologically. One must understand that *any* man filling this role is father of the child. Suppose, then, that a grasp of generality entails ability to imagine instances one has never observed or conceived. Still, this ability need only imply minimal imagination. Perhaps a recognitional ability suffices for minimally grasping generality: one might be able to recognize instances one could not antecedently imagine, and perhaps the requisite degree of that ability need not imply imagination. Compare comprehendingly thinking of a triangle in the abstract: one must in some way grasp that it is an enclosure with three sides, can be of any size, and can have any angles within the appropriate range; but one need not be able to *picture* an instance. That point holds even if one could not have *acquired* the concept without exposure to some instance.

Merely seeing, whether physically or in the mind's eye, an instance of a concept does not entail understanding that concept. Mere seeing does not assure a grasp of generality, though that may begin with seeing. Here and elsewhere, exercising imagination may assist in achieving a sense of generality but does not guarantee success. Exercising imagination might also be needed for an adequate understanding of a self-evident proposition to yield actually believing it. Justification for believing *p* at a time during which imagination yields adequate (occurrent) understanding of it would be occurrent justification. That understanding might also be manifested in an occurrent intuition that *p*.

IV. Major Elements in the Understanding of Propositions

With Sections I to III in mind, we might explore the variables essential for an account of the nature and degree of understanding of the intellectual kind in question. We might speak here of comprehensional variables to refer to those important for explicating adequate understanding. Many variables figure in determining how well someone understands a concept or proposition, and some of what is said here applies to understanding propositions in general. Given that concepts are apparently essential constituents of propositions—at least of propositions that are good candidates for self-evidence—both concepts and propositions will be considered.[10]

Recognitional Range

Consider first the range of cases someone who adequately understands a self-evident proposition must take to instantiate it or illustrate it, in the way that an animal that is both a fox and female instantiates the proposition that all vixens are female.[11] The crucial cases in this range are such that one must see some relation between or among the proposition's constituent concepts: some relation that both accounts for its truth and is such that seeing it inclines a rational person to believe it. One can see, in a certain non-inferential, apprehensional way, *how* it is true. This is often simply a matter of seeing a truth-sufficing relation between the concepts figuring in the proposition. Recall the proposition that all vixens are female, which is semantically like many other propositions. The relation underlying its truth, a kind of conjunctive "containment," is formal (since everything that is *F* and *G* is *F*); but seeing the relation need not be "reachable" only by using definitions, though *exhibiting* it may require that. Adequately understanding the relation should be

10. I do not take concepts to be the only candidates for a constitutive role here, and my overall view allows for (among other things) universals (assuming they are different in kind) to be constituents.

11. This raises the question of how to construe abstract singular propositions, say that 4 is even. Presumably in these cases concrete quadruples serve as a *kind* of instance.

manifested in also seeing that *young* vixens are female, and so forth for similar modifiers.

A different kind of self-evident truth is that if *p* entails *q*, and *q* entails *r*, then *p* entails *r*. Here adequate understanding should lead to readily seeing instances of it as such. By contrast, that nothing is round and square seems virtually as clearly self-evident, but is apparently neither analytic nor formal.[12] For these two cases, comprehensional adequacy would lead us to expect a tendency to endorse inferences in the indicated pattern of entailment and to accept propositions constituted by affirmations of the mutual exclusion relation between roundness and squareness. Taking the truth to depend on the size of the figures, e.g., and so rejecting an instance of the proposition that nothing is round and square applied to huge circles, would tend to indicate at best defective understanding.

The normative realm has apparently self-evident propositions that are highly substantive but also not analytic, e.g. such epistemic principles as

> *The visual principle*: If a person, *S*, has a clear and steadfast visual impression as of something *F* before *S*, then (at least given concepts adequate for believing there is something *F* there), *S* has prima facie justification for believing this.

The force of 'as of something *F* there' is not statistical, e.g. meaning *as is usual when something F is there*. I have in mind a kind of appropriateness to there being an *F* there, and I take this appropriateness to be determined by the properties figuring in *S*'s conception of an *F*. What these are is of course a major determinant of the content of *S*'s belief. How this appropriateness is to be explicated is no simple matter, but nothing I say (at least in this chapter) demands further specificity.

The self-evidence of such normative propositions is controversial, and the reasons for this may be in part why they need not figure in the recognitional range—or at least in the *acknowledgment range*—of the self-evident for everyone who adequately understands them. People can withhold or even disbelieve generalizations that guide their own

12. The nature of analytic truth and reasons for denying that this truth is analytic are discussed in the chapters of my *Epistemology* (2010) devoted to the a priori. For other examples of apparently non-analytic self-evident propositions, see the diverse group indicated by Conee (2010). The term 'self-support' should not be taken to imply his considering self-evident propositions self-supporting; he takes support (as I do) to be asymmetrical.

parlance. This, as we shall see in considering disagreement, is one reason some self-evident propositions can be rationally rejected.

The Sense of Rejectability

This variable is related to recognitional range. My counting as round a circle I'm shown indicates little about my understanding of the proposition that nothing is round and square if I also count as round all polygons with eight or more sides (visible to me). Given an understanding of the concept of a circle, one should reject these descriptions of circles and deny that what satisfies them is circular. The phenomenon illustrated here is conceptual rejectability.

Propositional rejectability—applying to propositions as candidates for equivalence with a self-evident proposition—is wider and also important. Suppose someone considers the epistemic principle just stated and does not see that we must reject a candidate for equivalence in which 'may assert it' replaces the prima facie justification clause. This would tend to show inadequate understanding, likely centered on the notion of what constitutes prima facie justification, which is defeasible and need not be strong.

Adequate understanding of the visual principle should lead at least to withholding the suggested substitute for it; but disbelieving it would tend to show more about the adequacy of the understanding of the principle. In cases like this, disbelief, as believing a negation, tends to imply better understanding of *p* than merely withholding, if only because it usually comes from apparently seeing why *p* is false, or from understanding an objection to it. Withholding may reflect mere abstension from taking *p* to be true, and that may come from mere uncertainty. (The relevant kind of withholding is not the sort that may result from skepticism due to philosophical reflection, since that may reflect good understanding—in certain skeptics, even comprehensional adequacy regarding a self-evident proposition does not assure believing it.)

Explicative Capacity

In people who, like well-trained teachers, can normally in some way articulate their understanding, explicating a proposition tends to indicate much about degree of understanding of it. Done well, explication implies adequate understanding. One kind of explication is provision of an analysis, but requiring this as for adequate understanding would be over-demanding. A more plausible adequacy requirement is having a kind of potentially articulable explanatory insight, even if it is mainly a matter of seeing *how* the proposition is true, say by apprehending the inclusion relation between being a vixen and being female.

Explicative capacity is normally in part constituted by ability to give a range of examples that illustrate the truth in question—something expected of good students conversant with a concept or proposition. This illustrative capacity is also important for adequate understanding, and it is normally accompanied by an ability both to rule out "look-alikes" and, often, to indicate why they are only that. Someone who adequately understands the proposition that first cousins share a pair of grandparents should be able to devise an example of two people who are cousins, note that their parents are siblings, point out that they would then have the same parents, and explain why these would be the cousins' grandparents. One would expect explication to proceed partly in terms of the kinds of examples we have cited, e.g. analytic versus synthetic cases, depending on the target proposition.

With readily definable concepts, such as being a circle, we might expect a description that corresponds to the definatory elements. With concepts such as obligatoriness, which are highly complex, we might expect only a certain way of citing paradigm cases. Comprehensional adequacy with respect to <Nothing is round and square> might imply only an ability to illustrate, in some appropriate way, (a) being a certain kind of uniform closed curve, (b) being right-angled and four-sided, and (c) the incompatibility between them. Drawing rough approximations of the shapes in question, given appropriate comment on their relevant properties, might suffice for adequate understanding.

By contrast, understanding the self-evident sufficiency of promising for prima facie obligation or of visual impressions for prima facie justification is more difficult to achieve. It cannot come from awareness of approximate "definitionally" sufficient conditions for the several crucial concepts (such definitional descriptions are apparently unavailable); nor is there any analogue of producing a simple illustration that characteristically manifests comprehensional adequacy. Even producing narrative examples would require special features to show adequate understanding of these rich concepts. For describing explicative capacity we might perhaps speak of *basic* kinds of examples appropriate to explication of the proposition in question. If so, I do not want to take the few kinds cited above as the only ones there are.

Logical Comprehension

This variable is connected with those so far considered, but nonetheless distinct. Particularly important is recognition of entailments and non-entailments. Suppose Jones purported to see that if *p* or *q* holds and *p* is false, then *q* holds. If Jones thought that if *p* or *q* holds, and *p* is true, then *q* is false, this would strongly count against adequacy of understanding of the self-evident conditional. To be sure, if Jones indicates taking the 'or' to be exclusive, we might then try some other "test," but it is significant that we might properly consider further testing necessary.

The case may be more complicated. Consider the proposition that if *p* entails *q*, and *q* entails *r*, and *r* entails *s*, and *s* is false, then *p* is false. Suppose someone is given time for reflection on the antecedent and denies the consequent. This strongly suggests inadequate understanding of the proposition, and to conclude otherwise would require special explanation. Granted, as in other cases, withholding is commonly less informative regarding kind or degree of understanding than is disbelieving. Withholding, may, e.g., come from thinking, truly or mistakenly, that one does not adequately understand, whereas disbelief requires a basic understanding and, especially where *p* is complex, may come from reflection on it. There is no simple rule here, but much can be learned about how well *S* understands a proposition by determining why *S* believes, disbelieves, or withholds.[13]

Certain analogies are also relevant to determining degree of logical comprehension. Suppose we provide a set-theoretic analogy for the logical conditional just cited. We note how set-theoretic inclusion is analogous to entailment, and we then draw concentric circles with the smallest, the *p* circle, inside the *q* one, the *q* circle inside the *r* one, and *r* one inside the *s* circle. We then draw an *x* outside the *s* and note that it is outside the *p* circle. If this does not help someone unfamiliar with such diagramming to see the truth of the conditional, that provides evidence of lacking not only a certain kind of imagination but also adequate understanding of at least some essential element in that proposition.

13. Withholding is far less well understood than generally realized. For extensive discussion, see Richard Feldman and Earl Conee (2018). Further analysis, focused partly on the question whether withholding is properly considered a propositional attitude is provided in Audi (forthcominga).

Confirmational Sensitivity

Logical comprehension and confirmational sensitivity are kindred phenomena. To be sure, for the self-evident what counts as confirmation is less clear than for many other kinds of proposition (especially empirical generalizations). But philosophy itself presents cases. Indeed, is not a presumptive and intuitive instance of a philosophical claim broadly confirmatory (roughly, epistemically supportive), whereas a presumptive and intuitive counterexample is broadly disconfirmatory? Related to this, intuitive induction, as illustrated by Ross following Aristotle, works by a kind of (non-enumerative) confirmation: a kind of ascent from particularity to generality. (Ross's main example concerns counting matches, joining disparate pairs, and recounting, as a way to produce understanding that 2 + 2 = 4.) Intuitive induction may occur through a certain kind of apprehension of a single instance, but it could require more such apprehensions than some cases of enumerative induction require for justification of the relevant generalization.

For another illustration, consider a counterpart of the visual principle stated above. Suppose someone who affirms it fails to see that it can be questioned for cases of artificial light. Suppose I view white paper I am unaware is under red light. Does my impression as of red paper provide any justification for believing there is something red before me? The proponent of the principle should see this case as needing comment—it may appear to disconfirm the principle and challenge my justification. Adequately understanding the principle, however, would yield a sense that *prima facie* justification is defeasible. Now consider confirmation. Suppose I said, to a person who wanted red paper, that there is a piece of red paper on the table and then was chidingly corrected by somebody aware of the red lighting. An apposite reply is 'I'm sorry—I had no inkling that there was red lighting'. *Rejecting* the reply as irrelevant or inapposite would tend to show some deficiency in understanding the visual principle—though (for reasons to emerge shortly) we cannot automatically rule out a different possibility: adequate understanding combined with philosophical disagreement.

Discriminative Acuity

A high degree of satisfaction of the variables so far described suggests a high degree of sensitivity to differences between *p* and propositions one might call near-equivalents. But this acuity is apparently not reducible to any of the other variables that tend to indicate degree of understanding of a self-evident proposition. Consider the generalization that altruistic people as such tend to do good deeds toward others, which, given a natural reading of 'tendency', seems self-evident. Could someone adequately understand this without ability to see that the converse is not true, or at least need not be considered true on the basis of its content? For someone who adequately understands the concept of altruism, the discriminative acuity I am describing should be manifested at least by recognizing that doing good deeds can be self-interestedly motivated.

This point should be confirmable by reactivity to concrete cases described in detail. For instance, seeing the truth of the original tendency proposition about altruists would likely lead one to deny that altruistic people as such tend to do good deeds that are self-interestedly motivated. Someone who understands altruism should see that doing a good deed toward someone solely for money is uncharacteristic of altruism. What should occur here is discrimination of altruistic deeds from merely beneficent ones.

Discrimination of such differences is correlated (though imperfectly) with ability to clarify them in different ways, from exemplification to explanation. Here we may compare the instructor's ways of explaining with the novice's; they differ, but both are relevant. Instructors tend to be better at framing examples and at explaining differences even of a kind novices may, with equal acuity, notice.

Related to the capacity to distinguish self-evident propositions from near-equivalents is the ability to see a difference between the equivalence of propositions and their identities. Consider the proposition that (1) All justifiably believable propositions are rationally believable propositions. This seems self-evidently equivalent to (2) All non-(rationally-believable-propositions) are non-(justifiably-believable-propositions). Now imagine asking a student who sees these points, and has learned to assess the usual kinds of confirming instances for such universal propositions as (1), to consider, as supporting (1), a piece of white paper, which, as a non-proposition, is obviously a referent of both predicative terms in (2). We would expect at least doubt regarding whether the paper instantiates (1) and related hesitation concerning whether the contrapositive of (1) is the same proposition. If the student finds no ground for hesitation here, we should suspect a lack of discriminative acuity or some other comprehensional failure (the case may also illustrate a deficiency in confirmational sensitivity).[14]

14. This is an a priori counterpart of the paradox of the ravens. Plainly, adequately understanding (1) does not imply an ability to explain *why* a piece

Translational Capacity

This capacity comes in degrees and is one kind of indication of adequate understanding. Imagine children asking their parents, or students of a foreign language asking their teachers, what a sentence means. Capacity to answer such questions correctly, or at least plausibly, for a self-evident proposition is an element in understanding it, at least for those who, like some native speakers of sufficiently rich natural languages, have the conceptual sophistication to translate the relevant sentences intralinguistically. (Intralinguistic translation seems to be the more comprehensionally significant kind.) Notice that translational capacity is not entailed by even a combination of the sense of rejectability and discriminative capacity, but it is related to both and tends to presuppose a good measure of each. Developmentally, they may be the best route to its achievement.

Translational capacity may be hypothetical given the possibility that the person is monolingual and knows only a language lacking any translation of the sentence in question. We have seen, however, that *mere* translational capacity, especially when interlinguistic, does not imply adequate understanding—even where it implies a level of understanding from which, by reflection, someone might progress to adequate understanding.

Adequate understanding may go beyond even good semantic comprehension, nor is it equivalent to ability to supply a logical equivalent, as seems to be indicated by the case of contraposition as apparently affecting confirmational range and certainly changing meaning. Vagueness is a different thing. A good translation need not (for every kind of expression figuring in it) preserve exactly the same degree of vagueness as the target sentence; but the further a translation is from preservation of vagueness, the less likely it is to reveal adequate understanding.

of white paper does not appear to confirm it, or to provide an approximation of a Bayesian account of how confirmation should be understood here; but we would expect ability to respond differently to instances of *p* and those of its contrapositive and a readiness to treat (2) as "saying" something different from (1).

Readiness to Meet Objections

For philosophers, degree of understanding is prominently associated with this variable, but it figures in degree of understanding quite generally. If, objecting to the promissory principle, someone says that one could turn out to be obligated to do the opposite of what is promised, 'prima facie' has likely been inadequately understood. Or suppose someone asks, regarding a person lauded as generous, 'If he's generous, why does he give nothing to charity?' The reply, 'He has little money, but he gives much time and energy to helping the sick' would suggest significant understanding of a predication of generosity, and denying its relevance would show some lack of understanding.

Granted, ability to meet objections is a case illustrating that there is no sharp distinction between the role of understanding and that of imagination. Exercising imagination, moreover, often tends to enhance one's justification. Given non-imaginative reflection in responding to an objection, there may be only a slight chance that one will find, e.g., a new premise, whereas imaginatively seeking premises to shore up a proposition objected to often expands one's evidence base. Recall the colored light objection to the visual principle: that it is disconfirmed by cases of red light's making white surfaces look red. With a little imagination one might reply to the effect that since the objection ultimately presupposes the visual principle, it is not cogent.

By contrast, if someone objects to 'She prefers the company of men to that of women' (said of a middle-aged woman) with 'No—she likes the company of girls as much as that of boys', there has likely been misunderstanding detectable with little imagination. There are contexts in which it is not presupposed that boys are not men or that girls are not women; but in the intended context, the presupposed propositions may be plausibly considered self-evident, and the example thus illustrate a deficiency in the kind of readiness to meet objections that is normally implied by adequate understanding of the self-evident.

Accessibility to Occurrent Thought

Given that the paradigms of the self-evident are formulable in sentences one can easily entertain without reliance on memory, as may be required with long formulations, it is natural to take a kind of entertainability of propositions as an element in adequate understanding of them. But a self-evident proposition can be such that a normal person can (1) read it comprehendingly yet (2) not hold it before the mind in a single "mental breath" but still (3) adequately understand it by (at least) all the criteria above. There the proposition, for that person, would not pass the mental breath test, which we associate with paradigms of the self-evident. This criterion—call it *thinkability*—will be relative to the capacities of different thinkers, but we need not discuss that separately. The thinkability of *p* (for *S*) is its being entertainable in toto at a single time—not necessarily instantaneously, to be sure, but in the "present," in the sense entailing no dependence on memory. Thinkability does not seem to be a strict requirement for adequate understanding. Let me explain.

We might first ask whether adequate understanding of a self-evident proposition (even if not of all self-evident propositions) can depend on memory. I believe so, but the dependence is limited and must be such as to permit, say, comparison with similar propositions, seeing entailments, and other achievements. Consider a multi-element conjunction that is not otherwise complicated. We might say of such cases that one can have them occurrently *in mind* even if not *before the mind*—focally in the eye of consciousness at a particular time. A related case is that of a multi-premise proof such that I cannot focally entertain the entire proof but have it in active memory in a way that empowers me to write it out on demand. Here, assuming each step is self-evidently entailed by the previous one, the conditional whose antecedent is the conjunction of the premises and whose conclusion is that of the proof, might be self-evident for me. I can adequately understand it by tracking the steps implicit in the antecedent, and that understanding would suffice to justify me in believing it and for my knowing it if I believe it on the basis of that understanding.

This kind of case confirms the hypothesis that the connection between adequacy of understanding and thinkability is contingent. This may not hold for the (phenomenal) *sense* of understanding; that *is* perhaps sometimes dependent on thinkability. The point is important since, when we lack the sense of something, such as remembering a person, where we expect to have that sense, we tend to think we do not have the thing in question at all. The sense of understanding by its very nature tends to diminish with distance from thinkability. Perhaps the same holds for degree of understanding itself, but it would not follow that every case of adequate understanding requires thinkability.

These reflections suggest an apparently necessary condition for comprehensional adequacy: *entertainability*, in the broad sense of *considerability*: the ability to have the proposition in mind—even if not before the mind—in a way that enables one to have the kinds of intellectual relations to it indicated so far. Take an example akin to that of the (self-evidential) proof described earlier. I am asked to consider this: *If A* entails *B, B* entails *C,* and so forth through <*Y* entails *Z*>, and yet not-*Z, then* not-*A*. Even if I cannot have this twenty-eight-element proposition before my mind, thus focally entertaining it, I can consider it under the simple description just given and can write it out on demand.

As indicated by the similar case of certain proofs, there are kinds of encapsulations that permit my account of the self-evident to include many cases with a significant degree of complexity of certain kinds. Some uses of 'entertain' apparently extend to considerability as I represent it, but there is a narrower sense of 'entertain' in which entertaining *p* requires having it focally in mind. This sense is too narrow to yield a condition for adequate understanding. Much as we can consider a painting without having its entirety in focus but with an overall visual sense of it, we can consider a proposition without having it fully before the mind as the content of a single thought, but with a grasp of it that enables such achievements as discriminating it from near equivalents. What we cannot consider, we cannot understand. But we can understand more than we can have focally before the mind.

Adequate understanding of a self-evident proposition, then, requires an ability to consider it with a certain degree of clarity and, accordingly, with a kind of recognition of its essential elements. Some propositions, however, are, for some people, more readily considered than others; and a fairly high degree of readiness to consider a self-evident proposition may, as a matter of contingent fact, often be necessary for a high degree of satisfaction of the other comprehensional variables we have explored that determine adequacy of understanding of that proposition. In any case, considerability of *p* for S comes in degrees, as does the clarity with which *S* considers *p*.

V. Degrees of Understanding and Propositional Justification

So far, I have been exploring elements that figure essentially in degree of understanding of self-evident propositions (though understanding of propositions in general appears similarly explicable). Contingent elements in understanding self-evident propositions (and others) are also significant, but they are both too numerous and too far from philosophical centrality for our topic to be a main concern here. Rapidity of responsiveness, e.g., might often be a significant measure of degree of understanding. We are often impressed by it, and many teachers nurture it in their students. Still, it is only contingently related to degree of understanding and, thereby, to degrees of (propositional) justification. A slow uptake may indicate deliberateness, and a depth of understanding may make speed uncomfortable. The slow often understand deeply, the quick can merely seem profound. Adequacy and depth are of course near equivalents here.

As in other cases, the comparative notion can help with the primary one. One case here is intrapersonal: understanding p better than one did before, yielding the question of what accounts for the improvement. There is also interpersonal comparison. Here is a first pass at clarification:

> *Intrapersonal understanding of a self-evident proposition*: Where *p* is self-evident, a person, *S*, who, at *t*, understands *p*, understands it better at *t* than at an earlier time t_e if and only if, other things equal, at *t S* more extensively satisfies, in an overall way, the nine comprehensional variables, than *S* did at t_e.

Similarly we might affirm, for interpersonal comparisons:

> *Interpersonal understanding of a self-evident proposition*: Where *p* is self-evident, a person, *X*, understands *p* better than does another person, *Y*, if and only if, other things equal, *X* more extensively satisfies, in an overall way, the nine comprehensional variables.

Consider, for instance, how these formulations apply to readiness to meet objections and to the range and number of objections seen to be relevant—or disconfirmatory. We commonly judge even ourselves in relation to these variables. We can also look in a more positive direction—toward how well one marshals supporting considerations, an ability that tends to indicate degree of (propositional) justification. A related idea regarding the interpersonal case is that *X* understands a self-evident proposition, *p*, better than does *Y* if, after a certain period and intensity of reflection on the part of both, *X* sees the truth of *p* and *Y* does not. I am inclined, however, to consider this speed variable both a contingent "measure" and, even if often useful, less important than the other variables.

Another illustration may help. Consider the proposition that *If X killed Y, then Y is dead.*[15] This proposition is intuitive but at least not clearly self-evident (though, if true, apparently a priori true). It is intuitive in

15. This has been called "as clear and obvious as anything" by Thurow in "Experiential Defeaters and A Priori Justification" (2006: 601). I believe I now understand this proposition better than I have before and better than some who are bilingual and affirm it with an understanding of it (expressed in

normally evoking, on comprehending consideration, the sense of non-inferential credibility, and it has this property at least in part because the common kinds of cases by which the term 'killing' is learned are such that learners become aware of killings only when they are also aware of the resulting and often immediate deaths. But consider this. You see *X* inject in *Y* a fatal dose of a poison that kills within hours and for which you know there is no antidote. Is it wrong to react with 'My God, *X* killed *Y*!'? Do you not see the act that is the killing? If you leave the scene before the death and are asked if *X* killed *Y*, as *X* threatened, would you not (justifiably) assent? Although you see the injection perceptually, you see it *as* a killing in an inferential way—this is a kind of property ascription based on your non-perceptual knowledge of the lethality of the action you see. But you can see the act that *is* a killing before you know that it is, and possibly even before your background knowledge enables you to see it, aspectually, as such.

On this view, killing is constituted by an act that in a certain (non-deviant) way causes death, and reluctance to call the poisoning a killing before the death is epistemic. It may, after all, be plausibly thought that we don't know for certain that an act is a killing until the victim dies.[16] Also supporting the view that killing may precede dying is the argument that since killing is at least in part doing something that causes death, and since a causative event can *have* occurred before the effect occurs, the causative act can be completed before the death occurs. This argument is not self-evidently sound, but it should nonetheless be apparent that the claim in question is not clearly self-evident.

VI. Comprehensional Adequacy

Do we now have an account of comprehensional adequacy? Suppose we take each of the nine variables as a criterion for understanding a self-evident proposition, in the sense of a consideration partly constitutive of such understanding. If these are the (or even the major) criteria, that is significant in itself. Suppose further that we take minimal satisfaction

English) easily good enough to translate it into another language which they know as well as they know English. Just how puzzling the issue is may be seen from Thomson (1971).

16. Killing may be overdetermined, and if poisoning produced death just when natural causes also do, we would hesitate to say unqualifiedly that the poison killed the victim. As to a case where someone is fatally shot before the poison produces death, there we should say that the fatal dose *would* have killed.

of each criterion to be satisfaction at or above the level implied by mere semantic comprehension. Satisfaction at this level seems roughly equivalent to the intellectual relation normally implied by the ability, for a bilingual person, to translate, with at least rough correctness, the relevant sentence from one of the languages to the other (I assume a person with minimal understanding of *p* must satisfy one or, normally several, of the variables, though this is not self-evident, and the question depends substantially on empirical data.)[17] On these assumptions, we can perhaps say this:

> *Comprehensional adequacy*: A person, *S*, adequately understands a self-evident proposition, *p*, if and only if, in relation to *p*; *S* at least minimally satisfies each of the nine criteria of recognitional range, the sense of rejectability, explicative capacity, logical comprehension, confirmational sensitivity, discriminative acuity, translational capacity, readiness to meet objections, and considerability.

If we are guided by this notion of comprehensional adequacy, we might say that, at least for self-evident propositions, understanding is minimally adequate where all nine are satisfied at least minimally. Our overall discussion suggests (but does not require holding) that minimal overall satisfaction must be just above the level expectable given mere semantic comprehension of a formulation of *p*. In typical cases of self-evidential justification the understanding exceeds the minimal level for most of the criteria, perhaps indeed for each, but I am inclined to leave open that a high level of satisfaction of one or more of the criteria may well offset a failure of minimal satisfaction of at least one other.

Comprehension may be at a very high level in some cases. Perhaps we can describe maximal satisfaction insofar as we can see what would constitute the highest degree for each criterion, but I doubt that in general we can see this. Perhaps only minds with certain infinite capacities could achieve it. Still, we have roughly specifiable end points with respect to which we can normally locate adequacy. It might help to think of it as a kind of mastery of the concepts figuring essentially in the proposition in question. It lies somewhere between the low comprehensional level of the beginner and the high level of the consummate expert.

17. One qualification here is that the person must be translating in the "normal way"—it would not do to have the person's brain manipulated so as to provide, even if the person is ignorant of one or both languages, what a translating computer dictates is the translation.

Here we must bear in mind that the account of self-evidence presupposes the concepts of justification and knowledge. These have vagueness of their own, but once we have an account of understanding and see how to ascertain its (approximate) degree, we can appeal to those concepts—indispensable in epistemology in any case—to help in determining whether an understanding is adequate. If we take justifiedness as internal and suppose that, in principle, it is connected with a potential process of justification, we have two dimensions of appraisal for it. If we take knowledge to be partly constituted by reliable grounding (which, where *p* is self-evident, will be clarified in Chapter 9), this gives a different anchor for the proposed account of self-evidence.

VII. Obstacles to Comprehension

An account of comprehensional adequacy can be enhanced by considering some of the factors that prevent it or tend to reduce one's degree of understanding. Here are some instructive examples.

Biasing background beliefs may obscure understanding, making it defective and certainly inadequate. Consider the proposition that if parental consent is required for a child's surgery, then either a man or a woman must give it. This may seem self-evident to many people. Many presuppose that a child's parents are a mother and father; most people (at this writing) presuppose that mothers are female and fathers male. But does the notion of a parent entail having sex (or even gender)? And can't a transgender person have changed in sex while remaining the same in parentage?

We also tend to presuppose, mistakenly, that a person's grandparent is not also that person's parent. Similarly, someone might tend to believe that *parent of* is intransitive (anti-transitive). Few people have even considered this question, but my experience discussing relevant cases suggests that there is a common tendency to agree that if, e.g., Tom is the father of Addie, and she is the mother of Carl, then Tom is not the father of Carl. A technical example would be the proposition that infinite sets are equinumerous, which might seem true on the assumption that any infinity of elements can be placed in one-to-one correspondence with the integers.

To be sure, for the incestuous proposition, as for many plausibly considered self-evident, it is not easy to say what kind of mastery of the constituent concepts is required for an adequate understanding of the proposition. Take those of being a father, being a grandfather, and being a person's child. Do these require having concepts such as producing offspring by fertilization through male-female intercourse? And if, as with a technology of the future, this common concept of parenthood is not required, does it nonetheless suffice? It presumably will suffice for ascribing parenthood (given the concept of a grandparent) on the presupposition that biologically normal fertile male and female human beings can jointly reproduce, and this does seem a normal presupposition even on the part of people who cannot initially see the truth of the incestuous proposition. However, must one see, on perhaps long reflection, that the relation *parent of* is not intransitive to have an adequate understanding of the key terms in the incestuous proposition? I am inclined to say so, given that no more than ordinary reflection on what constitutes a parent and child of that person is needed. We can of course regard the incestuous proposition as, *for* most people, only mediately self-evident, but this is consistent with treating it as self-evident simpliciter.

The domain of formal logic contains other examples of obstacles to understanding. A quite different bias that can block philosophical understanding of the self-evident is suggested by the mistaken idea, expressed by Moore and Ross among others, that the self-evident is unprovable. At that rate, it could not be self-evident that if p entails q, and q entails r, and r is false, then p is false.[18] Granted, for some people this is only mediately self-evident. I do not take non-inferentiality to rule out *internal* inferences (those using premises following from the self-evident proposition itself or from some constituent proposition in it), so I grant that adequate understanding may in some cases be achievable only through drawing inferences.

Understanding is multidimensional; and when its object is a self-evident proposition it will, if adequate and not merely semantic, ground justification for believing that proposition. Indeed, if the theory outlined in this chapter is correct, then (as will be explained in Chapter 9) any a priori (true) proposition can in principle be justifiedly believed and

18. We might grant Moore and Ross that the proposition is not a good candidate for an axiom in a formal system, but unprovability is not required for self-evidence. It may be mistakenly taken to be required, given the functions axioms are often taken to play, e.g. being somehow epistemically ultimate, as with Aristotle's indemonstrables, which may include simple paradigms of self-evidence; see, e.g., *Posterior Analytics* 72b.

known either on the basis of an adequate understanding of it, as is possible where it is self-evident, or on the basis of valid inferences from a justifiedly believed self-evident proposition. Not just any kind of understanding suffices for comprehensional adequacy. It is very difficult to specify what kind is adequate. This chapter indicates the main variables that determine what constitutes comprehensional adequacy. Even when we have these variables in clear view, however, there is no quantitative measure of adequacy. I have suggested that we might view the comprehensional adequacy in question as a kind of *intellectual mastery* of the relevant concepts. This mastery admits of degrees and connects understanding with degrees of justification, but some vagueness in the account of comprehensional adequacy remains. I have argued, however, that the vagueness we cannot eliminate is appropriate to that of 'self-evident'. In any case, the account provides a good intuitive sense of what kind of understanding goes with the sort of consideration of self-evident propositions that tends to yield justification and knowledge regarding them. The proposed account of adequate understanding also helps in explicating understanding in empirical cases, such as those of generalizations in science and even propositions believed on the basis of perception. In both cases, the variables constitutive of understanding apparently correspond to some of the dimensions of possible clarification and explication of the propositions in question—perhaps indeed of propositions in general. Regarding the broad notion of the a priori, if the self-evident is indeed the basic case of the a priori and is to be explicated as proposed here, we can see that the more generous our notion of adequate understanding, the wider and more substantive the a priori can be taken to be. These points are mainly conceptual. Further epistemological and ontological aspects of the self-evident remain to be explored.

9

APRIORITY, DISPUTABILITY, AND NECESSITY

This chapter extends the account of self-evidence offered in Chapter 8, with a view to clarifying how the account bears on the a priori broadly conceived and on knowledge and justification. Its main epistemological aim is to show how there can be rational disagreement even on certain important self-evident propositions. Its main ontological aim is to show how, if self-evident propositions (at least those that are not formal) are conceived as (in rough terms) expressing relations among abstract entities, then knowledge of the self-evident can be seen to be like knowledge of many ordinary empirical propositions—especially those known perceptually—in being a case in which the belief constituting knowledge is reliably connected to its truthmaker. Section I concerns the scope of the a priori. Sections II and III bring out the relevance of the account of self-evidence to the theory of disagreement. Doing this is particularly important given the way in which disagreement on purportedly self-evident propositions has been a source of skepticism about their knowability. Sections IV and V concern ontological issues besetting the view that the mind can grasp anything beyond the causal order.

I. Self-Evidence and Provability

Self-evident propositions are knowable both by reflection (including understanding-based intuition as a minimal case) and non-inferentially. In non-inferentiality they are like perceptually knowable propositions; but by contrast with those, their truth does not depend on the physical world. The domain of the a priori is, however, like that of perception in having a kind of hierarchical structure. In both realms, a kind of direct

Seeing, Knowing, and Doing. Robert Audi, Oxford University Press (2020). © Oxford University Press.
DOI: 10.1093/oso/9780197503508.001.0001

contact with the objects constituting truthmakers is the basic case. That idea will be clarified in this chapter, but we should first consider how self-evidence plays a basic role in the theory of a priori knowledge and justification.

Suppose *p* is self-evident and that the conditional <if *p* then *q*> is also. One might say, then, that *q* is in principle knowable by reflection on the basis of understanding. This does not make *q* self-evident, since it might be knowable only on the basis of *p*, and hence inferentially—it might be premise-dependent. It is a priori true that either (1) nothing is round and square or (2) tringles have four sides. But its knowability depends on that of (1), which entails it. Nonetheless, it would still be knowable, and justifiedly believable, where one reflects on it *with* an adequate understanding of its entailment by (1). Call such propositions *broadly* a priori: not self-evident but provable by a single self-evident step from a self-evident proposition. Calling this (a priori) provability presupposes that a self-evident proposition is an appropriate premise to transmit knowledge and justification, but that is highly plausible.

The broadly a priori, then, is provable. But the converse seems false. Imagine the likeliest counterexample: *p* is self-evident; *p* self-evidently entails *q*; and *q* self-evidently entails *r*. I am happy to call *r* provable, but whereas understanding alone together with a single inference suffices to see the truth of *q*, this need not hold for *r*. The reason is that although entailment is transitive, self-evident entailment is not. In the case imagined, nothing guarantees the self-evidence of the proposition that if *p* then *r*.[1] This yields a difference with the case of the broadly a

1. This point is difficult to prove, but consider this. Letting the variables be any readily understandable propositions (not necessarily self-evident ones), assume these self-evident entailments: (1) $p \rightarrow p \vee (s \,\&\, t)$; (2) $p \vee (s \,\&\, t) \rightarrow (p \vee s) \,\&\, (p \vee t)$; and (3) $(p \vee s) \,\&\, (p \vee t) \rightarrow {\sim}({\sim}p \,\&\, {\sim}s) \,\&\, {\sim}({\sim}p \,\&\, {\sim}t)$. If self-evident entailment is transitive, then it is also self-evident that (4) $p \rightarrow {\sim}({\sim}p \,\&\, {\sim}s) \,\&\, {\sim}({\sim}p \,\&\, {\sim}t)$. Is (4) self-evident? Consider it in isolation from (1), (2), and (3), which each entail it. Leaving aside a high level of logical proficiency, it appears that a person could understand (4), say expressed in English, well enough to explain its meaning and work with it in ways that show comprehensional adequacy, but *without* seeing how it is true, e.g. by 'thinking backwards' to (1) as equivalent to it. Suppose, however, that (4) *is* self-evident. Then, by increasing complexity in the illustrated way, we can proceed to another proposition—call it (5)—complicated as much as possible while preserving the self-evidence of each entailment in the chain. Now we will again *either* have a proposition, with p as its antecedent, that falsifies the transitivity hypothesis *or* we may continue the process until we do. Proposition (5) will be provable from p by self-evident

priori. Furthermore, where the number of self-evident steps required for proving *r* depends on an exercise of memory, knowing that *r* might even depend on memory. Still, so long as there is an a priori path from the self-evident to *r* as a theorem, it might, like many theorems in logic and pure mathematics, be provable. Some propositions are *both* self-evident and provable from what is self-evident. This is compatible with the idea that the concept of self-evidence is basic for that of the a priori and for treating provability (of the rigorous kind in question), which may or may not entail broad apriority, as a genuine case of the a priori.

II. Can Rational Disagreement Extend to the Self-Evident?

Contrary to the common view that the self-evident is obvious, people can have rational disagreements on a self-evident proposition: one person rationally believes *p* while the other rationally disbelieves it or withholds believing it. Here it is essential to see that even adequately understanding a self-evident proposition and considering it with such understanding is not necessarily (psychologically) *compelling:* it does not entail believing it. In rational persons, it at least commonly tends to yield both intuition and belief, but this is a different point. One reason why neither belief nor intuition is entailed is that this tendency can be inhibited by some biasing background belief.

The Permissiveness of Rationality

A philosophically important case of rational disagreement on a self-evident proposition occurs where both parties adequately understand it and are thereby justified in believing it, yet one believes it and the other disbelieves it. Such a disagreement may be considered rational because the rejection might be supported by plausible though unsound arguments—arguments just good enough to prevent the disbelief from being irrational and, often, to inhibit the normal tendency to find the proposition intuitive.[2] On the assumption that some philosophical

steps, but that does not entail its self-evidence—or that of the *n*th element in such a series. Compare arriving by helicopter at an alpine destination reachable by very clear paths; even from a good view of the whole place, we may not see how to get there from the ground.

2. In, e.g., my 2008b I have indicated in more detail how such a disagreement might occur, cited an apparent case in ethical theory, and indicated one way to approach resolution, but there is no need to reintroduce the details.

theses are self-evident, their being rationally disputed makes them an important source of possible examples of precisely what I am describing. Chapter 8 showed both how biasing considerations can lead to denying something self-evident and also how appeal to the dimensions of understanding introduced there can be a route to achieving agreement. This possibility implies a dilemma. If the self-evident is by its very nature obvious and unprovable, no one who understands it should fail to believe it, and it needs no proof. If, however, the self-evident need not be obvious or unprovable, then rational persons can disagree about its truth, and those who deny or doubt it may demand proof and may reject it if proof is not forthcoming. The first horn was wielded by H. A. Prichard and has led many philosophers to view ethical intuitionism, which construes certain moral principles to be self-evident, as dogmatic.[3] The second horn yields a challenge that must be met if philosophical intuitionism is to be sustained, whether in ethics or in epistemology. We have seen errors in the stereotypes that underlie the first horn. As to the second, I will argue that neither dogmatism nor skepticism need result from an intuitionism that employs the moderate conceptions of self-evidence and intuition I have proposed.

Many philosophical theses may be conceived as self-evident if true. Consider a basic epistemic principle: It is not rational to believe something having what we can see has the form of '*p* and *not-p*'. We tend to presuppose this, and even if we can think of ways to argue for it, we do not take it to need argument. We can of course illustrate it by citing propositions of similar status, e.g. that believing that I am reading and it is not the case that I am reading. One could call this kind of support of a self-evident proposition intuitive induction, as did Ross. But this kind of argument does not work as supporting arguments usually do, by adducing premises knowable, or justifiably believable, wholly independently of the conclusion they are meant to support. It works mainly by enhancing the understanding of the proposition it supports. Here it may parallel the way certain self-evident propositions are learned. But the order of argumentation need not match the order of learning. Suppose we argue for *p* by appeal to *q* and *r*. This does not imply that

3. For Sidgwick's view of "dogmatic intuitionism" (his term) see his 1907 (pp. 100–101). Prichard (1912) gives this impression in the way he stresses "the mistake of supposing the possibility of proving what can only be apprehended directly in an act of moral thinking." The view that intuitionism is dogmatic is reiterated in points made by Korsgaard (1996).

these premises lay on our route to believing *p*. We may have discovered them only in our search for reasons.

To focus the question of how we should conceive rational disagreement on the self-evident, recall a basic point about self-evidence: that, although adequately understanding a self-evident proposition entails having justification for believing it, even comprehendingly considering it does not *compel* believing it. Clearly, then, one can understand a self-evident proposition and reject it—withhold or disbelieve it—in disagreement with someone affirming it. A central point is that adequacy of understanding goes beyond basic semantic comprehension. As we have seen a bilingual person who can immediately translate 'A child can be borne by its grandmother' may still need reflection or even Socratic questioning to achieve understanding of the kind that justifies accepting the claim. Mere semantic comprehension of that proposition need not justify believing it. But seeing its truth through an adequate understanding of it enables one to believe it non-inferentially, presumably on the basis of apprehending the concepts figuring in it and the relations among them in virtue of which the proposition is true.

An adequate understanding of a self-evident proposition, *p*, moreover, does imply (at least in a rational person) a *disposition* to believe it, indeed, one strong enough so that non-belief *given* one's comprehending consideration of *p* calls for explanation. Two possible explanations are constitutional skepticism and commitment to a theory clearly implying the negation of *p*. With disagreements on complex propositions, finding such an explanation is often possible, but it may not be easy. Moreover, in some cases it is unclear whether a person lacks adequate understanding. Understanding comes in degrees. With Rossian moral principles (Ross's and similar ones) and counterpart epistemic principles in mind, let us explore how these points about the self-evident bear on rational disagreement.

Peer Disagreements on Self-Evident Principles

If, like the major intuitionists from Moore on, one takes moral properties to be consequential (hence supervenient) on non-moral properties, one might think that rational persons who disagree on a moral proposition either do not share all the relevant non-moral information or do not each see what that information indicates. This view is highly plausible, but its applicability is limited by the impossibility, in many cases, of specifying *all* the information indicating the non-moral properties on the basis of which there is a truth of the matter in dispute.

Recent epistemological work has raised a challenging problem that does not presuppose our having such comprehensive knowledge: how to deal with possible disagreements one has with someone who seems, in the relevant matter, an *epistemic peer*: roughly, a person who (1) is as rational and as thoughtful as oneself (in the relevant matter, the assessment of whether *p* is true), (2) has considered the same relevant evidence—which need not be all the relevant evidence—and (3) has done so equally conscientiously.[4] By contrast with most descriptions of epistemic parity, this one requires that the parties *consider* the relevant evidence and do so *equally* conscientiously. If parity requires only sharing the same relevant evidence and having the same epistemic virtues (or being equally rational in the matter, which is a similar condition), nothing follows about the extent to which these virtues are *expressed* or "operative" in the cognitions central in the disagreement. Parties having the same evidence might devote very different amounts of time or effort to appraising the proposition. That disparity is common in philosophical controversies.

Given the complexity and idealization in the notion of epistemic parity, one would at best rarely be justified in considering a disputant an epistemic peer. This point alone explains how one might justifiedly adhere to a view one knows someone rationally denies and how rational disagreement as I have characterized it is possible (as we would expect) without parity of the parties to it. Suppose, however, that we *are* justified in believing that a disputant is, by and large, an epistemic peer on the relevant subject, such as ethics, and so meets conditions (1) to (3) for many important propositions of mutual concern. Rational disagreement still seems possible. This can be seen in relation to disagreement on the status of Rossian principles. (Since adequately understanding a self-evident proposition implies having a justification *for* it but does not entail believing it, one could rationally believe that a disputant can adequately understand a self-evident proposition, be justified in believing it, and still not believe it).

Take a counterpart of the strong "particularist" case against Ross's intuitionism.[5] Using examples such as promises whose fulfillment would kill innocent people, some have denied that promising to do something entails any prima facie moral reason to do it. Let us take a perceptual principle as a counterpart example. If, like Macbeth, I have a

4. I discuss and apply this characterization in my 2011; for further discussion see Christensen and Lackey (2013).

5. The most influential statement of this view is probably Dancy's. See, e.g., his 1993. I have replied in detail in ch. 2 of my 2004.

clear steadfast visual experience as of a dagger before me, I have prima facie justification for believing there is one there. One might hold that only in particular cases viewed holistically can one tell whether such experiences yield *any* justification. Suppose that, quite reasonably, epistemological intuitionists do not allow that one can be justified in believing *p and* in simultaneously believing *not-p*. They must then deny either that the particularist adequately understands the visual principle (where adequate understanding implies justification for believing) or that the particularist's arguments justify rejecting it. Intuitionists may deny the latter even while granting that the arguments provide *some* reason to accept strong particularism.[6] Let me explain.

A major point here is that lack of overall justification for believing *p* does not imply that believing it is *irrational*. Being sometimes unjustified—in the sense of lacking overall justification—is common in rational persons in matters requiring rigorous reasoning. This point may also be seen in perceptual cases, as where *S* forms a perceptual belief upon an insufficiently sharp view of a crime or in certain cases requiring aesthetic judgment on a complex artwork.[7] Irrationality, by contrast, is a lapse rational persons do not often suffer. In any event, failure to use reason adequately does not entail flying in its face. That failure is compatible with having *some* degree of justification; but the question here is overall justification of the kind that normally suffices for knowledge when the relevant belief is true and, in broad terms, appropriately grounded. This point is important in appraising disagreement. It implies that even justified confidence that a disputant is unjustified does not automatically warrant attributing irrationality. In many cases, an unjustified but not irrational disputant can offer *some* reason to doubt a proposition at issue, even if not sufficient reason.

In the light of these points about rational disagreement, we can see how philosophical tolerance calls for resisting, so far as possible, attributing inadequate understanding where disagreement provides a better explanation of linguistic or inferential behavior that is evidence of inadequate understanding. In some cases we cannot distinguish between failing to accept a self-evident proposition owing to inadequacy of understanding and failing to accept it owing to holding a theory that

6. This is my strategy (in my 2006) in responding to a strong version of ethical particularism proposed by Dancy (1993), e.g. 60–62 and 66–68.

7. For a treatment of aesthetic judgment that is instructive for both the theory of perception and the contrast between moral principles and such counterparts as exist in aesthetics, see Lopes (2018).

requires rejecting it. Granting this does not make it impossible to get progressively greater clarity about what constitutes inadequate understanding as opposed to theoretical disagreement. Each can be clarified by comparison and contrast with the other. The comparison and contrast is significant given how important it is to determine what constitutes reasonable theoretical disagreement on a self-evident proposition, as opposed to the common kind based in part on some inadequacy in understanding a relevant concept that figures in the disagreement. For surely our assessment of whether such disagreements are reasonable will depend in part on adequately understanding disputants' views and their reasons for them.

These points do not imply that self-evidential justification is indefeasible. Self-evidential justification is defeasible because comprehensional adequacy is vulnerable. How it is vulnerable—say to confusion or misleading argumentation—is clear given the many variables that determine it. Many factors, including philosophical discussion, can impair it. If, however, *S* adequately understands a self-evident proposition, then *S* is justified in believing it and capable of knowing it, even if, on the basis of plausible but unsound arguments, *S* disbelieves it at the time.

III. The Self-Evident, the Obvious, and the Credible

Related to the disagreement issue is another question the account of self-evidence raises. How *unobvious* can the self-evident be to those with enough understanding to translate a formulation of it? Here we need a theory of rationally believing, and of having justification, that leaves open their not entailing, and even being at quite a distance from, occurrent justification, where (roughly)

> *S* has occurrent justification, at *t*, for believing *p* at *t*, if and only if, at *t*, *S* has *in mind* (in the right, adequately comprehending way) some element, e.g. an evidential ground for *p*, that provides justification for believing *p*.

One can have occurrent justification for believing *p* without believing it occurrently—or at all, as with "refusal to believe" in the face of excellent evidence. Moreover, if one believes *p* without occurrent justification, as where one believes it simply on the basis of memorially retaining a justified belief that *p*, one could have an occurrent justified belief that is not *occurrently justified*, since we can occurrently believe *p*, as where we assert it in discussion, without at the time having in mind anything constituting an occurrent justification for believing *p*.

We have not so far considered whether adequate understanding is sufficient to justify not only believing self-evident propositions but also believing certain *non*-self-evident propositions. Despite appearances, nothing said here clearly entails that where adequately understanding *p* is *sufficient* to justify believing *p*, *p* is self-evident. This might apply not only to propositions, such as some in logic, that are plausible and seem self-evident though they are false, but also to controversial cases like *cogito* propositions and others whose *consideration* entails their truth. Those propositions and others whose consideration entails their truth should be briefly considered here.

Think of my contemplating, with adequate understanding, the proposition that I exist, or even simply that something exists. Adequate understanding certainly seems to guarantee my justification and indeed the truth of the proposition. Are they self-evident? The central question here is whether understanding *these truths* is the justifier—what grounds the justification—or simply suffices for justification, which is something quite different. Perhaps one is justified by seeing *introspectively* that one exists (by a kind of inner self-perception) or by identifying a referent for 'something', a procedure that yields existential knowledge of that entity. One problem is that if there is a *proposition* that I exist, in the ordinary, non-Russellian sense in which propositions are objects of thought that more than one person can entertain, then what I understand in having the thought that I exist is the same thing you do when you entertain this. But surely what you understand here does not justify your believing the (presumably *de re*) proposition that I exist, one I could know by self-acquaintance and even without having a descriptive concept that yields a definite description co-extensive with 'I'. It would seem that it is my acquaintance with myself as considering the matter, and not my adequate understanding of the proposition in question, that justifies my believing it. Something similar is at least as plausible for the proposition that something exists.

The case of *cogito* propositions—a subcase of *de se* propositions—indicates a category of empirical propositions with a characteristic we might call *intrinsic credibility*: being such that, if one comprehendingly considers them, one has both (1) justification for believing them and (2) at least a strong tendency to believe them. Even (1) does not apply to all a priori propositions or to self-evident ones on which *S*'s comprehension is short of adequacy (since inadequate understanding does not suffice for justification). We have seen that (2), as an ostensible condition on self-evident propositions, does not apply to a priori propositions in general; some are provable without being self-evident. Condition (2) is also falsified by the possibility of rational disagreement on self-evident propositions. By contrast, (1)—roughly, justifiability for *S* upon comprehending consideration—typically holds for consideration of paradigms of the self-evident. But neither (1) nor (2) holds for all cases. Intrinsic credibility of the kind in question is not necessary for the self-evident in general.

IV. Apprehension of Abstract Entities

My main epistemological points are supported by a certain account of the ontological commitments of the theory of self-evidence and understanding presented here. Ontologically, understanding as I have explicated it might be argued to be explicable without positing abstracta. But suppose, as seems more plausible, that the concepts that figure in self-evidential justification are abstract and that their relations ground the truth of the propositions in question.

A Perceptualist Conception of the Ontology of the Self-Evident

Suppose, then, that a priori knowledge of the self-evident is significantly analogous to perceptual knowledge. Empiricists will ask how the facts in question can causally yield the purported knowledge. So might anyone who considers knowledge dependent on some reliable connection between the fact that *p* and any belief that *p* constituting knowledge that *p*.[8] The idea is that knowledge must meet a reliability condition, which is plausibly considered in some way causal: in rough terms,

> *A causal reliability condition*: A belief constituting knowledge must be reliably *fact-based* in some causal if indirect way.[9]

Given the conception of the a priori now sketched, what can be said to the objection that my view of self-evidential knowledge precludes its meeting this condition?

8. This problem was forcefully raised by Benaceraff (1973, pp. 661–79). For a recent response supporting my approach to the problem but less perceptually oriented, see Fischer (2018).

9. This condition may imply that beliefs constituting knowledge that *p* are in some way explainable by the fact that *p* or appropriately connected facts, as with knowledge of the future (which may be explained by facts that cause both the belief constituting the knowledge and the future state of affairs it "foretells"). Some such explanationist view has been widely defended. For a recent detailed defense, see Bernecker, forthcoming.

In addition to leaving open—at the outset, at least—the possibility of a contingent self-evident truth, my account is moderate in not requiring any special faculty for knowing the self-evident. Proponents of an external causal condition on all knowledge might deny this. Imagine, e.g., that to know that *p*, one must be causally affected by some object(s) it is about. Then it might seem that knowledge can be grounded in understanding *p* only if some abstract entity, such as a constituent in *p*, causally affects the mind.

Such a causal condition, requiring that abstracta be in the causal order, is not necessary for a priori knowledge, even conceived "perceptionally" (as will become apparent). But might *some* kind of causal condition be required? I assume that apprehension of abstract entities is like perception of concrete ones in not being intrinsically doxastic. One need not have beliefs about the apprehended entity. This is consistent with holding that to understand abstract entities *is* in part to be in some kind of contact with them. Such contact presumably manifests a basic capacity of the mind, not some special mental faculty, whether the capacity is in some sense causal or not. Consider some important similarities to physical perception.

First, apprehensional knowledge of abstract entities is direct in being non-inferential. As with ordinary perceptual knowledge, no inference is needed for formation of beliefs about the apprehended entity, say the proposition that desires are not activities. Second, and related to this, apprehension has both *de re* and *de dicto* forms. In the *de re* case, it has a phenomenology in which acquaintance with the relevant object, such as the concept of a desire or, in the two-dimensional realm, a circle, is an element, and it also entails a discriminative sensitivity to the kinds of elements we noted in considering how understanding figures in justification for believing self-evident propositions.[10] In the *de dicto* case, occurrently believing a self-evident proposition on the basis of understanding it (which includes understanding the abstract entities that are constituents in it) commonly has the same kind (though not the same vividness) of the sense of presented truth that is often experienced in having an (occurrent) perceptual belief.

10. This approach may well be consistent with that of Chudnoff, e.g. in chs. 4 and 7 of his wide-ranging 2013, though the two approaches are very different. In part following Husserl, he sketches an account of how relations among abstract elements are apprehended. See especially Husserl's treatment of "presentive consciousness" in ch. 2 of (1982).

Two further points, related to those made so far, are also important. One is that apprehension exhibits both referential and propositional factivity, as does ordinary seeing. If you apprehend a concept, say *triangularity*, there is such a concept, and if you apprehend *that* triangularity entails three-sidedness, then it does. Another point (my fourth) is that apprehension may, like ordinary seeing, be aspectual—as where you might apprehend a relation *as* transitive. Aspectual apprehension is fallible, as illustrated by the possibility of uncritically apprehending a proposition as identical with its contrapositive. None of these points implies that a belief can constitute a priori knowledge without meeting *any* causal condition.

Guises of Abstract Entities

A fifth point concerns the presentational aspect of apprehension. This opens the way for a further similarity between apprehension and physical perception. In apprehension, as in perception, we instantiate a kind of phenomenal property: a kind that enables us to characterize physical objects in the perceptual case and abstract ones in the apprehensional case; e.g., for plane figures, enclosing a space. In both cases, acquaintance with instances of the concepts in question seems crucial, at least developmentally. In the abstract cases, the instances may be considered a kind of *guise*. Different size circles, e.g., are guises in which the concept can be presented to us—imaginationally or physically—say in diagrams. For normative propositions, agents and act-types may figure in the guises, as in reflections on the concept of promising. Once we have acquired a concept, having it in mind does not entail having in mind an instance, such as a red circle; but in human development as we know it, something like intuitive induction seems needed for acquisition of concepts—or at least the basic ones. Given the basic cases, complexification may come readily. If you have conceptions of the eagle and the lion, conceiving a griffin is no challenge.

What makes the causal condition on knowledge plausible may be more than its apparent application to all empirical knowledge. Perhaps the condition is best conceived as a way—perhaps theoretically not needed here—of satisfying the wider requirement that knowledge must be based on something appropriately connected with that in virtue of which a belief constituting that knowledge is true. We might call this the *external requirement on knowledge* provided we note that *self*-knowledge (which includes knowledge of one's mental states) can be based on something not external to the *mind* but only to the belief in question. If the properties and relations of abstract entities are external to the mind, knowledge of self-evident propositions meets the external requirement. On the other hand, because those properties and relations are *accessible* to the mind, justification, conceived on epistemologically internalist lines, is also possible for self-evident propositions. The proposed characterization of self-evidence thus connects it with both internal and external epistemological requirements; and in the light of the previous sketch of adequate understanding as a ground of justification, it should be clear how, for self-evident propositions, both are possible on the basis of internally accessible grounds.

A further point can be made here. Suppose that understanding abstract entities and their relations—say, understanding of circles, spaces, and the enclosure relation between them—does entail a kind of direct contact with them, indeed, a kind such that these entities form an essential part of the very content of the kind of understanding in question. These entities, which may be presented in a phenomenally apprehended guise, can then play an indispensable, if indirect, role in sustaining beliefs that are justified a priori or constitute a priori knowledge. These beliefs have understanding as a causal sustaining ground, and the relevant understanding in a sense contains—by virtue of embodying a direct apprehension of—the abstract entities that ground the truths known. The causal basis of such beliefs, then, guarantees the presence of their truthmakers.[11] Through this apprehensional causal grounding of the beliefs, they are *reliably* connected to the facts they represent.

The Explanatory Power of Adequately Understanding Self-Evident Propositions

Given that the relevant causal sustaining relation is explanatory, the understanding also *explains* why the self-evidentially justified belief is held. This explanatory connection is a sustaining relation between

11. One could say here, as Bengson does in his detailed study of apprehension, that the truthmaker is a constituent in the apprehension. Perhaps this makes no difference in what propositions are considered self-evident. See his 2015. I prefer the relational view in part because I take apprehension to have different degrees of clarity in the way perception does, and this is perhaps best explained by conceiving the object apprehended not as a constituent in the apprehension but as something to which access may, as with perception, be better or worse and have varying degrees of clarity.

psychological elements that are not themselves events. *Reaching* an occurrent understanding, however, is an event and may yield an occurrent intuition with the self-evident proposition as content. Simply *having* an occurrent understanding may underlie an occurrent intuition with this content. This intuition, as an occurrent conscious element embodying a phenomenal sense of truth or at least of non-inferential credibility, can explain, in a broadly causal way, the event of belief-formation.

Comprehensional events of a related kind may yield knowledge of a self-evident proposition. Consider having a sudden insight, e.g. realizing the possibility that a man could produce a grandchild with his daughter, and thereby seeing how the incestuous proposition is true. This apprehensional event may be a case of knowledge-acquisition (and will be if the belief in question is based on, and not just caused by, the occurrent adequate understanding of a self-evident proposition).[12] One forms the belief constituting the knowledge on the basis of directly apprehending its truthmaker.

There is also a kind of *normative* explanation where adequate understanding of a self-evident proposition, *p*, grounds justification for believing it. This understanding explains, *non-causally* and in what seems an a priori way, why the person has justification for believing p. In the abstract, that *S* has justification for believing *p* is explained by *S*'s adequately understanding *p*. Adequate understanding of self-evident propositions has this power in part because it guarantees comprehensional access to abstract entities whose nature or relations account for the truth of *p*. Such access, moreover, as enabling understanding the essential elements in the proposition, makes possible in principle the person's *justifying* the proposition by appropriately manifesting the understanding, e.g. in providing an explication of the kind indicated in Chapter 8.

The relevant kind of understanding is in some sense conceptual (and so differs from perception as such), but it is not reducible to understanding terms in any particular language. The conceptual knowledge in question, say that nothing is round and square, may, however,

12. May we posit a causal sustaining relation between relational phenomena such as understanding an abstract entity and believing a proposition in which it figures, where one relatum is abstract? I believe so. Both understanding and believing are temporal and (arguably) in some way spatial. That the mind has direct access to abstract entities does not entail that its *accessing* them is not spatiotemporal in an appropriate way. In any case, the same kind of question about causality seems at least as important for the constitution view.

be reached *through* linguistic understanding and perhaps even through a certain kind of mental imaging. But it is not constituted by understanding any particular language (and arguably is not essentially linguistic). Moreover, the knowledge based on adequate understanding is not groundable in a definition of any linguistic expressions. This calls for explanation.

If anything may be properly said to be true by definition, this is not because its truth is grounded in that of any linguistic definition but because of some epistemic relation, such as knowability through knowing—in what may be a complicated way—the truth of some such definition. Knowability through a definition does not entail being grounded in that definition. Moreover, the conceptual knowledge in question, including a priori knowledge of self-evident propositions, need not be groundable through the kind of analysis of concepts that (apparently) enables us to reduce the proposition that all vixens are female to the formal truth that all female foxes are female. As we have seen through examples, no parallel analysis is available for the concepts central for substantive a priori truths, such as the concepts of roundness, of redness, and, arguably, of moral obligation or of justification for belief.[13]

This view of apprehension does not entail that abstract entities have causal power. They do not play a direct causal role in producing or sustaining justified self-evidential beliefs. But they do play an essential role in what constitutes a causal basis of such beliefs: they are essential objects of the kind of understanding that does the ordinary causal work of producing or sustaining belief. The role of abstract entities as essential in the understanding that causally grounds the relevant knowledge can guarantee true belief as well as can any ordinary causal role played by physical phenomena; and it is the need for a reliable basis of truth that chiefly motivates the causal requirement in the first place.

Despite all the analogies to ordinary perception now sketched, one may wonder how the apprehensional conception of knowledge of

13. The possibility of reduction of such normative concepts (and properties) as obligatoriness is critically considered in "Toward an Epistemology of Moral Principles" (my forthcoming b). A full discussion of the idea that some propositions are true by definition would explore whether it holds for real definition. That raises metaphysical issues I cannot pursue here, where the focus is on linguistic and conceptual definitions.

self-evident truths reflects the presentational element in perception. One natural answer is supported by the developmental perspective introduced earlier: we might think of the concrete things on which intuitive induction works as guises in which abstract entities often present themselves. Consider drawing a triangle to represent "any triangle" and thereby learning that, say, any enclosed angle must be smaller than 180 degrees. The object is concrete, yet its representational function is general.

It is noteworthy that even in ordinary perception there is a kind of generalization and abstraction. Sounds, e.g., do not invite the same picture of instantiation as do visibles. Sounds are presented only to hearing and do not even presuppose space, at least in the way triangles and other visibles do. Nonetheless, the pitch A 440, presented pianistically, may still be a basis for recognition of the same pitch represented by a violin. With notions like entailment, which are not instantiated by concrete entities, we may still take linguistic representations—whether in writing or in thought—to be, or at least to elicit, kinds of presentations (when they are in writing they are of course not phenomenal or even mental presentations). A reasonable conclusion here is that for apprehension, as for ordinary perception, the objects are phenomenally presented in multiple ways, and in *both* cases an understanding of something abstract (such as properties) is needed for presentational occurrences to ground knowledge.

Must abstract entities be presented to us by concrete guises in order for us to understand them adequately? This could be developmentally normal in human life. But even if it is, philosophical dialectic seems to show that at almost any time in our adult lives we can think, conceptually and abstractly, about, say, the concepts of knowledge and obligation. Suppose, moreover, that a perfect duplicate of me has exactly the understanding I have of the abstract. At the first moment of his creation, he will not have encountered anything. Understanding, then, does not entail *prior* acquaintance with any object.

If this ontic picture is on the right track, we also have a way of *both* extending a version of reliabilism to the a priori and saving a causal reliability condition on belief as a condition for its constituting knowledge—an epistemic success condition, where 'epistemic' is understood as pertaining to knowledge and not taken to concern justification as well. Let me sketch further how the extension works for knowledge and, on the basis of what we can see there, for justification.

V. Apriority and Necessity

I here assume that self-evident propositions and indeed a priori propositions in general are necessary. If there are exceptions, as Kripke and others have argued,[14] we may take my points to hold for those cases that are necessary, which surely include the paradigms and at least many logical, mathematical, normative, and philosophical propositions. I also assume that self-evident propositions are constituted by abstract entities and that their truth is determined by the interrelations of those entities. If we take understanding (at least of abstracta) to be a kind of direct apprehension, we can treat adequate understanding analogously to the way we treat adequate sense-perception in the case of seeing. You see an object of perception adequately relative to obtaining knowledge of a proposition about it when your sensory representation includes the properties and relations crucial for the truth of the proposition. To see that a figure is (approximately) pentagonal, e.g., we must see the five straight lines together with their relation of contiguity and the five equal angles at their joints. To see the truth of the proposition that first cousins share a pair of grandparents, one must apprehend the concepts and relations *child of, sibling of, parent of,* and *grandparent of* and also apprehend at least the entailment between *being a child of a child of* and *being a grandchild of.*

Such apprehension may be assisted by picturing, e.g., some parent-child-grandchild combination, but this is not needed for even occurrent adequate understanding. It may be a contingent truth that one could not *acquire* these concepts apart from experiencing some such combinations—and in the case of geometry and perhaps basic arithmetic some similar genetic condition seems contingently necessary. But understanding can float free of its developmentally necessary roots. When we discuss the a priori, our sensory experience and mental images may be entirely determined by our conversation partner and our physical setting. This need not interfere with intellectual focus on propositions and concepts under consideration. The apprehension we achieve here is a major element in adequate understanding, and when adequate understanding of a self-evident proposition is occurrent, as where one comprehendingly considers the self-evident proposition in question, it tends to yield an intuition whose content is that proposition.

14. I refer to Kripke's widely discussed meter bar case (1980), in which the truth of 'the length of the Meter Bar [in Paris] is one meter' is treated as both a priori and contingent.

The phenomenology of such experiences varies in different cases and, doubtless, between different persons. But it does not entail imaging or even imagining concrete objects that may serve as guises of (certain) concepts, even if these psychologically familiar elements are in fact developmentally essential.

Where believing a self-evident proposition is based on an adequate understanding that is in direct contact with the truthmakers for the proposition, the belief is reliably grounded. There is no threat of a wayward causal chain between the truthmakers and the belief, which is non-inferentially based on a psychological state "containing" them (I take the basis-relation to be intrinsically non-wayward). Now suppose one assumes that abstract entities (at least the kind in question regarding a priori knowledge) have all their properties (monadic and relational) essentially and is thereby committed to

> *A constancy assumption regarding abstracta*: The relations of abstract entities are constant across all possible worlds.[15]

This assumption would explain why the a priori (if solely about abstracta) is also necessary, but my overall theory of self-evidence either does not *require* the constancy assumption or may restrict it to a subcase of the abstract. It also does not imply that adequately understanding self-evident propositions that *are* necessary entails also grasping their necessity—though in some cases *dis*believing that a proposition is necessary might suggest one's inadequately understanding it. Self-evident propositions can be accounted for as I propose even if they are not only adequately understandable without exercising the concept of necessity but are also not all viewed as necessary.

The case of self-evidential justification is similar, but we must remember that being justified *in* believing *p*, whether or not *p* is self-evident, does not entail believing it. Positively speaking, we might hold something close to

> *Epistemological presentationalism*: Much as (given sufficient understanding of the relevant propositions) (1) we are (prima facie) justified in

15. I am assuming that, for reasons indicated early in the chapter, the self-evident is the base case of the a priori and that entailment (which links the self-evident to the remaining a priori propositions) preserves both truth and modality. What is entailed by a necessary axiom is therefore itself necessary. The constancy assumption does not entail that abstracta are in all possible worlds but only that if they are ever related to one another in a given way this does not change.

> believing propositions sensorily presented to us, (2) we are (prima facie) justified in believing a priori propositions apprehensionally presented to us.[16]

This hypothesis apparently holds for a priori propositions, whether self-evident or not; but given that I am taking apprehension of propositions—a kind of intuitive presentation—to be a kind of non-inferential impression of truth, a similar principle might apply to certain empirical propositions that, though false, seem true on the basis of their conceptual content. It does not apply even to all a priori propositions, such as those we can be justified in believing only through proof. But it seems highly plausible as applied to self-evident propositions apprehensionally presented to us and adequately understood by us. In occurrent cases of self-evidentially justified belief, moreover, a kind of intuition is normally parallel to a sensory seeming.[17] Given the apprehensional relation that a belief *based on* adequately understanding a self-evident proposition bears to its truthmakers, the presence of an intuition that p should be no surprise, and we can also see why such a belief constitutes knowledge. But the question whether self-evidence, or the a priori in general, entails necessity is still left open.

This chapter and the previous one indicate the main variables that determine what constitutes comprehensional adequacy, the kind required for self-evidential justification. Given my account of the self-evident and, by extension, of a priori propositions, we need not, but may, consider the a priori a realm of necessity. Conceived as I propose, however, self-evident and other a priori propositions are best taken to have, as truthmakers, abstract objects and their interrelations. Moreover, although we need not consider those and other a priori propositions necessary, the a priori domain is most plausibly considered a realm of necessity. On my view, moreover, the a priori may be plausibly taken to extend to certain normative truths and to many propositions that, like the perceptual principles I have cited, belong to philosophy itself. As the case of philosophy well illustrates, when a priori propositions

16. This may be fruitfully compared with Husserl's "principle of all principles" (1982: 44; cf. 36–37 and 41) and Chudnoff (2014: 94).

17. Only normally because skepticism or disbelief can prevent its formation. A philosopher who rejects a self-evident principle is not likely to have an intuitive seeming that favors it; but it does not follow from this that the philosopher does not adequately understand the proposition.

are substantive, it may be very difficult to determine or, especially, to show, that they are a priori. This is confirmed by the possibility of widespread rational disagreement in philosophy even on certain self-evident propositions. Nonetheless, even a clear account of what constitutes a self-evident proposition need not make it easy to acquire higher-order knowledge about such propositions. It is, however, possible in some cases to have such knowledge. Nonetheless, on the view developed in this book, even when we have it we may not use it to silence opposition or dogmatically retain our apparently self-evident claims. Rational disagreement may arise at almost any point. But to say that need not dampen our efforts to resolve it, and the account of the a priori given here indicates many of the elements of understanding that provide a route to resolution.

PART THREE

PRACTICAL KNOWLEDGE

10

KNOWLEDGE, BELIEF, AND ACTION

Parts One and Two provided a picture of how knowledge arises in experience, grows by reflection and inference, and guides our thinking. Perception is central for knowledge, and it provides a model for understanding intuition, which is like perception in being experiential and non-inferential. Perception also constitutes, in many instances, a basis for inference, which often requires at least one perceptually justified premise, and perceptual experience is instructively parallel to apprehension of abstract entities and their role as truthmakers. How perception guides action, both through the beliefs and knowledge it yields and even without them, has been suggested, especially in Chapters 1 to 3; but more must be said to provide a wider conception of major connections among perception, knowledge, and belief, on the one hand, and action on the other. In broad terms, the need here is for an adequate account of practical knowledge. One question in particular has been left open: why, for guiding our action, is knowledge any better than true belief? This is an action-theoretic version of part of the "value problem," the general problem of explicating the value of knowledge beyond that of true belief. One question here is this: If cognition gives us a true map of the world, what difference does it make how well grounded are the beliefs that provide the indicated routes? A related question for this chapter is whether, given reliable perceptions, knowledge or even propositional belief is needed for the guidance of action.

Seeing, Knowing, and Doing. Robert Audi, Oxford University Press (2020). © Oxford University Press.
DOI: 10.1093/oso/9780197503508.001.0001

I. Belief and Action

There is no need here for fully comprehensive accounts of belief or action, and much has already been said about belief. For our purposes, it should suffice to think of actions as doings that have a description under which they are intentional (this holds with at most a few exceptions). This is not equivalent to saying that there is a description under which they are *intended.* Intentional action may arise simply from a hope, as where we hit a target we had only a faint hope of hitting, but, having made a good try under normal circumstances, did hit intentionally.[1]

A further point is that if, as is common, 'intend*ed*' implies the formation of an intention prior to action (or even at the time of action), the condition would be too strong. As Chapter 11 will show, many things we do in the course of intentionally carrying out a routine are intentional but not separately intended. It should also be stressed that even if all the clear cases of doings are actions, 'do' is highly elastic. Not only can we speak of someone as doing well when we mean living healthily, or of a patient as doing well when we mean recovering satisfactorily; we can describe someone's movements while asleep in bed as doings. And to 'What did Sander do?' one can answer 'He believed a confidence man's story, and we were afraid he'd lose his savings'. In these cases, 'intentionally' seems clearly inapplicable.[2]

I assume that intentional action is explainable by appeal to a set of beliefs and desires.[3] This does not require positing beliefs in every case in which *S* would sincerely affirm the propositions in question. If, for instance, I had been asked whether the rug beneath my chair has flown to the top of Mount McKinley, I would immediately have said no, but it is not plausible to maintain that I was expressing a belief already possessed. I have long criticized such overascription of beliefs. It manifests a tendency I call *doxasticism,* stemming from assimilating beliefs to dispositions to form them.[4] If, however, we take action as requiring that the agent has at least one belief relevant to it, are we guilty of doxasticism in the practical realm? This turns out to be a difficult question whose pursuit reveals much about both action and belief.

1. I take this example from my 1973, where much is said to distinguish intending to *A* from hoping to *A.*

2. For discussion of the general question of doxastic voluntarism, see, e.g., Steup (2001).

3. I explained and argued for this in my 1986a.

4. Detailed explanation of this tendency and a proposal of a more economical view is given in my 2019 and reflected in many points here.

The Teleological Paradigm

Paradigmatically intentional actions are those performed *in order to* bring something about. Suppose I apply my brakes (in order) to stop. Must I not believe doing that will achieve this—or, more broadly, believe it to bear some instrumental connection to achieving it? Such instrumental belief might be *de re,* but our purposes do not require dealing with that case separately. It is plausible to conceive action, at least when intentional, as belief-guided, and few have questioned whether (as I have argued elsewhere[5]), when *S A*-s *in order to* bring something about, *S* has an instrumental belief connecting the envisaged act with *S*'s goal. This chapter brings to the fore the question whether intentional action can instead be guided by dispositions to believe. These are, after all, cognitive, and they often reside in elements that can both justify the beliefs in question and explain their formation. Might dispositions to believe have much the same action-guiding power as the beliefs they are a disposition to form?

A short answer would be that we can always explain *S*'s intentionally *A*-ing by citing a belief to the effect that *A*-ing will realize the relevant goal of the action, but we cannot (or cannot in general) do so by citing a disposition to form such a belief. Such an instrumental belief might be that one must brake in order to stop. But the fact that such belief-ascriptions *would* explain the action does not entail that their applicability is necessary for explaining it nor that, even when they do, a disposition to form them could not have sufficed. Perhaps, however, *some* instrumental belief, even if *de re,* is necessary. Certainly the case is one in which the agent does something that responds to salient perceptible facts of a belief-eliciting kind. Perhaps the appearance of a red light or, especially, an obstacle, tends to evoke the realization (hence belief) that one must brake.

Another spontaneous purposive action is reaching for grapes on a plate in order to eat them. This seems possible only given a belief to the effect that eating them requires reaching for them. Might the action be merely done from habit? At least two cases of habit are relevant here.

5. In my 1986a. As also explained there, one might believe depressing the brake *to be* a way to stop the car without having in mind the specific conception(s) of the brake, the kind of stopping, and the car needed for a *de dicto* belief, such as that jamming the brake now will quickly stop the car. Another possibility I leave open is that *taking* one's braking to be a way to stop may have a non-conceptual, property-ascriptive force that does not entail even *de re* belief about the braking.

In one, there is a doing that is not intentional—*non*-intentional, as opposed to unintentional. Biting one's fingernails can be such a case. In the other, an intentional action is triggered without forethought but is still belief-guided, if only by *de re* belief, e.g. believing the grapes to be reachable and good. Similarly, on meeting somebody, one might believe shaking hands to be the thing to do. Here we enter the domain of conventional, rehearsed behavior. These and other cases require a broad conception of the content of intention.

The Indefinite Scope of Intention

The role of habit in relation to intentional action raises a question concerning the scope of instrumental belief and, correspondingly, of intention. Consider learning a piano piece. At first one may consciously aim at a certain fingering. Here it is plausible to posit instrumental beliefs regarding ways of moving one's fingers. Once the piece is memorized, one may be able to play it upon deciding to do so while having the quasi-indexical belief that *this* is how it goes, where a single cognitive picture or "script" carries the content of the instrumental belief. In cases like this, the whole performance is intentional and its actional parts are each either (1) automatic in a sense that does not entail being intentional (or unintentional, of course) or (2) intentional in something like the following way: *as de re* believed to be necessary, or (consistent with that) *as* non-intentional doings believed, *de re*, to belong to the intended overall performance. On either interpretation, we can account both for surprise at mistaken movements and for the presence of an appropriate instrumental belief; yet we need not posit individual instrumental *beliefs* governing each finger movement anticipated as part of the performance. We need not, but my view leaves open that we may. A pianist might be self-consciously trying to render every note expressively and so focus on each finger movement. This might lead to forming many action-guiding beliefs during the performance. Here, by contrast with much complex behavior, positing the usually unneeded beliefs would explain aspects of the performance and is itself explained by the pianist's particular focal aims.

The first case—that of the *automaticity* of scripted behavior—might be understood in terms of something like a program. The details of such programs—which likely differ considerably in different people and for different activities—require empirical investigation that would take us outside philosophy. The philosophical point is that once a pattern of behavior is sufficiently familiar and, especially when it is remembered clearly, it may be governed by an intention whose content is a *script,* in the sense that (1) if *S* is unimpeded and fully successful in doing what *S* intends to do on the occasion in question, then what triggers the intention to realize the scripted content—a kind of *global intention,* we might say—yields the entire sequence of doings without the formation of intentions having focal contents corresponding to each constituent doing that is a basic act-type for the agent (i.e., a type of act, *A*-ing, *S* can perform "directly" at will, without *A*-ing by doing something else); (2) *S* is disposed to believe, and may virtually know, of each element in a suitable subset of these doings, that it is part of the intended behavior; (3) *S* is disposed, on the basis of the governing intentional script, both to correct errors, such as playing a wrong note, and to consider the erroneous doing unintentional and the corrective action intentional; and (4) the entire behavioral sequence is guided by the scripted intention and one or more related instrumental beliefs. Those beliefs guide the behavior by creating non-doxastic pathways from perception to action, including both scripted and corrective action, e.g. following a wrong note by emphatically rendering the right one. Beliefs, then, have an indirect as well as a direct guiding role. They can empower non-propositional information, such as the sight of a piano key far to one's left, to guide action.

If, as I hold, intention embodies a kind of expectation, we can bring that notion to bear in clarifying scripted intentional contents. If you play a piece you have well memorized, you expect it to sound as you're used to. Such expectation does not entail a separate belief regarding each note you expect to hear, yet you are disposed to be surprised or unsettled if you miss one or play the wrong one and, if you do miss a note or err, disposed to form the belief that you did so. Here expectation is a forward-looking counterpart of presupposition. Expectation need not be doxastic, though it may be and may constitute foreknowledge. If I discover, regarding an ordinary conference room, that it has only four chairs in it, I will be surprised, even if I had no specific numerical belief, say that it had more than four, or had three rows of five, or, more likely, that it had an adequate number. The scope of our expectations, like that of our presuppositions, is wider than that of our beliefs. But expectation plays an important role in explaining the often automatic way in which those cognitive elements guide or constrain our behavior.

Giving expectations as non-doxastic cognitions a role clarifies my sketch of global intention and helps in refining the belief-desire model of intentional action so as to explain complex behavior without yielding to doxasticism or other kinds of intellectualism. A further advantage of the proposal is that it avoids attributing a kind of causal power to dispositions to believe which they apparently do not have: the power to produce actions in the way the corresponding beliefs do. Something should be now said to indicate why they apparently lack it. Part of the answer concerns orders of psychological properties.

II. Two Orders of Cognitive Disposition

Dispositions to believe are higher-order properties, being dispositions to instantiate the dispositional property of believing. This does not entail lacking causal power, but at least the typical cases of dispositional properties serving as causes of events (such as actions) require, for fulfilling that role, both an event elicitor, such as the thought of a proposition, *p*, that is the content of the belief *S* is disposed to form, and an event manifestation, such as affirming that *p*. For dispositions to believe, the constitutive event manifestation is forming the relevant belief. This event seems the best candidate to explain why dispositions to believe might be thought to explain actions—though only indirectly by a manifestation—say, changing behavior in the way one's newly formed belief calls for. There is no need to deny that such indirect explanations are possible, but even if they are, we must not assume that the formation of a belief can explain what a belief itself can.

It should be clear that forming a belief at a given time entails the presence of that belief then. This may seem to imply that belief-formation explains what belief itself explains. The action-explaining role of belief, however, commonly requires its persisting as a sustainer of actions over their duration; but belief-formation is momentary and cannot play a temporally extended role, hence cannot sustain temporally extended actions. Take an example. Believing I ought to phone an ageing aunt may, upon my noting a phone, cause (or figure essentially in what causes) my phoning her. This deed is temporally extended and a constitutive manifestation of the belief. By contrast, being *disposed* to believe I ought to phone her has no action as a constitutive manifestation,[6] and, in part for this reason, is causally further from producing

6. What of "deciding to believe?" If there is such an action, it is not equivalent to belief-formation: that is its result. Suppose belief-formation can occur through something we may call "deciding" to believe; it does not follow that a *belief's forming* is an action. Supporting considerations and a partial account of the relation between belief and will are provided in (1999a). For one of the best statements of a view more sympathetic to doxastic voluntarism, see Steup (2001).

action than dispositional belief with the same content. Dispositional beliefs, then, can be seen as potential causes or partial causes of action; dispositions to believe are at best potential causes of the genesis of such "direct" causes and are best seen as affecting action mainly through those causes.

There is a wider action-theoretic perspective for determining whether belief is required for intentional action. Consider the plausible view that intentional action is action performed in order to achieve something and is explainable by appeal to the agent's wanting to achieve that and having an instrumental (possibly *de re*) belief to the effect that the action conduces to achieving it. In this light, two kinds of variables seem needed to explain intentional action: a motivational variable to explain the energy in some sense underlying it, and a cognitive one to explain its "direction." Neither the energy nor the direction need be physical. The former is "measured" by such variables as the vigor or enthusiasm with which the agent acts and the strength of the agent's resistance to giving up the effort; the direction is a matter of where and how the instrumental belief leads the agent, which may be a direction in thought alone. In broad terms (and with certain exceptions), desire without belief would be directionless; instrumental belief without desire would be powerless.

Desires, then, are to be understood partly in terms of yielding action given a belief indicating how their object is realizable. Beliefs—most notably those with instrumental content—are to be understood partly in terms of their tendency to yield action given appropriate desires.[7] The very conception of desire (wanting) requires a connection to belief and vice-versa. This is a systematic consideration. One cannot account for the role of desire in action (or intention) without positing instrumental beliefs, nor understand instrumental beliefs apart from connecting them with the desire(s) to which they are subordinate.

A supporting epistemological consideration is this. It is part of the concept of both beliefs and desires that actions of a certain kind (including at least those that seem goal-directed) are evidences of their presence. It is also part of the concept of intentional action that it is explainable by appeal to certain desires and beliefs. This does not by

7. If there are intentional actions that need not be belief-guided, the best candidates arise from desires to perform acts basic for the agent and familiar in the way moving one's limbs is. If I want to stretch, need I believe that (say) *this* is how to do it? After paralysis, I might have such a belief, but perhaps in that case the action is a deliberative response to volition, as where the physician tells me to breathe in and, with the thought that this will enable me to stretch, I breath in.

itself entail that dispositions to believe *cannot* also play the instrumental role of cognitively guiding behavior. But it is difficult to see how they can do this given that they are not propositional attitudes. We might at least say that the concept of intentional action is implicitly tied to cognitive propositional attitudes that have a kind of instrumental content. Figuratively, whereas beliefs represent lines drawn on our map of the world, dispositions to believe represent our inclinations to draw them; but they provide no path to follow until the inclination is realized in drawing one, and there may be obstacles preventing that realization, whereas even erasable lines are actual.

It is true that we *identify* dispositions to believe by the propositional content of the beliefs whose formation manifests them. This may create the impression that they themselves *have* instrumental or other propositional content. But they are not representational states, whereas even dispositional beliefs are—those need only come into consciousness, as in simply becoming occurrent, for the representation to be a contentful state of mind and in that way an element of awareness. A disposition to believe *p* may reside either in non-representational elements such as bodily sensations or in representational elements with very different content, such as beliefs whose propositional objects would, if conscious, yield formation of a belief of the quite different content in question. One might, e.g., believe *q* and *r* but never bring them together, though doing so would produce a belief that *p*, which might have very different content and might or might not follow from *q* and *r*. Dispositions to believe may be non-cognitive and may lack representational content.

Even when dispositions to believe are cognitive, as just illustrated, they are unfit for the guiding role that instrumental beliefs play in action. Given this point together with the other considerations in this section, it is reasonable to conclude that although intentional action requires a doxastic basis, it requires far fewer beliefs than would be posited if dispositions to form beliefs are assimilated to actual beliefs. Intentional action (including activities) may be scripted. That indicates the potential complexity of the content of the underlying propositional attitudes, but it does not support the view that mere dispositions to believe may play the causal and explanatory role played by those attitudes.

III. Belief and Knowledge, Intention and Action

The conception of perceptual knowledge developed in this book provides ample room for understanding its connection with action. On my view, perception can guide action even apart from producing beliefs.

This is not to deny that where *S* acts intentionally, *S* must have a belief that in some way indicates a direction in which to seek the goal. The point is rather that there need not be, for every action we intentionally perform, a belief having both a content concerning precisely that action, e.g., each step in climbing a staircase, and a causal effect on that action. Once we see how perceptual beliefs are based on perceptions, which is through an appropriate causal connection with the underlying facts, we can understand how action is guided by perception. Let me elaborate.

Take paradigms of full-blooded actions, which are performed intentionally (and in many cases also deliberately). The agent acts in order to achieve some end; the end is represented in the content of the agent's motivation (say desire); a "route" to it is indicated by an instrumental belief; and (for physical action) perception commonly serves to guide action toward that end. If I want to avoid stepping into a stream as I cross it, I might step only on dry stones that rise above the water. I may be so practiced that the mere sight of accessible, conveniently spaced dry stones guides my steps. If concentration is required, I may have to believe a stone to be dry and stable before, guided by that objectual belief, I step on it. If I am new at this, it may be only when I cautiously form the belief that a stone is dry and stable that I feel secure enough to step forward. Given the perceptual hierarchy, behavioral guidance may occur either from the bottom level, e.g. my simply glimpsing the stones, or from higher up, as where one must scrutinize each stone for safety. Guidance may vary from case to case in a single person and, in the same kind of situation, between different people.

This is a point at which we can see the importance of the indeterminacy in the perceptual hierarchy viewed from the bottom up. Merely seeing a stone in my path may or may not lead to an objectual (*de re*) belief or simply to a property attribution. It may or may not result, at the next level up, in a propositional belief. This partly accounts for individual differences: some of us may need to rehearse instructions before crossing a stream; others may be so practiced at it that perceptions of a path feed into action directly or with only the minimal intermediaries of property attributions, as where something relevant, such as moss on a stone that would otherwise provide a safe footing, is sufficiently salient to attract attention.

These points should be connected with a conception of how belief guides action. Belief, but not knowledge, is required for intentional action. Why isn't belief rather than knowledge enough in general? One plausible answer is that to navigate the world successfully, we have to get a lot right, and this is unlikely apart from perception, which, in the context of intentional action, will yield at least *de re* belief of a kind that characteristically constitutes knowledge. This point is important. If only *de dicto* beliefs (of the non-Russellian kind, which are usually designated by 'believes-that' locutions) emerged from perception, then conceptualization would be needed for the cognitive guidance of behavior through perception: one might have to conceive, say, moving aside a wild rosebush branch as such, rather than just believe *that* to have to be moved aside. The mental effort (or anyway episode) of conceptualizing the object might reduce speed in action and perhaps even accuracy in belief.

It is plausible, then, to suppose that only *de re* belief that amounts to knowledge would be at all likely to produce the high rate of success we find in much normal action and activity. In following a wooded path I form *de re* beliefs, as just illustrated, and, where perception grounds them, they commonly constitute knowledge. These referential beliefs can often play their guiding role without one's having to conceptualize the objects they are about. It may be easy to see, and know, that I must get *that* out of my way even when I must think a moment to conceptualize it in the way I most naturally would, say as *that poison-ivy vine.* But even referential beliefs may often be bypassed; the better I know a path, the more likely it is that perceptual cues are enough to guide me. A single intention can govern a large sequence of cue-guided actions given appropriate perceptions.[8]

Nothing said here entails that the guidance of action *always* requires knowledge. True belief that does not constitute knowledge may be good enough on many occasions. But could we be built so that we have only true beliefs and never knowledge? The supposition is implausible given our psychology and the world as we know it. How could we be cognitively adjusted to our environment in the way our perceptual belief-formation requires *without* a high proportion of our beliefs being, by virtue of the causal connections we have seen

8. From a diachronic point of view (including an evolutionary one—it matters greatly whether we are correct by accident, or by the outputs of merely somewhat probable mechanisms, or by reliable processes. Given how cognition arises from perception and that in turn from external stimuli, it is hard to see how nature could select for survival without selecting for cognitive reliability. Could we even get 99 percent accuracy without a reliable route? And mustn't complex beings have to be self-corrective to prevent errors' fatally multiplying? Cf. the debate among Alvin Plantinga, Elliott Sober, and others regarding the fitness value to be attributed to truth-seeking tendencies.

operative in perception, not only true or at least approximately true but also formed in a way that goes with a discriminative sensitivity to sensory inputs? Wanting to stay dry in the rain, I look for an umbrella; seeing it, I know its location. Hearing someone enter downstairs and expecting no one, I listen to determine who it is; hearing a familiar voice tells me who it is and sets me at ease. If I did not acquire beliefs of the kind that characteristically constitute knowledge as I traverse a forest path, or did not correct my outlook when my perceptions call for it, I might die on a routine hike.

Would *justified* true belief that does not constitute knowledge suffice in action guidance? This may depend on what does the justifying. If it is the normal sensory inputs, then, as many of our examples indicate, the justified true beliefs will tend to constitute knowledge. If what prevents my justified true belief that a vine is poison ivy from constituting knowledge is my not taking a slightly closer look, I may as carefully avoid touching it as I would upon a better view of it. But suppose my sense-experience justifying the true poison ivy belief depends on the directives of a Cartesian demon. I would be at its mercy. That agential dependency would be a distinct liability in relation to guiding action, by contrast with its guidance by knowledge. It is one thing for what justifies an action-guiding belief to come from facts not quite evidentially strong enough to yield knowledge; it is another for it to come from the wrong kind of fact. (This is a point accessible to both internalist and externalist accounts of justification.)

We might also consider lottery cases. Justified true belief that one will lose might yield the same practical results for guiding action as knowledge that one will. Ordinary lottery cases, however, are importantly different from cases of action-guiding perceptual beliefs. The belief that one will lose may be true owing to "chance" even when one holds only one ticket in a billion-ticket lottery. This seems implicit in the point that one's evidential position matches that of the person who holds the winning ticket but also believes it will lose. Compare my evidential position in perceptually believing there is typeface here. First, there is surely a causal connection, and there may even be a lawlike generality linking the stimuli with my typeface belief by an exceptionless causal connection. Second, even apart from this, my belief is not true by chance, even if there should be no greater probability of its being true than in the billion-ticket lottery case. Both points indicate, moreover, a difference between me and someone clearly hallucinating the same typeface. Even internalists about justification can say that although there can be the same degree of justification in these cases, there remains a normative difference. In an overall way, knowledge can still be a normatively better cognitive state to be in than justified true belief that does not constitute knowledge.

In suggesting that knowledge is, in an overall way, preferable to justified true belief in guiding action, I have made room for cases in which it is not. If we change the context to a comparison simply of cognitive states, then there may be some cases in which a justified true belief is normatively preferable to knowledge. Compare an idiot savant's knowledge of a mathematical truth with your justified true belief of the same proposition, based on a quickly constructed proof which is sound but, to qualify as knowledge, needs rechecking or, alternatively, has an almost undetectable error yet is good enough to justify your believing its conclusion. The first state manifests epistemic *power*, but the second may express a good measure of epistemic *virtue*. The former state reflects a natural gift; the latter bespeaks responsiveness to normative standards.

What we have seen in this chapter goes well with the contrast, nicely suggested by Elizabeth Anscombe,[9] encapsulated in the idea that belief and intention—and with it intentional action—have different "directions of fit," applicable to us as knowers on the one hand and as doers on the other. Beliefs should fit the world; the world, or the part of it we act to change, should fit our intentions. The 'should' must be taken normatively rather than probabilistically: falsehood is a critical standard applicable to beliefs, as failure is for intentions; and, for the most part, it is only when beliefs are justified that they should (normatively) fit the world and only where intentions are rational (perhaps also morally permissible) that the world should (normatively) fit them. What I have been doing in this book is largely to provide accounts of perception and apprehension with a view to outlining how they can map the world for us—including the abstract realm of objects that apparently exist in any world. What this chapter has done is largely to show in outline how that mapping, as achieved through perception, guides action in bringing about the changes in the world that successful actions—in the sense of actions fulfilling our intentions—achieve. In explicating the connection between perception and belief, I have said much about the kinds of things we ought to believe, in the sense (roughly) of being well justified in believing them. I have not discussed the kind of thing

9. See her *Intention* (1957).

we ought to intend—a topic for the theory of value and obligation and needing another kind of inquiry. What remains in this book is to consider further how mind and action are connected in other ways and whether the theoretical side of our nature, the intellect and the knowledge that cognitively structures our thinking, determines the practical side of our nature.

11

KNOWING, REASONING, AND DOING

Part One developed accounts of perception and perceptual knowledge, and Part Two connected both with a priori knowledge and a priori justification. In doing this, those nine chapters provided a partial picture of the human intellect. They also described many parallels between the theoretical and practical realms. These are extensive and important. The overall questions I now want to pursue are, in very broad terms, these two: To what extent is the intellect more basic for understanding human persons than the will, and related to this, to what extent do action and practical reasoning depend on knowledge? That intellect is more basic in this way goes with the idea that knowing is more basic for persons than doing, at least in the sense that doing—or at any rate rational doing—requires knowing, whereas knowing does not require doing.

I. Intellectualism as a Perspective on Action

The term that most readily describes the main perspective this chapter examines is 'intellectualism'. For what I call intellectualism—in application to the philosophy of action—theoretical knowledge is more basic than practical knowledge, and action, at least if performed for a good reason, must be knowledge-guided and not just guided by otherwise appropriate beliefs, such as true beliefs indicating what action will satisfy a desire. Indeed, on some views currently considered intellectualist, practical knowledge *is*, despite appearances, a kind of theoretical knowledge with behavioral content. Moreover, on some intellectualist views, rational action must be guided not only by cognition—which is

Seeing, Knowing, and Doing. Robert Audi, Oxford University Press (2020). © Oxford University Press.
DOI: 10.1093/oso/9780197503508.001.0001

essential in directing the will in ways we have seen in exploring how perception guides action—but also by knowledge. Knowledge, by contrast with cognition as simply a manifestation of truth-valued mental content, is a kind of intellectual success.

Action, like knowledge, often occurs on the basis of reasoning. From an intellectualist perspective, just as beliefs based on reasoning constitute knowledge only if the essential premises of the reasoning are knowledge, actions based on practical reasoning are rational only if any essential cognitive premise in the reasoning is known. An intellectualist may or may not hold an inferentialist view, on which, in a very broad form, genuine knowledge is inferential and rational action is based on practical reasoning, which is a kind of inferential episode; but intellectualists strongly tend to hold that both rational action and knowledge are reason-based and, commonly, that reasons are facts, and that these facts must be known in order to render actions based them—performed for the reason(s) in question—rational.

Some of the elements of intellectualism have been examined in earlier chapters. This chapter examines intellectualism mainly in the theory of action, but with some comparisons to relevant points in epistemology. My point of view here is that of both epistemology and the theory of action, each conceived as integrated with the philosophy of mind. Here two major intellectualist claims are of special interest for exploring intellectualism. One is that practical knowledge, conceived as *knowing how*—a notion of major concern in both action theory and epistemology—is reducible to propositional knowledge, a kind of knowing *that.* The other is that reasons for action are constituted by what is (propositionally) known by the agent.

II. Practical Knowledge and Knowledge of the Practical

Knowledge plays a central role in guiding human action. It provides crucial raw material for both theoretical and practical reasoning. Reasoning, in turn, provides premises that may yield new beliefs or fresh deeds and, quite independently of this, may be later invoked to support what is already believed or already done. But these points leave open the question whether *knowing* one's premises, as opposed to justifiedly believing them, is *required* for practical reasoning or for rational action by the agent. And is propositional knowledge the basic kind of practical knowledge, or is there another kind, knowing *how,* that is not reducible to propositional knowledge?

The most widely discussed case of practical knowledge is knowing *how*, say how to swim. But *knowing what to do*, say what to do given a flood warning, is also practical knowledge. There are several similar cases of practical knowledge, such as *knowing one's way* home, *knowing when* to come in with the piano part in a concerto, and knowing *the habits* of another person. Perhaps in good part because, among knowledge-locutions, 'knowing *that*' and its cognates dominate much ordinary parlance, we might wonder whether knowing *that* is more basic than knowing *how*. It is also true that knowing *how to A* and knowing (propositionally) *how A-ing is done*, are closely connected, partly because the former usually implies *some* grasp of the latter. But is know-how reducible to propositional practical knowledge of this sort, or even entailed by it?[1]

Given the common understanding of the terms of the discussion, *this* reduction will not work. Consider knowledge of the practical, and take swimming as an example. Knowing propositions that, even in detail, indicate how this is done does not entail knowing how to swim. If this does not seem obvious, imagine observing swimmers carefully and writing down a good and highly detailed description of how swimming is done. Knowing the descriptive propositions in question surely does not entail knowing how to swim. Even the purported converse entailment from knowing *how* to knowing *that* is questionable: conceivably, one could come to know how to swim simply by imitation, or by certain brain manipulations, without knowing that it is done by . . . where the dots are replaced by a comprehensive description.

Perhaps, for agents with an adequate battery of descriptive concepts, the possibility of such cases of know-how entails an ability to *acquire* knowledge of how swimming is done, say by reflecting, after the fact, on how one does it. But this possibility does not show that knowing such propositions is an *element* in knowing *how*; on the contrary, it indicates a way in which practical knowledge, in the form of knowing *how*, underlies certain theoretical knowledge, knowledge of what is the case. That practical knowledge is made possible by actual practice shows a significant

1. Among the attempts to achieve a kind of reductive account is Stanley and Williamson (2001). For a detailed and plausible negative assessment of the former (with several points that support this paper), see Hornsby (2011). Further critical discussion is found in the *Philosophy and Phenomenological Research* symposium on Stanley's *Know How* (2011), with papers by Imogen Dickie, Mark Schroeder, and Robert Stalnaker and with a precis and replies by Stanley (2012: 733–778). For a critical discussion of intellectualism that particularly supports my conception of know-how, see Setiya (2012).

intellectual receptivity to acquiring knowledge of the practical, but it does not support the reduction of knowing *how* to knowing *that.*

A very different kind of case, concerning practical knowledge in the animal kingdom,[2] also casts doubt on whether knowing *how* entails a relevant kind of knowing *that*—an implication that is important for appraising intellectualism but has received less philosophical attention than its converse. A rat confronted with a bar-pressing apparatus that dispenses food may be described as learning, through pressing the bar, and thereby as knowing, *how* to get food. The rat may learn this using its right paw, but if that is tied, it will (or some rats will) use the left. With both tied, it may use its nose. And suppose one could prevent that maneuver. The animal might use another part of its body. Must knowing *that* be involved, say knowing that the bar is to be pressed with *some* body part? Even if so—and this quantificational cognition seems more sophisticated than required to explain the behavior—knowing that proposition does not entail either knowing *which* body part to use or knowing how to press the bar.

Suppose, however, that the animal's know-how does imply having a true instrumental belief about how to get food, and that having such a belief entails ability to *learn* how to get food from the device. Still, knowing something that enables one to learn how to *A* does not entail one's already knowing how to *A*. It is possible, moreover, that any such instrumental beliefs acquired by the animal may come only through the *exercise* of the ability. We may even plausibly suppose that by *doing,* and by a kind of response generalization, the animal can discover some instrumental connection between moving the bar and certain causative bodily motions. Whatever we say about such instrumental learning, the data apparently indicate (for certain animals, at least) that performance precedes cognition in such cases and that the acquired know-how is the basis of whatever instrumental propositional knowledge the animal gains, and not equivalent to it. This is knowing by doing, not doing as manifesting prior knowing, or know-how as equivalent to propositional knowledge.[3]

2. The example to follow is suggested by experiments described in Tolman's classic (1948). A "cognitive map," in the sense illustrated in that paper and my text, may be taken to be mainly a set of beliefs.

3. One may wonder here whether knowing *that* is reducible to knowing *how,* as argued by Hetherington (2006). Exploring this view is beyond the already wide scope of this chapter. For a valuable survey of many of the issues, see Fantl (2016).

Compare human agency. I know how to use a cook's knife and my know-how includes using it with my left hand, though I have never done that. I believe, moreover, that I have never even thought of doing this or formed a belief about it before writing on this topic. It is true that in knowing how to use the knife and having the propositional knowledge I do, I was *positioned* to believe that I *can* do this. But must a right-hander actually have such a belief in order to know how to slice left-handedly? If not, as seems the case, then far from my knowing *how* being reducible to a kind of propositional knowledge, instances of the former are apparently often the basis for instances of the latter.[4]

This is a good place to stress something implicit already. The plausibility of any reduction project can be enhanced by broadening the reducing concept(s) in a way that narrows the sense of difference between what is to be reduced and the presumptively more basic elements to which it is claimed to reduce. Consider, for instance, the thesis that "knowing how to do something is the same as knowing a fact," where "facts are true propositions" and when you learned how to swim "The fact you learned is the proposition that answers . . . 'How could you swim?' "[5] One might initially think the reference is to the kind of fact illustrated by 'You can swim by . . .' where the dots stand for a detailed description of a set of movements sufficient for swimming. But given how much detail would be required and how unlikely it seems that even an able-bodied person would, on the basis of knowing it, know how to swim, I doubt that the view so understood has been seriously defended.

4. My points in this paragraph and indeed elsewhere are supported by the case made by Carter and Pritchard for the view that, in relation to epistemic luck, knowing *how* and knowing *that* come apart in a way they should not on the reductivist view. See Carter and Pritchard (2015: 449). For a contrasting view defending an unorthodox intellectualism against Gettier-style counterexamples, see Cath (2015).

5. Stanley (2011: vii). I find it unclear what to make of 'How could you?' versus the natural 'How do you?', which, unlike 'How could you swim?', normally presupposes your knowing how. 'How could you?' may also mislead here in that it in some contexts (e.g. 'How could you find a cab around here?' seems answerable by describing how the thing in question is or might be done, which does not entail knowing how to do it. The question is anyway difficult to interpret without some context. In what seems the most natural kind relevant here, illustrated by 'How could you swim against such a strong current' or '. . . if you were drugged?', asking it presupposes knowing how, and correct answers do not support the reduction in question.

In any case, the intent here is to represent "Knowing how . . . [as] first-person knowledge. It is knowledge about oneself, or knowledge *de se*."[6] Is this true? Granted, in some cases *de se* knowledge would entail knowing how to swim. Suppose that, in exercising swimming ability in a favorite pond, I know that *I myself* am swimming. I might know this by doing . . . , where the dots stand for whatever actions are designated in my appropriately answering 'How could you swim?' If I have this particular *de se* knowledge at the time, then I know how to swim. But such knowledge is not a basis for reduction of knowing how to swim to knowing that some fact obtains. The entailments hold on the basis of the swimming: it is my awareness of my swimming itself that enables me to know the fact that *this* is how I do it.

Perhaps the spirit of the proposal is partly captured by the idea that if one knows how to *A*, then one (agentially) *knows A-ing* in a referential sense. Some of us, e.g., know canoeing, somewhat as a pianist may know a Bach Invention. This use of 'know' apparently implies knowledge of some facts. I suggest, however, that if this is how the reduction is understood, then the *de re* knowledge of (say) canoeing does the reductive work, even if the agent must have *de se* knowledge of canoeing as well. To see this kind of case for reducing knowing how to knowing that, we might take the relevant knowledge of propositions—a kind of intellectual knowledge—to include such things as my knowing that the way I swim is *like this*, something I might say to a learner as I demonstrate, by swimming, what I refer to. Saying this would, in the context of demonstration, answer 'How could you swim?' But here, to a *de se* self-reference we have added a *de re* reference to actual swimming. If this is what the reduction comes to, then its success (if it does succeed) is much diminished. Insofar as knowing that one swims "like this," where one can (normally) demonstrate swimming at will given available water, is taken to be knowing *that*, it is not "intellectual" propositional knowledge. It does, to be sure, entail knowing how to give an actual demonstration under favorable conditions for swimming,[7] but the order of clarification is reversed. Far from knowing *how* reducing to a kind of knowing *that*, a kind of propositional knowledge, this is surely a case in which practical *de re* knowledge *that*—which does not seem "intellectual" or even propositional in any clear sense—presupposes knowing *how*.

6. Stanley (2011: 98).

7. Compare Stalnaker (2012: 754): "The thesis [that "knowing how is a species of knowing that"], as I think it should be understood, would be more accurately labeled "anti-intellectualism"."

It is worth noting that we could substitute 'like *that*', applied to *others'* swimming, for 'like *this*' applied to one's own. But there, ability to swim would not be implied by the indexical knowledge. Ability to identify a kind of activity ostensively—say, as doing *that,* where one points at the swimming—has practical importance, but it does not entail knowing how to do the relevant kind of thing. Suppose I see a swimmer cross the pond. If, by observing, I know (the fact) that the way I can do such a swim is like *that,* I may well be in a position to *learn* how to swim, or perhaps even to do it by imitation, but it does not follow that I now know how to swim.[8]

III. Virtual Knowledge: A Neglected Category

Our examples should make clear that for at least normal adult human agents, even if knowing how to *A* implies a strong disposition to believe many propositions about how *A*-ing is done, such know-how entails no propositional knowledge that is a good candidate to constitute know-how. But suppose the reductivist view that know-how is a kind of propositional knowledge is correct in one important claim: that in knowing how to *A*, agents in some way possess comprehensive information about how *A*-ing is done. That information need not all reside in the agent's *knowledge,* as opposed to residing in beliefs and other cognitive dispositional elements. If so, then even if the claim captures much of what a reductivist would seek to show, it would be quite weak. Knowing *how* (for normal adult human agents) could be equivalent to having information in the way one does in having a disposition to *acquire,* at least on suitable reflection, detailed propositional knowledge of how *A*-ing is

8. My points concerning what might be called a linguistic approach to the intellectualist view of knowing *how* do not take full account of all the valuable data *Know How* presents, but I doubt that anything in it sustains the thesis with which Stanley opens, as opposed to a number of points independent of it concerning propositional knowledge and practical abilities. A less sympathetic appraisal of intellectualism is given by Hornsby (2011). Her more recent work (2017) argues plausibly and in great detail against Stanley's case for intellectualism from linguistic evidence. A quite different line of objections comes from the point that knowing *how,* unlike knowing *that,* is not transmissible by testimony in the way one would expect given intellectualism. For a development of this critical line, see Poston (2016); and for a defense of intellectualism pertinent to these critical papers, see Pavesi (2017).

done. It would not follow that knowing *how* is equivalent to that knowledge itself.

These points suggest a weaker, less intellectualist position. Might knowing how to *A* be equivalent to this: *either* knowing an appropriate set of propositions about *A*-ing, say about how it is done, *or virtually knowing* this, in the sense that one is disposed to *form* true beliefs of the relevant propositions, where each would (normally) be knowledge? Recall the case of knowing canoeing. Such practical knowledge implies a readiness to come to know much that one need never believe—say that one's hands are never more than six feet apart. One could say that the rower "implicitly knows" this; but this move would force us either to give up the plausible view that propositional knowledge entails belief or to attribute to ordinary agents myriad beliefs of numerous even more far-fetched propositions that they surely do not believe.[9] Similarly, if someone asks me to explain how to swim, I will quickly form beliefs many of which *will* be knowledge—arguably, enough of them to constitute propositional knowledge of a kind that might manifest knowing how to *A*. It is doubtful, however, that this knowledge or the disposition to acquire it *suffices* to yield such know-how. What we have seen suggests instead that know-how commonly embodies much virtual knowledge and thereby much raw material for intellectual knowledge of the kind that makes reduction of knowing *how* to knowing *that* seem promising. Still, that know-how embodies, even in a constitutive way, much virtual knowledge does not support the view that it reduces to knowledge *that* or even to that together with virtual knowledge.

Rejecting the intellectualist reduction does not preclude accepting something intellectualism puts in high relief. Given that the question how to do something is answerable by citing facts, the very possibility of asking how to do something may seem to presuppose that a correct answer can indicate propositional knowledge constitutive of the know-how. The possibility does not in fact presuppose this, but only the unsurprising point that in many cases a good description of an action or activity can immediately *produce* knowing how to perform it. This sketch of a route to an equivalence thesis illustrates the danger of backing into a view on how much we know by assimilating actual knowledge to virtual

9. This is argued in detail in my 1994 and further in my 2019. Both also indicate how the idea of implicit belief invites the view that we "implicitly" believe all the propositions comprehensible to us that are obviously entailed by what we "explicitly believe." This would of course hold for any intellectually perfect being.

knowledge. Here the temptation is to exaggerate how much propositional knowledge is required by knowing *how* by assuming that the agent knows all that one *would* know on considering how one *A*-s *and*, with that in view, forms true beliefs that describe *A*-ing in a kind of "practical detail," a kind readily applicable to teaching someone how to perform the action.

What we have seen strongly suggests that, far from being reducible to any kind of knowing *that*, knowing *how* is, in at least many cases, more basic and explains why we know as much as we do, and have as much potential, virtual knowledge as we do, about how the things we can do are done.[10] The intellectualism of propositional reduction seems lost in the indefinitely rich concrete details of doing, recalling, envisaging, or other elements closer to doing, perceiving, or imagining than to propositional knowing.

IV. The Place of Knowledge in Practical Reasoning

Intellectualism in the practical domain goes far beyond the view that knowing *how* reduces to (or is at least equivalent to) a kind of knowing *that*. Another question in this domain is whether knowledge is required for practical reasoning, at least where that reasoning shows an action to be rational. The view that knowledge is required in such cases constitutes another aspect of intellectualism regarding the practical domain.[11] Broadly speaking, the idea is that an intellectual success is required for even the limited practical success manifested by satisfactory practical reasoning. Perhaps one source of the attractiveness of this view is the

10. Here one might think of the "objectual intellectualism" proposed by Bengson and Moffet (2011). They deny that knowing *how* reduces to knowing *that* but argue that "to know how to act is to understand a way of so acting, where such understanding involves grasping a (possibly implicit) conception that is poised to guide the successful intentional performance of such an act—hence, to possess a cognitive state with a distinctively practical character" (p. 161). Clearly, knowing how to *A* requires some conception of how to *A*. But how "cognitive" must the "possibly implicit" conception be? They do not address this in a way that leaves me confident that their view should be considered genuinely intellectualist.

11. Cf. Stanley's defense of the view that "an action is done for a proper reason only if it is knowledge" (2011: 175). His defense of this concerns chiefly skilled action, for which it seems more plausible than for action in general.

idea that reasons are facts.[12] For one thing, it is natural to think that we do and should reason from facts to various conclusions, including practical ones. Moreover, if reasons are facts then they will be expressible by that-clauses and such that one might think practical reasoning has some defect if a crucial premise is either false or not known—in either case manifesting some kind of intellectual failure. But, quite apart from whether, when reasons are expressible in that-clauses, they constitute knowledge, there is (as argued in Chapter 5) good ground for denying that reasons are *necessarily* facts. Two considerations will suffice here. Both are broadly epistemological. One concerns the kind of evidence required for knowledge, as opposed to what is needed for justified action. The second concerns whether knowing a proposition is necessary for its constituting a reason for action.

First, consider what kinds of belief are eligible to express reasons for action. Take a well-evidenced belief that apparently does not constitute knowledge. For many epistemologists, even if one holds just one ticket in a fair lottery with a million tickets, one does not know one will lose. Even those who contest this may accept the following for the case of ten thousand tickets, where one's chance of winning is much greater. Suppose I am offered a fine car for half its value. If I know I can afford it *only* if I win the lottery and I have a justified belief that my chance is very slight, may I not reason: I'm not going to win, and without a win, refusing is my only sensible option, so I should refuse? Granted, I might also reason from my chance of winning being only 1/10,000—something I know—to the same conclusion. But suppose I don't work with numerical probabilities and simply have the categorical belief that I won't win, whose truth is only highly probable (as I may realize). I need not also believe (even if on reflection I would believe) that I do not *know* I will lose. My not knowing an important premise surely does not vitiate my reasoning or render irrational the refusal based on it, even if the (accepted) *thought* that I don't know might do so.[13]

12. This view has long been held by Parfit and others and defended by him in, e.g. his 2011 (pp. 31–38).

13. It should be granted that if I went into debt to buy the car and then lost in the lottery, a natural complaint would be 'How could you do that?! You knew you would lose'. This is a use of 'knew' akin to that in 'I just knew we would win the game' where even experts were on the edge of their seats wondering who would win. In each case, we would expect withdrawal of the knowledge-claim given evident facts, e.g. that there was a *chance* that one would win. The pragmatics of language use allow that in actual conversation many kinds of things can be said, given the special context, that are not a good basis for theory-building.

Lottery cases are not the only challenge to the intellectualist view in question. Imagine apparently reliable testimony given in such a way that the recipient has good justification but not knowledge regarding what is said. This might occur *either* where the testifier has no evidence but is highly credible and (luckily) correct or even where the testifier is amply justified but in error. Can this response to testimony not also lead to rationally adequate practical reasoning?[14] Surely we need not independently verify credible testimony in order to reason in quite acceptable ways from one or more propositions credibly attested to by people we know.

To be sure, where we cite *p* as our reason for doing something and are *warned* that that we don't know that *p*, we should see the relevance of this reproach. Indeed, we may reasonably infer from it that caution is warranted—and this reasoning can be good even if the warning is false and we really do know that *p*. But the relevance of such a criticism does not entail the intellectualist view that *only* propositions an agent knows are appropriate for practical reasoning. If that were so, citing a proposition one is amply justified in believing would not normally be an adequate response to a challenge to a premise in practical reasoning But it is, at least where the proposition clearly entails that premise, and this holds even if the speaker's justification for the proposition does not suffice for knowledge.

V. Factivity versus Pluralism in the Theory of Reasons for Action

A third kind of case is easily overlooked by those who think of reasons as facts or indeed as anything (such as a true proposition or correct judgment) expressible by a truth-apt that-clause. In the case of actions, this view of reasons is too narrow, and here, as in Chapter 5, I stress a neglected mode of reason-ascription.[15] If *S A*-s for a reason, there is an

This does not preclude taking account of them, but that requires caution, and at least often hypothetical conversations are not as conceptually significant as descriptive non-conversational uses of the terms in question.

14. This case does not require denying that it might be better in some way to *know* what is said (*p*); but the rationality of accepting credible testimony is not undermined simply by the attester's not knowing that *p*. Nor need a testimony-based reason fail to be "proper" (Stanley's term) because it does not represent knowledge—even if knowledge would be more desirable.

15. One indication of this neglect is that in a paper devoted to answering the question whether (motivating) reasons for action are facts known to the agent, there is, as in other papers addressing it, simply no mention of infinitival

infinitival expression of the reason. Roughly, where we *A* for a reason—schematically, in order to bring about a state of affairs, *R*—our reason can be specified not only as <*that A*-ing will bring about *R*> but also as (in order) <*to* bring about *R*> (or the state of affairs corresponding to *R*, say getting revenge). The content of the infinitive clause is not plausibly taken to be a fact, nor need it *be* a fact that the goal in question is realizable by *A*-ing.

It is also instructive to consider the *kinds* of instrumental facts that can constitute (normative) reasons for action. Suppose I know that helping with renovations will expedite them. This knowledge can motivate action, and believing the proposition can be a motivational reason for helping. But suppose the renovation is a bad idea and there is no value at all in expediting it. Then the knowledge does not provide a normative reason to contribute. Granting, then, that some instrumental facts, say that an action will prevent a disaster, *do* provide normative reasons for action, it does not follow that they can do so independently of an apparently different kind of consideration.[16] If there is any priority relation between normative reasons expressible with true instrumental that-clauses and normative reasons expressible in a value-indicative infinitive clause, it would appear to be in favor of the latter.

What important conclusions follow from the proposed pluralistic view of reasons? One is that there are cases of good practical reasoning whose premises are justifiedly believed but not known. It is true and important that at least in these cases knowledge is superior to mere true belief or even justified true belief. But explaining that does not require regarding reasons as factive. Another point here is that rejecting the factivity view is neutral regarding whether knowledge is the "norm of assertion." It may be true that if I *assert* a premise in practical reasoning, I am subject to criticism if I do not know that premise to be true. But we do not assert all the premises of our reasoning. We need not assert any in silent reasoning; some premises may be tacit; and practical reasoning as such may be hypothetical. One may suppose certain things

expressions of reasons or the question whether reasons for action must be considered facts. See Locke (2015).

16. Granted, infinitively expressed reasons may constitute normative reasons only if it is a normative fact that the relevant state of affairs is in some way good; but this is a different kind of fact from the relevant instrumental kind. Moreover, even if there *being* a reason to bring about a state of affairs depends on that fact that it is (normatively) good, it is far from clear that *having* a normative reason to bring it about entails knowing that it is good.

and infer consequences, even if one neither knows nor even believes the suppositions.

Whether or not (propositional) reasons one has for action (or belief for that matter) are facts, practical reasoning remains subject to objective intellectual standards. It has an inference—a practical one in some sense—as an element and may be valid or invalid. It also has a cognitive element, whose content is broadly instrumental, even if that content need not be a fact or represent knowledge. But we must not allow either the importance of cognition in practical reasoning, or the importance of practical reasoning itself in understanding action, to move us toward another kind of intellectualism in the theory of action: *inferentialism*—the view that every intentional action is based on practical reasoning. Inferentialism is intellectualist in implying that an intellectual performance is required for full-blooded action. More broadly still, an underlying idea here might be that the will moves us to intentional action only given the guidance of reasoning. This view yields too narrow an understanding of action, even rational action.

What may partly motivate inferentialism is a *correspondence thesis*—that for every intentional action, there is corresponding practical reasoning whose premises express the relevant aim and an appropriate instrumental belief. We can grant this without accepting inferentialism, which requires a process (however short) of reasoning underlying every intentional action. Not every action for a reason—such as quickly placing a lid on a pan with burning oil—is a reasoned action: based on a process of reasoning. *Structurally*, action may be reason-based, with cognition and, in that weak sense, "intellect," playing a role, without identifying reasons for action with facts or taking all intentional action to be based on practical reasoning as a process that requires some element of consciousness beyond what is required to perform the action itself.[17] Being reason-based does not entail being reasoning-based. The exercise of agency apparently does require guidance by belief, as well as sufficient rational structure for the content of belief and motivation to play a rationalizing role in the sense that they at least render actions explainable. But the kind of intellectualism that requires either knowledge status for the action-guiding beliefs that express reasons, or an inferential process as mediating between action-guiding beliefs and action, is too narrow.

---

17. A full-scale account of practical reasoning, inference as understood in relation to it, and related criticism of inferentialism is provided by my 2006.

In the light of the examples and arguments presented in this chapter, it seems clear that intellectualism in the theory of action fails on at least three counts. Knowledge how is not reducible to knowledge that; knowledge is not required for the premises of practical reasoning; and (normative) reasons for action need not be factive, much less constituted by known propositions. Indeed, (normative) reasons for action are to be understood pluralistically, both because they include propositions that are not true (though not irrationally believed) and because they need not be propositions as distinct from states of affairs conceived as *to be realized.* These conclusions by no means imply that knowledge is not important for understanding action and practical reasoning, especially rational action and good practical reasoning. How this is so is evident in some of the points made so far and will be further illustrated in the next chapter.

12

INFERENCE AND ITS ROLE IN RATIONAL ACTION

A fully comprehensive epistemology must address not only the nature of non-inferential knowledge and justified belief but also how these are transmitted from (or made possible by) such "basic" cases as those of perceptual knowledge, which we have explored in detail. On any plausible epistemology, propositional knowledge from any of the basic sources of it can provide premises for inference (as can testimony, which I have argued is an essential though not a basic source of knowledge[1]). There are substantive criteria that govern the connection between beliefs on the basis of which one believes *p* and the belief that *p* itself. These are intricate and controversial and need not be discussed now.[2] Here I want to begin with a prior question: how we should characterize inference and, in that light, action based on practical inference.

I. Inference and Inferential Belief

If we understand belief and its possible basis in "theoretical" inference, that will help us in understanding action and its possible basis in practical reasoning. Of special interest here are justified beliefs and beliefs constituting knowledge. One source of resistance to the idea that some knowledge and justified belief is non-inferential may come from the view that we cannot simply know truth or be justified in believing truths,

1. E.g. in my 2013c.

2. I discuss in detail the conception of these criteria for practical reasoning in my 2006, and, for theoretical reasoning, in my 2010.

Seeing, Knowing, and Doing. Robert Audi, Oxford University Press (2020). © Oxford University Press.
DOI: 10.1093/oso/9780197503508.001.0001

but must know or be justified in believing them on some *basis*. When we seek to explain how we know—and, as skeptics never tire of reminding us, we may always be intelligibly asked this—we commonly cite, for instance, a basis in perception, memory, or indeed propositions we take to be known or (in the context) justifiably assumable. But citing this basis typically takes the form of adducing propositions, such as <I see it>. In adducing those as an explanation or justification, we provide one or more premises from which the proposition we take ourselves to know can be inferred. How then, can it be reasonably held that we have non-inferential knowledge, say intuitive knowledge?

Here I must emphasize that although justified (doxastic) intuitions and other non-inferentially justified cognitions are not *premise-dependent*, it does not follow that they are not *epistemically* dependent at all. They are *ground-dependent* (the basic kind of ground being awareness of a relevant set of properties or, with self-evident propositions, understanding of the relevant concepts and certain of their relations). An inferential cognition, however, is "mediated" by at least one premise and is in that way indirect. It is psychologically, not just epistemically, ground-dependent. A premise-belief, e.g., must ultimately trace to a (non-doxastic) ground if it is to be justified (I assume a moderate foundationalist view here), though a premise may itself be premise-based.

Intuitions, by contrast, are (in their common occurrent forms) epistemically direct responses to something presented. Functionally, they save us from needing a premise. They do not, however, make premises impossible or protect us from refutation by considerations that cogent critics may adduce. In this way, intuitions are analogous to visual beliefs grounded in visual experience, which also provides non-inferential but defeasible justification for those beliefs. But the analogy to seeing must be carefully interpreted: much as a mere glance at a tree may not yield justified visual belief or indeed any belief, a mere passing thought of even an intuitive proposition or concept may yield no intuition. Reflection may be needed to see even what, once it is clearly seen, is intuitive.[3]

3. The point that what is intuitively known may be knowable only through reflection though still known non-inferentially is defended and developed in my response to Sinnott-Armstrong (2007) in my 2007b. Cf. the misleading idea, commonly attributed to twentieth-century intuitionists (as I noted in my 2004), that we "just see" the truth of self-evident and many other kinds of intuitive true propositions.

I have so far spoken of inferential belief, but not of inference. There is wide agreement that a belief which is premise-dependent is inferential, but there is less agreement on what constitutes *an inference,* in the common sense in which inferences are *made* and making an inference entails *reasoning.* As indicated in Chapter 3, an inference, whether theoretical or practical, is roughly a kind of passage of thought from one or more propositions to another, in part on the basis of (or at least causally assisted by) a sense of some support relation between the former and the latter. I take inference to be roughly equivalent to a mental *tokening* of an argument, if we may assume that arguments may be both logically and epistemically bad and that tokening, though in consciousness and in some way symbolic, need not occur in a natural language.[4] This characterization leaves open whether an inference is valid and whether it is (1) belief-forming—in which case the conclusion belief is at least characteristically based, wholly or in part, on the premise belief(s)—or (2) proceeds from propositions already believed to another that is believed, or indeed (3), as with disproofs by deductions of absurdities, from propositions only supposed, to another proposition that may be only considered and quickly rejected. The notion of inference is both psychological and, at least on an objective conception of support-relations, epistemic.

The notion of inference in question (perhaps capturing a conception of inference prevalent until rather recently) is also *phenomenal*: inference (in the sense in which inferences are drawn or made) is episodic and manifested in consciousness, though there need be no consciousness *of* the inference under any particular description. This point is easily missed because the related notions of *inferential belief* and of inferential (dispositional) judgment are not episodic or even phenomenal, though they are psychological. A belief that p can be based on a belief that q *without* the person's inferring p from q. I could, for instance, discover

4. The notion of inference and related notions, such as inferential belief, and tokening—sometimes enthymematically—of arguments, are explicated in my 1986b, and esp. in chs. 4 and 8 of 2006. I should add that I assume that a *belief* that the premises support the conclusion may be taken to be a special (perhaps phenomenally thin) case of the sense of support in question. Unfortunately, my 2004 did not refer to 1986b or other works in which I explicated the notion of justified belief, nor reproduce the account. It is understandable, then, that Shafer-Landau (2007), in reviewing my 2004 missed the inclusion of such an account in that book. For related discussion of inference, with bearing on a number of issues treated in this chapter, see Malmgren (2018).

q, which is evidence for *p*, only after *already* believing *p* on testimony. I could then begin to believe *p* inferentially, on the basis of the new evidence, *q*. This is possible even if there is no related phenomenal element, such as a sense of forming the belief that *p*, or even my consciously connecting *p* with *q*, as where I have a thought of *q* as supporting *p*. The kinds of phenomenal elements essential in drawing an inference are not needed for a belief to acquire a supporting role: the inferentiality in question is not episodic or even phenomenal; it is a *structural relation* between beliefs. It implies nothing about what occurs in consciousness. We often *make* connections between propositions by drawing inferences; but the mind is capable of responding to such connections more spontaneously, without our drawing inferences. Because inferential belief need not arise from inference, and because inferentiality need not be phenomenal, showing that intuitions are not inferential is difficult.

II. Inference, Reasoning, and Premise-Based Belief-Formation

So far, I have left temporal considerations implicit. But they are epistemologically significant. The epistemic principles most commonly discussed are synchronic, applying at a given time. We have seen principles saying that *given* a certain visual experience at *t*, one has, at *t*, justification for certain propositions (those appropriately connected with the content of the experience). Epistemologists considering conditions for knowledge normally focus on, say, justified true belief at the time of the supposed knowledge. Inferential principles may, moreover, also presuppose a single time. Here I want to show the importance of the distinction between synchronic and diachronic principles. The former apply to a time slice of the agent; they take no account of change. Incoherence is possible at a given time, and there are sound principles that prohibit it; but considering a proposition or prospect *and* forming a belief (or intention) on the basis of it (or an intention to bring about a goal indicated by the belief) is at least normally not possible at a single time. In this case the mind may have to pause a moment on one step (or on one ground) before taking another step. Even simply moving from one step to another requires time.

Instantaneity is certainly not possible for reasoning if we take reasoning to include very common cases, particularly when reasoning occurs in the course of practical thinking. Consider the case of *beginning* to consider a proposition, or prospect, as where it occurs to one that doing something would be good, and *then*, on that basis, one inferentially forms the relevant belief or intention. Call this case *episodic inference.* This is the kind that constitutes a tokening of practical reasoning in at least the normal cases of such reasoning. By contrast, it does seem possible at a single time to draw a conclusion *while* still considering a belief or prospect that had already come to mind. Call this *instantaneous inference.* (One could also call it *emergent* inference, given that the concluding element emerges from a "static" basis and is not the final element in a process.) Here the premise set is already in mind, possibly even long reflected on, and we focus just on the formation of a conclusion on the basis of it. The inference is a momentary movement of thought, not a process of which that is a part.

If it turns out that although reasoning, whether theoretical or practical, need not involve episodic inference and is barely possible at a single time (a matter that can be left open here), the common kind of inference that qualifies as at least a minimal segment of *reflection*—is not possible without some elapse of time. It is such reflection that is a characteristic element in *practical thinking*; and at least the vast majority of our practical reasonings either occur as part of a stretch of practical thinking (even if a short stretch) or at least require time for us to consider one or more propositions and, on that basis, to conclude in favor of some action. Thus, thinking about how to help a student, I may come to want to discuss her paper. The thought that meeting next week would be best may lead me to conclude my thinking by, say, forming a judgment in favor of doing that, and a normal upshot of so judging would be intending to do it.

An important general point implicit here concerns an agent's consideration of a possible action, particularly where the action is already intended. Consideration of one's options may lead to change in desires or other psychological elements, and such change, in turn, may alter the rationality status of an intention. Thinking of discussing a paper next week might lead me to realize it would be better to wait for a revised draft, and this may make it unreasonable to intend to discuss it next week, and I may cease to intend to do so. This point bears on standards governing practical reasoning.

It is doubtful that reasoning is commonly instantaneous, if it ever is. It is certainly not instantaneous if we think of a piece of reasoning as at least a minimal case of reflection, as opposed to just the constituent inference conceived as an unreflective passage of thought from the premise(s) one already has in mind to the conclusion. But suppose a piece of reasoning can be instantaneous. This would *still* allow that at the very moment one considers *B*-ing in the light of intending to *A* and of believing that *B*-ing is necessary and sufficient for *A*-ing, one could have the thought that *B*-ing is morally repugnant just as quickly as one could form the intention to *B*. How much the mind can do, or respond to, at a given time, is largely a contingent matter. But if a mental phenomenon as complex as reasoning *can* be instantaneous, so can the occurrence of the thought that *B*-ing is morally repugnant together with its eliminating the intention to *A*.

More generally, if it is theoretically possible for reasoning—whether practical or theoretical—to be instantaneous, it is also theoretically possible that, at the relevant time, a thought or realization can occur to an agent and provide reason *not* to form the intention (or belief), or do the deed, in question. This bears on how one can avoid certain kinds of incoherent triads of propositional attitudes, for instance believing that *p*, that *p* entails *q*, and that not-*q*. If concluding practical reasoning in the usual way that favors the act figuring in the minor premise can be instantaneous, acquiring a reason to reject one of the premises that favor so concluding can be also. The need to avoid inconsistent triads does not, however, necessarily favor one pattern of reasoning over the other. If, wanting to help someone with a draft, and believing that offering assistance would bring this about, I consider actually offering it and immediately judge that this would, in the context, be considered patronizing, I may either cease to want to help or cease to believe that offering assistance would lead to helping.

There is another way to put one of my conclusions. Even if reasoning need not be diachronic, it is *dynamic*. It entails a developmental change, at least when it is belief-forming. That change can bring with it new reasons, as where we arrive at a new justified practical judgment. These reasons in turn can alter what the agent ought to (and does) intend (or believe). There is a sense, then, in which the assessment of reasoning—theoretical as well as practical—is holistic. This is why so many criteria figure in its proper assessment and why it is defeasible in the light of new considerations.

III. Reasoning and Rational Action

We have seen that practical reasoning is much less epistemically constrained than it might seem to be. Simply as an inferential tokening of an argument, it may be rational without the person's knowing or even having strong justification for its premises. I have shown how we can resist the temptation to parley epistemic conditions for ideal reasoning into conditions for reasoning simpliciter, for instance by allowing that instrumental beliefs underlying rational action need not be true or, if true, knowledge. I have also maintained that intentional action need not emerge from reasoning at all. From here it is a short step to the conclusion that not all rational action need emerge from it either. This calls for explanation.

Suppose that, as I suggest, we distinguish between reasoned action and action for a reason, which does not entail the former. Add to this that an action may be performed for *the same reason* whether or not that reason is expressed in a piece of *reasoning*, conceived (appropriately) as some kind of inferential process. We can then maintain the plausible view that the rationality of an action is determined by the character of the reason(s) it is based on and simply grant that this basis relation need not be mediated by reasoning—*ratiocinatively instantiated*, we might say. Contrary to an intellectualist conception of rational action, the support given to an action by reasons favoring it does not depend on those reasons yielding it by any particular process, much less one that requires mental activity distinct from whatever mental events (say perceptual ones) guide the action itself. In very global terms, one could say that although the mind is required to ground rational action, the *intellect* is not.

One could qualify an inferentialist view by being selective, for both practical and theoretical reasoning. Inferentialism might be maintained for normal cases of rational action but restricted to the genesis of only the *initial* action of the type in question, say slicing a watermelon into equal wedges having equal parts of the heart. One might initially have to reason about how to slice so that each share has the same proportion of the heart, but then one might simply carry out the slicing without reasoning. One can throw away the ladder one climbed on—or traverse it quickly and unnoticed (or even imperceptibly). If this example is insufficiently representative, the realm of testimony provides a more common case. Consider receiving information from someone on how to reach a destination. Once the recipient takes the attester to be credible, which is often virtually immediately though it may require inference, the information-receiving channel is open. Not just anything will fit through it, but not everything that can needs scrutiny. This moderate initial-case inferentialism is more plausible than the constant inference view of belief-formation, but it is not needed to account even for intellectually cautious recipients of testimony, and it does not reflect common experience in either the formation of beliefs or the performance of actions.

For testimony, then, we can surely believe directly (non-inferentially and thus without reasoning) what someone tells us, much as we can at will follow an order to do something in our repertoire of basic act-types, such as raising our right hand. Indeed, can't I acquire testimony-based knowledge when I accept testimony from someone who does indeed know *p* and is honest but is also such that I do not have justification for assuming credibility? Surely we learn from strangers on matters concerning which we have no credible evidence either way regarding their character or reliability. I do not say that the inferentialist thesis on which we must infer credibility in order to acquire testimony-based knowledge is obviously false.[5] But one way to see its implausibility is to consider tiny children's acquiring knowledge on the basis of parental testimony before they even have the conceptual resources to make the credibility assumptions an inferentialist needs.

Whatever the ultimate verdict on whether action for a reason must be based on reasoning (and I do not claim that this chapter by itself justifies the more economical view favored here), we should countenance information-processing that does not constitute reasoning. Consider a readily generalizable example. Regarding the kind of information-processing that may be outside consciousness, a clear case is facial recognition. We cannot recognize a face we know when too much of it is covered. We need a certain (situationally variable) minimum of visual information, such as adequate light. But even if facial recognition normally requires much visual information, it is characteristically neither inferential nor a result of reasoning—not, anyway, if reasoning is propositionally constituted and requires occurrent thought. For much facial recognition, no such process is needed. It *can* be: where, for instance, there is a distinctive tattoo from whose presence one must infer the person's identity. But, however much the brain does, facial recognition is typically immediate, non-inferential, and unreflectively automatic.

Compare catching a ball that the wind is blowing to our right. Must we do a quick unconscious calculation? If the know-how is ingrained, the visual system can "project" location with no accompanying intellectual operations.[6] Even if the system provides projective information, must every propositional piece of information that can guide action do so via a propositional tokening in "unconsciousness?" Some of our

5. For a careful attempt to show it for testimony-based beliefs, see Malmgren (2007).

6. On some views, inference is apparently not intellectual at all. For Mitchell Green, even perception may be inferential given that "The inferences . . . will not in general consist in the derivation of one proposition from a set of others . . . they will more commonly take the form of a positioning of an object

examples, such as that of cautiously crossing a stream by choosing only safe-looking rocks to tread on, suggest that no such intellectualist view is forced on us by the need to account for the relevant discriminative perceptual responses to the environment or their guidance of behavior.

Might we not consider other cases in the practical realm analogous? There appear to be rational actions, as there may be rational beliefs, that (perhaps in some Bayesian way) are guided by information, yet are not reason-based. I have not implied precisely that conclusion regarding action, but it may be true, depending on whether every rational action must be intentional. That rational actions must be based on reasons in the way characteristic of what we do intentionally is a position one would expect in an intellectualist perspective on action. Let us explore the view.

IV. The Scope of Rational Action

We have seen good grounds to reject the intellectualist view that rational action must be based on reasoning and the associated view that *good* reasoning can have only premises that constitute knowledge. A weaker, perhaps more plausible thesis suggested by these views is that rational action must be intentional. Here I continue to make the plausible and widely accepted assumption that intentional action is equivalent to action for a reason, in the sense that it has a description under which it is explainable by appeal to intentionalistic elements, presumably at least one belief and at least one desire, that instrumentally connect it with the content of the description. Few would deny that this view holds for at least the vast majority of actions plausibly considered intentional—a weaker assumption sufficient for my purposes. Take a case of appointing *x* to a post. The agent wants something, *G*, and believes something to the effect that appointing *x* will realize *G*. Appointing for this (compound) reason might well be rational. But can an action also have a description under which it is *not* performed for a reason, yet is still rational?

in egocentric space, an attribution of absolute and relative trajectories, and so forth." See his 2010 (pp. 48–49). If inference is taken so generally and includes information-processing the brain can do without agential consciousness of any element in the process, proponents of this inferentialist picture may hold that the ball catcher in some way infers the position of the ball as it approaches the awaiting hands. Cf. Clark (2014, e.g. ch. 11, esp. 229–237), which explicate the "perception-as-inference" view of Richard Gregory, emphasizing "predictive processing" as "essentially a process of bottom-up feature detection."

Suppose I realize (and regret) that nominating *x* to chair a committee will offend *y*. Under the description, *offending y*, I have no reason to appoint *x*; indeed, I have a reason to avoid offending *y* even if it is an inevitable consequence of nominating *x*. Suppose it is inevitable. Surely, if appointing *x* is rational and sufficiently valuable, then offending *y* may also be rational—*derivatively rational.* It could even be a reasonable cost to bear—indeed, even necessary. These terms contrast it with actions that are either instrumentally rational or inherently rational, say as enjoyable. My offending *y* is of course only prima facie (and defeasibly) rational; it would not be rational overall if it would obviously cause a disaster, but that need not be so in such cases.

One could say that there is an *oblique reason* or a *consequential reason* to offend the bypassed candidate (or at least not to avoid the offense by failing to make the intended nomination). But the offending is not done for a reason. One might say that it is *indirectly based* on a reason, but not performed *for* one. It is foreseen as a consequence of what is intentional and thereby indirectly reason-based. Moreover, unlike accidentally spilling a drink, it is not *un*intentional.

Should we say that similarly, it is not, in the imagined case, irrational but merely non-rational rather than rational? That would not do justice to the extent to which it is *supported by reasons,* such as the necessity of nominating *x* as the best candidate. The case shows, then (as do other kinds of case), that reasons can psychologically support and indeed causally explain an action without motivating it. As with offending the candidate not selected, the agent neither aims at it nor even wants it as a means to something further. It may be merely acquiesced in because it results from something that is wanted (say selecting the best candidate), but it may have so much psychological support from the motivation driving the action of which it is regretted consequence that even powerful resistance to the regretted deed is overcome.

This case shows something else that may be surprising. Without being intentional, an action may be not only rational but also justified. I surely have a justification for offending *y*—that it is unavoidable given what I must on balance do—nominate *x*. That justification is in part why the act is rational. To be sure, I do not offend *y* on the basis of my justification, as would be expected if I did so intentionally (and in part for this reason some would prefer to say I have an excuse, but this is the sort of excuse compatible with the kind of justification I would have). The most general conclusion here is perhaps that justification, like rationality and moral responsibility, is attributable to what is in the scope of the will, as with acts we permit but do not intend; acts in the scope of the will are not limited to those the agent purposively aims at. These non-intentional rational and justified actions are performed—non-waywardly—*because of* a reason but still not *for* it.[7]

Another category should be considered here: mere doings, as distinct from non-intentional actions that are performed knowingly but not intentionally. Can these be rational? Consider moving one's feet during a long flight, where this is simply a natural response to being confined, as opposed to being aimed at getting comfortable. The distinction between such doings and mere bodily movements is not sharp. Presumably, if there is no description under which the doing is intentional, it is not action, hence is not minimally rational action. Still, the doing is both voluntary and not *irrational*, and the doing-*type* is rational *for* the agent at the time. Thus, intentionally making the same movements might be a good idea, and even likely to occur, if one thinks of making them. This is one reason why, if the doing is neither unintentional nor disconnected with the agent's interests, there is some pull toward calling it rational even if it is not intentional under any description. (I do not, however, claim that, simply as described, it should be considered rational behavior.)

There is yet another behavioral category important for understanding rational behavior: a kind of action, or at least doing, that is automatic and might be considered *cue-guided*. Recall the case of stepping over stones on a hike. If this is action, it might be considered avoiding an obstacle. But suppose one has learned to step over obstacles and this becomes automatic—part of knowing how to hike in rough terrain. Might there be a non-doxastic instrumental connection? Perhaps one's background knowledge of how to hike in such terrain, together with seeing the stone, yield a sense of the need to step over it. The question is empirical, but the relevant concepts at least make room for the view I have proposed: that an action may be cue-guided, and in that sense information-guided by perception, rather than belief-guided by a focal instrumental belief—and in that way guided by knowledge or some other intellectual element describing the consequences of one's action.

7. Must we now say not only that a non-intentional action may be not only rational and justified *for S* but also rationally and justifiedly *performed by S*? They are not *irrationally* performed, but that term is a contrary, not the contradictory of, 'rationally performed', and it is preferable to use other adverbs, e.g. 'knowingly', 'consentingly', and 'regretfully', that indicate the relevant non-intentional action's being in the scope of the will, but do not imply that it is intended.

Granted, in such cases there is likely a background of experience and indeed of instrumental beliefs of the right kind. A hike would normally be belief-guided in an overall way, say such that its direction is determined by beliefs about the whereabouts of a friend. But a cue may yield a kind of action based on, e.g., perception, without doing so by way of a belief to the effect that the thing constituting the cue (say) indicates what one should do. Background experiences and standing beliefs may pave the way for a cue to govern, or at least trigger, the action; they need not yield an instrumental belief such as that one must step over the stone to avoid tripping. The automatic action here is more like catching a ball in the wind than like counting cash for groceries. Note, too, that automatic doings that manifest knowing *how* can be rational—as well as, say, deft or clumsy, fast or slow, novel or routine—even if they are not intentional.

None of the points made here implies that the intellect has no role in the grounding of rational action. But that role need not fit an intellectualist model of grounding in *reasoning*, where we have an analogy to belief or knowledge based on an argument that corresponds to one's reasoning. The role need not even exhibit the action's being *directly* supported by reasons at all. And the role of the intellect may be as indirect as occurs where rational action (or at least a rational kind of doing) is based on information that, even if accessible to the agent by reflection, is not expressed in specific action-guiding propositions the agent believes or knows. Rational action may instead derive from such cues as perceived obstacles in one's path that, given the agent's overall know-how, guide action.

V. Intentionality, Knowledge, and Agency

What we have seen so far makes it quite plausible to hold that rational action need not be intentional.[8] As rational, such action is evaluable in a way accidental doings are not (though they may of course also be negligent and evaluable in certain other ways appropriate to accidental doings). Rational non-intentional actions (or doings, at any rate) may

8. Being non-intentional does not entail being unintentional, as shown by doing something knowingly and willingly but not intentionally, as in the nomination case. There is also no question that something one does unintentionally, such as leaving water running, can be *rational for one*, even when not rationally performed. But I am not claiming (and doubt) that an act *un*intentionally performed can also be rationally performed.

be, for instance, voluntary in being fully under the control of the will, and they may be part of a behavioral pattern, such as hiking, that is intentional. Hiking, moreover, is *activity*, in a sense entailing constituent actions normally envisaged as parts of the behavior in question. Here it is useful, as in Chapter 10, to speak of scripts: roughly, regularized ways of doing the things in question, normally acquired by rehearsal or training, as with playing a part in a drama or rendering well memorized music. Although in principle scripts could be induced instantaneously by brain manipulation, they commonly arise by learning through multiple repetition. Some activities, like some rehearsed scripted behavior, may be "automatic" and still contrast with some instances of stepping over an obstacle, as is deliberately done in the unfamiliar hike portrayed earlier. There I knew how to hike, but had no script for traversing the new pathway I was following.

The most plausible understanding of certain activities—those that are fully or partly scripted—is that the intention to engage in them has a rich content that encompasses a wide range of the constituent actions. To see how this is possible, recall the distinction made in Chapter 8, between what is *before* the mind and what is simply *in* mind. Just as one can have a multiple-element conditional in mind and be able to write it out fully though it is too complex to be focally in consciousness at any one time, one could intend to recite a memorized poem though the entire work is too long to be focally in mind. Each word might be intentionally recited while also being spontaneously uttered and, as is often the case when responses are scripted or are cue-driven, automatic. Such actions (or in minimal cases perhaps only doings) can be intentional, and even rational, without being either reasoned or indeed performed for any reason besides whatever set of reasons governs the entire activity. Intentions can determine the scope of expectations without doing so by inducing beliefs for each expected element in the intended activity. For much of what we know how to do, we have apparently internalized a kind of script. But this is not a condition for knowing *how*. Indeed, some scripts can doubtless be "written" only after the fact. Some scripts may also have such indexicals as occur in 'Do it like *this*', and those that are purely intellectual may be learnable without at the time knowing how to do what they describe.

In the light of the considerations indicated in this section, we can see reason to resist a kind of intellectualism not so far directly addressed: a kind implying that acting requires a basis in knowledge. If the question concerns just the action-guiding knowledge operative in much of what we do, we have seen reason to doubt that all action is knowledge-based.[9] Even instrumental knowledge does not seem necessary: instrumental beliefs (roughly means-ends beliefs) can guide action without constituting knowledge. But we have not seen reason to give up the venerable view that action is in some way, even if indirectly, belief-guided. This holds even for scripted action once we allow for believing such propositions as that one simply *A*-s, where *A*-ing is sufficiently familiar, as in reciting a well-memorized poem. If intellectualism in the theory of action is too strong, an information-responsiveness view of action of the kind outlined here may still hold.

It should be apparent from Chapter 10 that knowledge *how* is another case in which, if cognitions with propositional content are needed, they need not constitute propositional knowledge. If you know how to swim, then normally you can simply swim when you want to (and have the means). A typical swimmer will doubtless have some propositional knowledge about how swimming is done, and arguably a measure of what I call virtual knowledge is, for agents with sufficient conceptual capacity, necessary for knowing how to swim. Someone who has just crossed the threshold of knowing how to swim might merely have evidence, rather than knowledge, about how swimming is done and may need more experience to *know* how it is done.

Abandoning the several intellectualist claims I have challenged need not lead to insufficiently appreciating the powers of intellect. For instance, simple activities like cutting out a rectangle from a sheet of paper and doubtless some far more complex activities can be such that, although an agent does not already know how to engage in them, instruction can lead to immediate success. Some people can do complex puzzles given just one good clue. Facts of this kind are perhaps one source of support for the idea that knowing how is (in principle) reducible to knowing that. Instructional learning of the right propositions can yield know-how. But from the possibility that knowledge *that*—say knowing *that* of the kind testimony can provide—may *produce* knowing

9. I leave aside the special case of agential self-knowledge. Here the most plausible intellectualist view is perhaps that, for everything we do intentionally, there is some description under which (at the time and given adequate conceptual resources) we know we are doing it. On the information-responsiveness view illustrated in parts of this book, a preferable view would be that one need have only virtual knowledge here, in the sense that, on grounds that characteristically suffice for knowledge, one is disposed to believe one is doing the thing in question.

how, it certainly does not follow that every case of the latter is a case of or, especially, based on, knowing the propositions describing how the thing in question is done (or other non-indexical propositions). It is a contingent matter what information will lead a person to know how to do something or indeed to do it. My point here is that the concept of propositional knowledge about how a thing is done does not guarantee that having such knowledge yields the corresponding know-how, nor does the concept of know-how guarantee that those possessing it have the corresponding propositional knowledge.

In much of this book I have sought both to clarify and to overcome a certain intellectualist picture of both perception and agency and of thinking and doing, a picture that (among other things) takes knowing *how* to be a case of knowing *that*, construes reasons for action as facts, requires the relevant facts to be known to the agent, tends to conceive intentional action inferentially, and encourages conceiving rational actions as necessarily intentional. Earlier chapters have undermined the counterpart intellectualist picture of theoretical reason, a picture like the former in, for instance, conceiving perception as inferential, reasons for belief as factive, and the relation in which one or more beliefs support another based on it—the "basing relation"—as requiring inference. The positive view partially sketched represents agency as both information-responsive and reasons-responsive—and indeed as appropriately governed by reason—without endorsing any of these intellectualist views. The examples provided in examining intellectualism indicate some ways in which information can guide action even if the information is not represented by knowledge, and to that extent intellectually possessed. They also show some ways in which reasons can underlie action even if they are neither objects of knowledge nor components in inference as an intellectual process.

Agency is exercisable where the information processing it requires occurs without inference; and beliefs or cues can guide action without constituting knowledge. I have not implied, however, and do not believe, that knowledge regarding the kinds of actions and activities in question is not desirable, and indeed more desirable than true belief with the same content. Nor have I implied that learning how to do many of the important things we do, say in speaking, playing instruments, gaming, and hiking, does not normally require gaining propositional knowledge along the developmental route. Nonetheless, some propositional knowledge is like a ladder that, once having climbed up on it, we can do without.

If the cases examined in this chapter are as representative as they seem, practical capacities are not reducible to theoretical capacities, nor does their exercise in what we know how to do necessarily yield detailed comprehensive knowledge about how the things in question are done: the kind of knowledge we would express to someone we hope thereby to teach, by instruction as opposed to demonstration, how to do these things. The role of knowledge in action and reasoning may in some cases be minimal. Rational action, moreover, may have immensely wide scope, extending to things we do, even intentionally, without our doing or depending on reasoning. Rational action at least typically results, in part, from realizing or trying to realize intention. This makes understanding intention particularly important for understanding rational action. Intention may have wide scope and complex content, much as belief can have a complex proposition as object, particularly if, as with scripted intentions, there is a background that enables the mind to encompass the full content in detail. In principle, the scope of intention can be as wide as is possible for the agent in relation to the kinds of activity that can become fully automatic for that agent and, in that sense, come under the control of a single intention.

The examples explored require some qualifications of the belief-desire view of intentional action, which has too often been developed atomistically in relation to "single" acts as opposed to activities. But we may resist concluding that no version of the belief-desire model of intentional action is sound. Maintaining the model, however, requires a wider conception, at least of action, intention, and practical reasoning, than has been traditionally dominant in the literature of action theory. Maintaining it also requires relinquishing at least some of the intellectualist views that, for many philosophers, seem required for understanding practical rationality. The broad idea of cognitive maps as crucial for navigating the world, however, is sustainable; and there is no need to deny that such maps are in certain ways better when their routes represent knowledge rather than even justified true cognitions that fall short of knowledge. This chapter, indeed the book as a whole, also does nothing to weaken the idea that knowledge and truth represent sources of critical standards for the domain of action, but it does indicate some ways in which we can understand the application of those standards to human agents without accepting intellectualism in either epistemology or the theory of action.

CONCLUSION

Perception, Apprehension, and Action

Perception is central in our engagement with the world. It is experiential, representational, and causally connected with its objects. It is a discriminative sensory response to multifarious phenomena in our experience of the world. Perceptual experience embodies phenomenally distinctive states. Those states, as phenomenally representational and discriminatively responsive to our environment, have a kind of content by which they guide us as agents in the physical realm. In these ways, and most prominently in its phenomenal elements, perception is mental, in the broad sense that entails some engagement of the mind. But I have distinguished the mental from the intellectual and argued that perception is neither fundamentally intellectual nor, in its simplest forms, belief-entailing.

My theory of perception is ontologically realist and phenomenologically pluralistic, but it is psychologically economical. It seeks to avoid positing any more mental processes or states than we need for a philosophical understanding of its subject. It is also epistemologically double-barreled: knowledge, whether perceptual or a priori, is external, justification internal. But my overall epistemology unifies these two notions: in relation to reasons and grounds on one side, as each essential for appraising either justification or knowledge, and, on the other side, as connected to truth conceived as an "aim" of both justification and knowledge. There is no compelling reason to be skeptical about whether we ever achieve justification or knowledge; but I have also made it easy to see that there is good reason for intellectual humility. Error is easy and sometimes inevitable.

Seeing, Knowing, and Doing. Robert Audi, Oxford University Press (2020). © Oxford University Press.
DOI: 10.1093/oso/9780197503508.001.0001

My view respects reflective common sense and is accordingly anti-intellectualist. In one way, it is also a kind of naturalistic view. Natural patterns—indeed patterns that represent causal connections—govern how events in the external world are related to our perceptions and our knowledge. They also govern the effects of our motivation and cognition on both our volitional activity and our overt behavior. A view that situates us in the world in this way, however—as perceptually affected by it and purposively altering it—gives us great latitude in accommodating scientific findings in psychology and cognitive science, but does not commit us to physicalism in ontology or empiricism in epistemology.

Information flows from world to mind with sufficient reliability to yield knowledge of our surroundings. Our perceptions, in one way or another and with varying degrees of accuracy, enable us to navigate the world, and our apprehensions of abstract entities, which are also phenomenologically presented in our experience, enable us to acquire a priori knowledge and justification. Causal, explanatory connections between what grounds knowledge and our minds as knowers also enable us to change the world. Our needs and wants yield motivation; our motivational energy is guided by our perceptions and knowledge; and we may, under good conditions, flourish. Action, like perception, has a structure in which some elements are basic; but even in their least complex cases the connections between mind and world are, in the multitude of ways illustrated in this book, causal and explanatory.

The theory of perception developed here is a basis for understanding major aspects of intuition. Like perception, intuition of the experiential sort most akin to perceiving is a kind of direct, non-inferential response to its object, phenomenally realized in occurrent forms. Intuition is also a ground of justification. Intuition may arise from comprehendingly considering the self-evident, which is commonly found intuitive when adequately understood, much as perceptions often become clear when conditions of observation are favorable. Adequate understanding is essential for our self-evidential knowledge, which is first-hand, non-inferential, and a priori. We have also seen how such knowledge is a basis for further a priori knowledge. In the a priori realm, inferential connections to that further knowledge may extend to a vast superstructure, as may also occur given inferences from perceptual knowledge. In both cases, moreover, a reliable connection between the objects known—physical ones in the perceptual case and abstract elements in the a priori case—grounds knowledge of those objects. The accessibility of those objects is possible through our phenomenological representational power, manifested in sense-experiences in perception and in comprehensional, often intuitional experiences in the a priori case.

Our practical knowledge, often manifested in our knowing how to do things, is commonly guided by perception and, often through perceptual experience, by perceptual knowledge. But perceived cues may also guide action without producing belief or knowledge, particularly where our beliefs or experiences have sensitized us to their relevance. Analogously, even rational action need not always emerge from reasoning, or be guided by it, or be based on reasons constituted by knowledge. In many aspects of our activity in the world, we are guided by scripts and realize our intentions with the automaticity that can grow from settled habits and constant practice. In a sense, our rationality, even if it is most robustly manifested in reasoning, frees us from needing to reason at every turn.

Overall, then, this book provides a theory of perception and its relation to thought, justification, and action; a pluralistic account of intuition; an account of perceptual as opposed to propositional content; a related account of normative reasons, theoretical and practical, and of their basis in experiential grounds of justification; and a theory of the a priori. I have developed distinctions between perceptual experience and mere sensory experience, between reasons and grounds, between justification and rationality, between epistemic dependence and inferential dependence, between the theoretical and the conceptual, between perception and cognition as mapping the world, and motivation guided by belief in changing the world. We can do justice to the complexity of perception and to the causal roots of perception and action without embracing reductive naturalism. We can account for cognitive diversity without intellectualism. And we can anchor human persons in the physical world while seeing ways in which we transcend it.

REFERENCES

Alston, William P. 1990. *Perceiving God.* Ithaca, NY: Cornell University Press.

———. 1971. "Varieties of Privileged Access." *American Philosophical Quarterly* 8(3): 223–41.

Anscombe, G. E. M. 1957. *Intention.* Oxford, UK: Blackwell.

Aristotle. 1915. *Posterior Analytics.* In *The Complete Works of Aristotle,* vol. 1, edited by Jonathan Barnes. Oxford: Clarendon Press.

Audi, Paul. 2012. "Grounding: Toward a Theory of the *In-Virtue-Of* Relation." *Journal of Philosophy* 109(12): 685–711.

Audi, Robert. Forthcoming a. "Intellectual Responsibility and the Scope of the Will." In *Epistemic Duties: New Arguments, New Angles,* edited by Kevin McCain and Scott Stapleford. New York: Routledge.

______. Forthcoming b. "Toward an Epistemology of Moral Principles." *Res Philosophica* 97, 1 (2020), 1–24.

———. 2019. "Doxasticism: Belief and the Information-Responsiveness of Mind." *Episteme,* 1–21. doi.org/10.1017/epi.2018.53.

———. 2018a. "Moral Perception Defended." In *Evaluative Perception,* edited by Anna Bergqvist and Robert Cowan, 58–79. Oxford: Oxford University Press. (Slightly revised version of the paper of the same title appearing online in *Argumenta* 1(1) (2015), 5-28.

———. 2018b. "Perception and Cognition: Structural and Epistemic Elements." In *Robert Audi: Critical Engagements,* edited by Johannes Müller-Salo, 3–39. Cham: Springer International.

———. 2018c. "Understanding, Self-Evidence, and Justification." *Philosophy and Phenomenological Research.* doi.org/10.1111/phpr.12492.

———. 2017. "On Intellectualism in the Theory of Action." *Journal of the American Philosophical Association* 3(3): 284–300.

———. 2015. "Intuition and Its Place in Ethics." *Journal of the American Philosophical Association* 1(1): 57–77.

———. 2013a. *Moral Perception.* Princeton, NJ: Princeton University Press.

———. 2013b. "Doxastic Innocence: Phenomenal Conservatism and Grounds of Justification." In *Seemings and Justification: New Essays on Dogmatism*

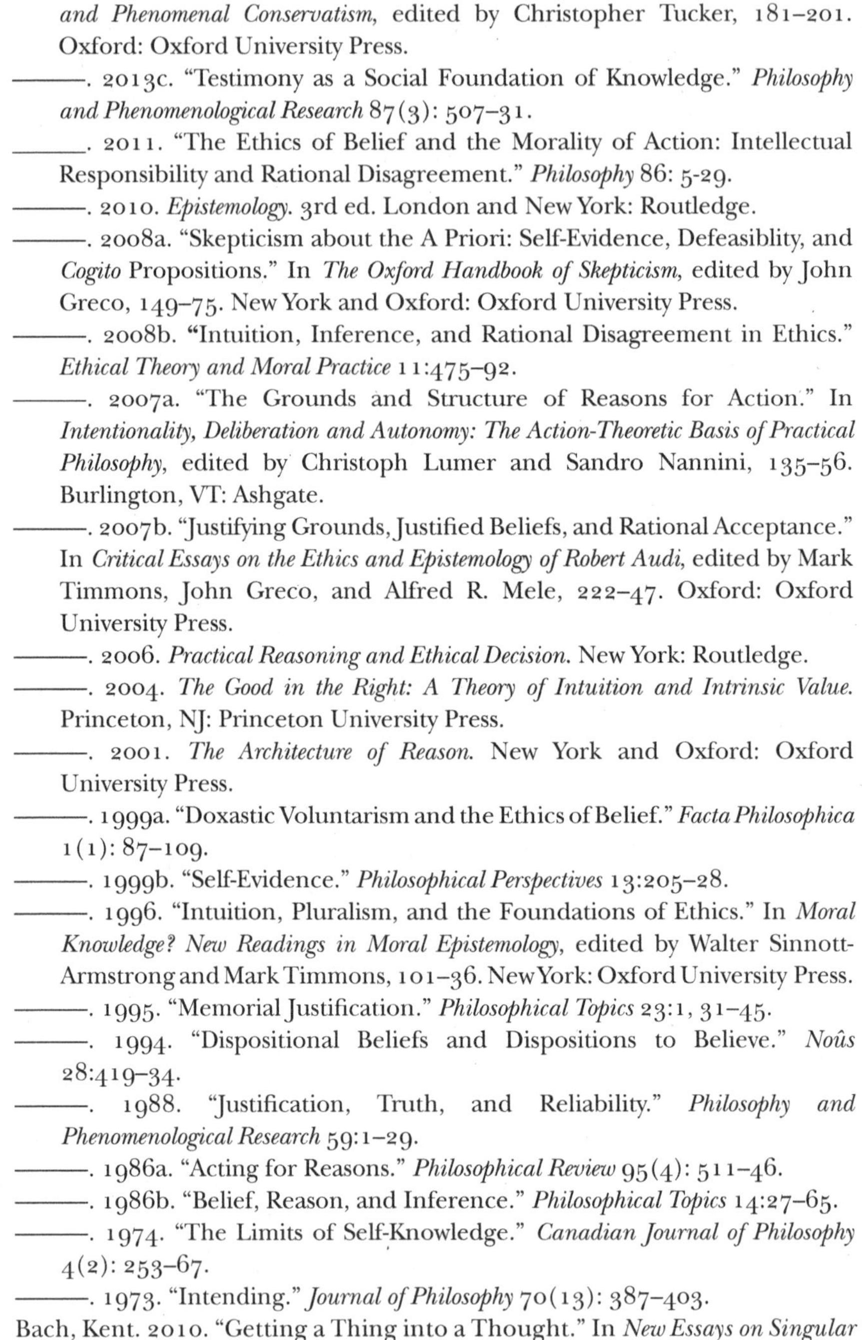

and Phenomenal Conservatism, edited by Christopher Tucker, 181–201. Oxford: Oxford University Press.

———. 2013c. "Testimony as a Social Foundation of Knowledge." *Philosophy and Phenomenological Research* 87(3): 507–31.

______. 2011. "The Ethics of Belief and the Morality of Action: Intellectual Responsibility and Rational Disagreement." *Philosophy* 86: 5-29.

———. 2010. *Epistemology*. 3rd ed. London and New York: Routledge.

———. 2008a. "Skepticism about the A Priori: Self-Evidence, Defeasiblity, and *Cogito* Propositions." In *The Oxford Handbook of Skepticism*, edited by John Greco, 149–75. New York and Oxford: Oxford University Press.

———. 2008b. "Intuition, Inference, and Rational Disagreement in Ethics." *Ethical Theory and Moral Practice* 11:475–92.

———. 2007a. "The Grounds and Structure of Reasons for Action." In *Intentionality, Deliberation and Autonomy: The Action-Theoretic Basis of Practical Philosophy*, edited by Christoph Lumer and Sandro Nannini, 135–56. Burlington, VT: Ashgate.

———. 2007b. "Justifying Grounds, Justified Beliefs, and Rational Acceptance." In *Critical Essays on the Ethics and Epistemology of Robert Audi*, edited by Mark Timmons, John Greco, and Alfred R. Mele, 222–47. Oxford: Oxford University Press.

———. 2006. *Practical Reasoning and Ethical Decision*. New York: Routledge.

———. 2004. *The Good in the Right: A Theory of Intuition and Intrinsic Value*. Princeton, NJ: Princeton University Press.

———. 2001. *The Architecture of Reason*. New York and Oxford: Oxford University Press.

———. 1999a. "Doxastic Voluntarism and the Ethics of Belief." *Facta Philosophica* 1(1): 87–109.

———. 1999b. "Self-Evidence." *Philosophical Perspectives* 13:205–28.

———. 1996. "Intuition, Pluralism, and the Foundations of Ethics." In *Moral Knowledge? New Readings in Moral Epistemology*, edited by Walter Sinnott-Armstrong and Mark Timmons, 101–36. New York: Oxford University Press.

———. 1995. "Memorial Justification." *Philosophical Topics* 23:1, 31–45.

———. 1994. "Dispositional Beliefs and Dispositions to Believe." *Noûs* 28:419–34.

———. 1988. "Justification, Truth, and Reliability." *Philosophy and Phenomenological Research* 59:1–29.

———. 1986a. "Acting for Reasons." *Philosophical Review* 95(4): 511–46.

———. 1986b. "Belief, Reason, and Inference." *Philosophical Topics* 14:27–65.

———. 1974. "The Limits of Self-Knowledge." *Canadian Journal of Philosophy* 4(2): 253–67.

———. 1973. "Intending." *Journal of Philosophy* 70(13): 387–403.

Bach, Kent. 2010. "Getting a Thing into a Thought." In *New Essays on Singular Thought*, edited by Robin Jeshion, 39–63. Oxford: Oxford University Press.

Bealer, George. 1998. "Intuition and the Autonomy of Philosophy." In *Rethinking Intuition: The Psychology of Intuition and Its Role in Philosophical Inquiry*, edited by Michael DePaul and William Ramsey, 201–44. Lanham, MD: Rowman and Littlefield.

Benaceraff, Paul. 1973. "Mathematical Knowledge." *Journal of Philosophy* 70:661–79.

Bengson, John. 2016. "Practical Perception and Intelligent Action." *Philosophical Issues* 26(1): 25–58.

———. 2015. "Grasping the Third Realm." In *Oxford Studies in Epistemology*, vol. 5, edited by Tamar Szabo Gendler and John Hawthorne, 1–34. Oxford: Clarendon Press.

———, and Marc A. Moffett. 2011. "Nonpropositional Intellectualism." In *Knowing How: Essays on Knowledge, Mind, and Action*, edited by John Bengson and Marc A. Moffett, 161–95. New York and Oxford: Oxford University Press.

Bergqvist, Anna, and Robert Cowan, eds. 2018. *Evaluative Perception*. Oxford: Oxford University Press.

Bernecker, Sven. Forthcoming. *Explaining Knowledge*. Princeton: Princeton University Press.

Boghossian, Paul, and Christopher Peacocke, eds. 2000. *New Essays on the A Priori*. Oxford: Clarendon Press.

Brogaard, Berit. 2017. "Seeing Things." *Philosophical Perspectives* 31:55–72.

Broome, John. 2013. *Rationality through Reasoning*. Malden, MA: Wiley Blackwell.

Burge, Tyler. 2010. *Origins of Objectivity*. Oxford: Oxford University Press.

Byrne, Alex. 2018. *Transparency and Self-Knowledge*. Oxford: Oxford University Press.

Carter, J. Adam, and Duncan Pritchard. 2015. "Knowledge-How and Epistemic Luck." *Noûs* 49(3): 440–53.

Casullo, Albert, and Joshua Thurow, eds. 2013. *The A Priori in Philosophy*. Oxford: Oxford University Press.

Cath, Yuri. 2015. "Revisionary Intellectualism and Gettier." *Philosophical Studies* 172(1): 7–27.

Chisholm, R. M. 1977. *Theory of Knowledge* 2nd ed. Englewood Cliffs, NJ: Prentice-Hall.

———. 1975. "Knowledge and Belief: De Dicto and De Re." *Philosophical Studies* 22:9–28.

———. 1942. "The Problem of the Speckled Hen." *Mind* 51:368–73.

Chudnoff, Elijah. 2014. *Intuition*. Oxford: Oxford University Press.

Clark, Andy. 2014. *Mindware: An Introduction to the Philosophy of Cognitive Science*. Oxford: Oxford University Press.

Conee, Earl. 2010. "Self-Support." *Philosophy and Phenomenological Research* 84(2): 419–66.

Cory, Therese Scarpelli. 2018. "Embodied vs. Non-embodied Modes of Knowing in Aquinas: Different Universals, Different Intelligible Spaces, Different Intellects." *Faith and Philosophy* 35(4): 417–46.

Crane, Tim. 2013. *The Objects of Thought.* Oxford: Oxford University Press.

Crisp, Roger. 2006. *Reasons and the Good.* Oxford: Oxford University Press.

Cristensen, David, and Jennifer Lackey, eds. 2013. *The Epistemology of Disagreement: New Essays.* Oxford: Oxford University Press.

Crowther, Thomas, and Claire Mac Cumhaill, eds. 2018. *Perceptual Ephemera.* Oxford: Oxford University Press.

Dancy, Jonathan. 1993. *Moral Reasons.* Oxford: Blackwell.

Davidson, Donald. 1963. "Actions, Reasons and Causes." *Journal of Philosophy* 60(23): 685–700.

Dretske, Fred I. 1981. *Knowledge and the Flow of Information.* Cambridge, MA: MIT Press.

Fantl, J. 2016. "Mary Shepherd on Causal Necessity." *Metaphysica* 17(1): 87–108.

Feldman, Richard, and Earl Conee,. 2018. "Between Belief and Disbelief." In Scott McCain, ed. *Believing in Accordance with the Evidence,* 71–90. Cham: Springer International.

Fischer, Bob. 2018. "C.I. Lewis and the Benaceraff Problem." *Episteme* 15:154–65.

Fish, William. 2010. *Philosophy of Perception: A Contemporary Introduction.* London and New York: Routledge.

Fodor, Jerry A., and Zenon W. Pylyshyn. 2015. *Minds without Meanings: An Essay on the Content of Concepts.* Cambridge, MA: MIT Press.

Goldman, Alvin I. 1976. "Discrimination and Perceptual Knowledge." *Journal of Philosophy* 73:771–91.

Goldman, Alvin I., and Joel Pust. 1998. "Philosophical Theory and Intuitional Evidence." In *Rethinking Intuition: The Psychology of Intuition and Its Role in Philosophical Inquiry,* edited by Michael DePaul and William Ramsey, 179–97. Lanham, MD: Rowman and Littlefield.

Gopnik, Alison, and Eric Schwitgebel. 1998. "The Role of Philosophical Intuition in Empirical Psychology." In *Rethinking Intuition: The Psychology of Intuition and Its Role in Philosophical Inquiry,* edited by Michael DePaul and William Ramsey, 75–112. Lanham, MD: Rowman and Littlefield.

Green, Mitchell. 2010. "Perceiving Emotions." *Proceedings of the Aristotelian Society Supplementary Volume* 84(1): 45–62.

Hagaman, Scott. 2015. "Content and Justification: Prospects for Epistemological Rationalism." PhD diss., University of Notre Dame.

Hetherington, Stephen (2006). "How to Know (that Knowledge-that is Knowledge-how)," in Stephen Hetherington, ed., *Epistemology Futures.* Oxford: Oxford University Press.

Hornsby, Jennifer. 2017. "Knowledge How in Philosophy of Action." *Royal Institute of Philosophy Supplement* 80:87–104.

———. 2011. "Ryle's *Knowing-How*, and Knowing How to Act," in Bengson, John, and Moffett, Mark A., eds. *Knowing How: Essays on Knowledge, Mind, and Action*. Oxford: Oxford University Press, 80-98

Huemer, Michael. 2005. *Ethical Intuitionism*. Basingstoke, UK: Palgrave Macmillan.

Hume, David. (1739) 1888. *A Treatise of Human Nature*. Oxford: Oxford University Press.

Husserl, Edmund. 1982. *Ideas Pertaining to a Pure Phenomenology and to Phenomenological Philosophy*. Translated by F. Kersten. The Hague: Martinus Nijhoff.

Johnston, Mark. 2011. "On a Neglected Epistemic Virtue." *Philosophical Issues* 21(1): 165–218.

King, Jeffrey C., Scott Soames, and Jeffrey Speaks. 2014 *New Thinking about Propositions*. Oxford: Oxford University Press.

Korsgaard, Christine. 1996. *The Sources of Normativity*. Cambridge: Cambridge University Press.

Kripke, Saul. 1980. *Naming and Necessity*. Cambridge, MA: Harvard University Press.

Locke, Dustin (2015). "Knowledge, Explanation, and Motivating Reasons." *American Philosophical Quarterly* 52, 215–232.

Locke, John. 1986. *An Essay Concerning Human Understanding*, edited by Kenneth P. Winkler. Indianapolis: Hackett.

Logue, Heather. 2018. "Can We Visually Experience Aesthetic Properties?" In *Evaluative Perception*, edited by Anna Bergqvist and Robert Cowan, 42–57. Oxford: Oxford University Press.

Lopes, Dominic McIver. 2018. *Being for Beauty*. Oxford: Oxford University Press.

Lord, Errol. 2015. "Acting for the Right Reasons, Abilities, and Obligation." *Oxford Studies in Metaethics* 10:26–52.

Lyons, Jack C. 2016. "Inferentialism and Cognitive Penetration." *Episteme* 13(1): 1–28.

Maddy, Penelope. 1980. "Perception and Mathematical Intuition." *Philosophical Review* 84(2): 163–96.

Malmgren, Anna-Sara. 2018. "Varieties of Inference?" *Philosophical Perspectives* 28:221–54.

———. 2007. 'Is There A Priori Knowledge by Testimony?' *Philosophical Review* 115(2): 199–241.

Matthen, Mohan, ed. 2015. *The Oxford Handbook of Philosophy of Perception*. Oxford: Oxford University Press.

McGrath, Matthew. 2017. "Knowing What Things Look Like." *Philosophical Review* 126(1): 1–42.

Milona, Michael. 2018. "On the Epistemological Significance of Value Perception." In *Evaluative Perception*, edited by Anna Berqvist and Robert Cowan, 200–218. Oxford: Oxford University Press.

Moore, G. E. 1912. *Ethics*. London and New York: Oxford University Press.

———. 1903. *Principia Ethica*. Cambridge: Cambridge University Press.

Morrison, John. 2016. "Perceptual Confidence." *Analytic Philosophy* 57(1): 15–48.

Nida-Rumelin, Martine. 2011. "Phenomenal Presence and Perceptual Awareness." *Philosophical Issues* 21(1): 352–383.

Noë, Alva. 2004. *Action in Perception.* Cambridge, MA: MIT Press.

Orlandi, Nico. 2014. *The Innocent Eye: Why Vision Is Not a Cognitive Process.* Oxford: Oxford University Press.

Pace, Michael. 2017. "Experiences, Seemings, and Perceptual Justification." *Australasian Journal of Philosophy* 95(2): 228–41.

Parfit, Derek. 2011. *On What Matters.* Vol. 2. Oxford: Oxford University Press.

Pavesi, Carlotta. 2017. "Know-How and Gradability." *Philosophical Review* 126(3): 345–83.

Prichard, H. A. 1912. "Does Moral Philosophy Rest on a Mistake?" *Mind: A Quarterly Review of Psychology and Philosophy* 21: 21–37.

Poston, Ted. 2016. "Knowing How to Transmit Knowledge?" *Noûs* 50(4): 865–78.

Prinz, Jesse. 2017. "Unconscious Perception." In *The Oxford Handbook of Perception,* edited by Mohan Matthen, 371–89. Oxford: Oxford University Press.

Pritchard, Duncan. 2012. *Epistemological Disjunctivism.* Oxford: Oxford University Press.

Rescorla, Michael. 2017. "Bayesian Perceptual Psychology." In *The Oxford Handbook of Perception,* edited by Mohan Matthen, 694–716. Oxford: Oxford University Press.

Ritchie, J. Brendan, and Peter Caruthers. 2017. "The Bodily Senses." In *The Oxford Handbook of Philosophy of Perception,* edited by Mohan Matthen, 353–70. Oxford: Oxford University Press.

Ross, W. D. 1930. *The Right and the Good.* Oxford: Clarendon Press.

Russell, Bertrand. (1912) 1959. *The Problems of Philosophy.* New York and Oxford: Oxford University Press.

Scanlon, T. M. 1998. *What We Owe to Each Other.* Cambridge, MA: Harvard University Press.

Schellenberg, Susanna. 2017. "The Origins of Perceptual Experience." *Episteme* 14(3): 311–28.

Sellars, Wilfrid. 1956. "The Myth of the Given." *Minnesota Studies in the Philosophy of Science,* 1, 253–329.

Setiya, Kiran. 2012. "Knowing How." *Proceedings of the Aristotelian Society* 112(3): 285–307. https://doi.org/10.1111/j.1467-9264.2012.00336.x.

Shafer-Landau, Russ. 2007. 'Audi's Intuitionism. *Philosophy and Phenomenological Research* 74 1: 250–61.

Sidgwick, Henry. 1907. *The Methods of Ethics.* 7th ed. London: Macmillan & Co.

Siegel, Susanna. 2017a. "In Defense of Perceptual Content." *Philosophical Perspectives* 31:409–47.

———. 2017b. *The Rationality of Perception.* Oxford: Oxford University Press.

———. 2010. *The Contents of Visual Experience.* Oxford: Oxford University Press.

———. 2006. "How Does Visual Phenomenology Constrain Object-Seeing?" *Australasian Journal of Philosophy* 84(3): 429–41.

Simmons, Alison. 2017. "Perception in Early Modern Philosophy." In *The Oxford Handbook of Philosophy of Perception*, edited by Mohan Matthen, 81–99. Oxford: Oxford University Press.

Sinnott-Armstrong, Walter. 2007. "Reflections on Reflection in Robert Audi's *Moral Intuitionism*." In *Rationality and the Good: Critical Essays on the Ethics and Epistemology of Robert Audi*, edited by Mark Timmons, John Greco, and Alfred Mele, 19–29. Oxford: Oxford University Press.

Sinnott-Armstrong, Walter, Liane Young, and Fiery Cushman. 2010. "Moral Intuitions." In *The Moral Psychology Handbook*, edited by John M. Doris and The Moral Psychology Research Group, 246–70. Oxford: Oxford University Press.

Smithies, Declan. 2019. *The Epistemic Role of Consciousness.* Oxford: Oxford University Press.

Sorensen, Roy. 2018. "Absences: A Companion Guide." In *Perceptual Ephemera*, edited by Thomas Crowther and Claire Mac Cumhaill. Oxford: Oxford University Press, 116-129.

Sorensen, Roy. 2008. *Seeing Dark Things.* Oxford: Oxford University Press.

Sosa, David. 2011a. "Perceptual Knowledge." In *The Routledge Companion to Epistemology*, edited by Sven Bernecker and Duncan Pritchard, 294–304. London and New York: Routledge.

———. 2011b. "Some of the Structure of Experience and Belief." *Philosophical Issues* 21(1): 474–84.

Sosa, Ernest. 2015. *Judgement and Agency.* Oxford: Oxford University Press.

Speaks, Jeff. 2015. *The Phenomenal and the Representational.* Oxford: Oxford University Press.

Stalnaker, Robert. 2012. "Intellectualism and the Objects of Knowledge." *Philosophy and Phenomenological Research* 55(3): 754–61.

Stanley, Jason. 2012. "Know How." *Philosophy and Phenomenological Research* 85(3): 762–78.

———. 2011. *Know How.* Oxford: Oxford University Press.

———, and Timothy Williamson. 2001. "Knowing How." *Journal of Philosophy* 98:411–44.

Steup, Matthias. 2001. "Epistemic Duty, Evidence, and Internality: A Reply to Alvin Goldman." In *Knowledge, Truth and Duty: Essays on Epistemic Justification, Responsibility, and Virtue*, edited by Matthias Steup, 134-48. Oxford: Oxford University Press.

Stokes, Dustin. 2018. "Rich Perceptual Content and Aesthetic Properties." In *Evaluative Perception*, edited by Anna Bergqvist and Robert Cowan. Oxford: Oxford University Press, 19-41.

———. 2014. "Cognitive Penetration and the Perception of Art." *Dialectica* 68(1): 1–34.

Stratton-Lake, Philip. 2002. *Ethical Intuitionism: Re-evaluations.* Oxford: Oxford University Press.

Sturgeon, Nicholas. 2006. "Moral Explanations Defended." In *Contemporary Debates in Moral Theory*, edited by James Dreier, 241–62. Malden, MA: Blackwell.

Thomson, Judith Jarvis. 1971. "The Time of a Killing." *Journal of Philosophy* 68(5): 115–32.

Thurow, Joshua. In preparation. "Understanding to the Rescue." Unpublished manuscript.

_____, Joshua. 2006. "Experiential Defeaters and A Priori Justification." *Philosophical Quarterly* 56(225): 596–602.

Tolman, Edward C. 1948. "Cognitive Maps in Rats and Men." *Psychological Review* 55(4): 189–208.

Tucker, Christopher. 2014. "If Phenomenal Dogmatists Have a Problem with Cognitive Penetration, You Do Too." *Dialectica* 68(1): 35–62.

Tye, Michael. 2010. "Attention, Seeing, and Change Blindness." *Philosophical Issues* 20:410–37.

Vayrynen, Pekka. 2018. "Doubts about Moral Perception." In *Evaluative Perception*, edited by Anna Bergqvist and Robert Cowan, 109–28. Oxford: Oxford University Press.

Williamson, Timothy. 2007a. "On Being Justified in One's Head." In *Critical Essays on the Ethics and Epistemology of Robert Audi*, edited by Mark Timmons, John Greco, and Alfred R. Mele, 106–22. Oxford: Oxford University Press.

———. 2007b. *The Philosophy of Philosophy*. Malden, MA: Blackwell.

INDEX

For the benefit of digital users, indexed terms that span two pages (e.g., 52–53) may, on occasion, appear on only one of those pages.